PEDAGOGIES FOR LEADING PRACTICE

Bringing together the experiences of professionals from around the world, this essential text explores the intersections between pedagogy and leadership to consider how effective Pedagogical Leadership can be used to foster the collaborative engagement of children and their families, staff and practitioners, and ensure high quality provision in early years settings and services.

Pedagogies for Leading Practice showcases a vast range of experiences and ideas which are at the heart of professional practice. Written to provoke group discussion and extend thinking, opportunities for international comparison, points for reflection, and editorial provocations will help students, policy-makers and others engage critically with wide-ranging approaches to leadership in early years practice. Considering varied forms of collaborative working, the challenges involved in becoming a pedagogical leader, and the role of management in meeting institutional demands and the needs of the wider community, chapters are divided into four key sections which reflect major influences on practice and pedagogy:

- Being alongside children
- Those who educate
- Embedding families and communities
- Working with systems

Offering insight, examples and challenges, this text will enhance understanding, support self-directed learning, and provoke and transform thinking at both graduate and postgraduate levels, particularly in the field of early childhood education and care.

Sandra Cheeseman is Senior Lecturer in early childhood policy, leadership and professional experience at Macquarie University, Sydney, Australia.

Rosie Walker is Senior Lecturer at the Department for Children and Families, School of Education, University of Worcester, UK.

THINKING ABOUT PEDAGOGY IN EARLY CHILDHOOD EDUCATION

Books in this series will serve as critical companions for senior under-graduate and postgraduate students conducting study and research in the field of early childhood education and care. As well as contributing to the thinking of teachers in a range of countries, these books will also be of interest to policy-makers and thinkers in a range of disciplines including health, welfare, sociology and community-building. Introducing new ideas and differing viewpoints from around the globe, texts take the reader beyond known cultural, ethical and geographical boundaries, to explore children's perspectives as a key component in early childhood pedagogy.

Each book in the series is divided into four interconnected sections: being alongside children, those who educate, families and communities, and policies and systems, to encompass the wide-ranging influences on contemporary pedagogical practice. Editors offer provocations to both link the chapters provided and offer directions for further thought. Grounded in sound empirical evidence, taking a global perspective, and born of critical and collaborative reflection, texts encourage readers to consider ideas which might be applied in their own learning, study and practice.

Series editors: Alma Fleet and Michael Reed

Titles in this series include:

PEDAGOGIES FOR CHILDREN'S PERSPECTIVES
Catherine Patterson and Laurie Kocher

PEDAGOGIES FOR LEADING PRACTICE
Sandra Cheeseman and Rosie Walker

For more information about this series, please visit:
www.routledge.com/education/series/TAPECE

PEDAGOGIES FOR LEADING PRACTICE

Edited by Sandra Cheeseman and Rosie Walker

Routledge
Taylor & Francis Group

LONDON AND NEW YORK

First published 2019
by Routledge
2 Park Square, Milton Park, Abingdon, Oxon OX14 4RN

and by Routledge
711 Third Avenue, New York, NY 10017

Routledge is an imprint of the Taylor & Francis Group, an informa business

British Library Cataloguing-in-Publication Data
A catalogue record for this book is available from the British Library

Library of Congress Cataloging-in-Publication Data
Names: Cheeseman, Sandra, editor. | Walker, Rosie (College teacher), editor.
Title: Pedagogies for leading practice / edited by Sandra Cheeseman and Rosie Walker.
Description: Abingdon, Oxon ; New York, NY : Routledge, 2019. | Includes bibliographical references.
Identifiers: LCCN 2018032999 (print) | LCCN 2018046520 (ebook) | ISBN 9781351266925 (eb) | ISBN 9781138577398 (hb) | ISBN 9781138577428 (pb) | ISBN 9781351266925 (ebk)
Subjects: LCSH: Educational leadership. | Early childhood education.
Classification: LCC LB2806 (ebook) | LCC LB2806 .P374 2019 (print) | DDC 371.2--dc23
LC record available at https://lccn.loc.gov/2018032999

ISBN: 978-1-138-57739-8 (hbk)
ISBN: 978-1-138-57742-8 (pbk)
ISBN: 978-1-351-26692-5 (ebk)

Typeset in Sabon
by Swales & Willis Ltd, Exeter, Devon, UK

FOR ALEC AND GRETA (SC)

FOR NICK, OLIVER AND CHRISTOPHER (RW)

ACKNOWLEDGEMENTS

VOLUME EDITORS' ACKNOWLEDGEMENTS

We warmly thank the children, families and communities who are central to this volume. Many rich stories come to life because people are prepared to share their lives and experiences. This volume is testament to those who courageously take on the challenge of telling those stories in interesting and authentic ways. It has been wonderful to capture the vastness of leadership experiences from many parts of the world.

Our thanks to series editors Alma and Mike for their initial inspiration in conceptualising this series about pedagogies in early childhood. We have gained from their hard work and meticulous eye for detail in looking over, under, backwards, forwards and through. Sincere thanks to the team at Routledge for their expertise and direction in moving from thoughts to print.

It has been a pleasure to work with each of the authors, who, over the time of writing this volume have each encountered life's tricks and turns, competing priorities and the incessant demands that come with working in early childhood. It has been a privilege to work with such great minds and generous spirits as we together have explored the complexities and nuances of early childhood leadership across nations. We appreciate and applaud the many acts of leadership and courage that were demonstrated in bringing this volume together.

We trust that all who read this volume will be enriched by the complexity of thinking, the provocations presented and the vision for leadership, now and beyond.

Sandra and Rosie

SERIES EDITORS' ACKNOWLEDGEMENTS

Children put their trust in those who hold their hands. From that perspective, we note that the Editorial team at Routledge believed in this book series from the start. They and the Production team transferred that belief into many small actions which taken together helped us make big decisions. Thanks to Alison Foyle and Elsbeth Wright and everyone who held our hands. The Volume Editors watched over the contributors' playground and made it a wonderful place. The contributors themselves generated energy, shared their knowledge and shaped the play space. As Series Editors, we very much enjoyed the opportunity to play with this collection of diverse, warm, supportive, intelligent and creative individuals.

Our thanks to all.
Alma and Mike

CONTENTS

CONTENTS

CONTENTS

FIGURES AND TABLE

Figures

Table

ABOUT THE SERIES EDITORS AND CONTRIBUTORS

Series editors

Michael Reed and Alma Fleet were the driving force behind the production of this six-book series involving over 85 editors and authors. The have shaped the direction of each volume and carefully considered which authors and editors would be best suited to bring their expertise to the project. Both are experienced university tutors and have previously collaborated on a number of projects, including a book on Pedagogical Documentation, a symposium at the European Early Childhood Education Research Association and an international conference on educational quality in North Africa.

Alma Fleet is an Honorary Associate Professor at the Department of Educational Studies, Macquarie University, Sydney, NSW, Australia. Formerly Head of the Institute of Early Childhood, her doctoral study was in the area of early childhood teacher education, with a focus on the practice teaching experience. She works extensively with educators across the early childhood sector, engaging those in schools and prior to school sectors in educational change initiatives, particularly through contextualised investigations. Recent publications include Fleet, DeGioia, Patterson, with contributions from colleagues (2016), *Engaging with educational change: Voices of Practitioner Inquiry*; Fleet, Patterson, Robertson (2017), *Pedagogical documentation in early years practice: Seeing through multiple perspectives*; Fleet (2017), *Planning, programming and embedding curriculum*. In B. Gobby and R. Walker (Eds.) *Powers of Curriculum: Sociological perspectives on education.*

Michael Reed is an Honorary Senior Fellow of the School of Education at the University of Worcester, England. He is also a Visiting Professor at the University of Ibn Zohr, Business School, Agadir, Morocco. He is a qualified teacher and holds advanced qualifications in Educational Inquiry, Educational Psychology and Special Education. The series editorship builds upon his experience of writing books, book chapters, research papers and co-edited textbooks. These include *Reflective practice in the early years* (2010), *Quality improvement and change in the Early Years* (2012) and *Work-based research in the early years* (2012). More recently, *A critical companion to early education* (2015) and, in conjunction with the Pre-School Learning Alliance in England, *Effective leadership for high quality early years practice* (2016).

Contributors

Tony Bertram is Director of the Centre for Research in Early Childhood (CREC) and Director of Amber Publications and Training Ltd (APT). He was a head teacher in infant schools before moving into higher education in 1987. He is Co-Founder of the European Early Childhood Education Research Association (EECERA) and was its elected President from 1992 to 2007. He was President of the British Association for Early Childhood Education from 2015 to 2018, and is now Vice President. He has been a member of the Ministerial Early Education Advisory Group (EEAG), which advised the government on the development of the Foundation Stage curriculum. He has a particular interest in cross-national, European early childhood projects and has worked extensively internationally for the British Council and the Organisation for Economic Cooperation & Development (OECD).

Sandra Cheeseman is a senior lecturer in early childhood policy, leadership and professional experience at Macquarie University, Sydney. She brings to this role extensive experience as an early childhood teacher, director and senior executive in a range of early childhood settings and organisations. Sandra was a member of the core writing team which developed the Early Years Learning Framework (EYLF) for Australia and has since worked on a number of related research and professional projects, particularly in the areas of pedagogical leadership. Sandra is co-author of the book *Leadership, contexts and complexities in early childhood* (2017), and sits on a number of Governance Boards including the Australian Children's Education and Care Quality Authority (ACECQA).

Gaynor Corrick led provision in a rural county of England for 15 years, graduating and gaining her qualifications whilst maintaining her lead practitioner role. She now contributes to Early Childhood Studies and Primary Outdoor Education undergraduate teaching as a tutor and has presented research papers at international events. She is currently completing an MA (Education). Her research interests are focused on developing pedagogic approaches to leading and managing provision.

Rebecca Dalgleish is the leader of an urban pre-school in England. Rebecca manages and leads a strong early education teaching team and holds a BSc Degree. She has gained further work-based qualifications over the past decade, culminating in an MA in Education. The focus of her research dissertation was the way children learn and how adults can enhance their experiences.

Alma Fleet is an Honorary Associate Professor at the Department of Educational Studies, Macquarie University, Sydney, NSW, Australia. Formerly the coordinator of a targetted Bachelor of Teaching for Aboriginal and Torres Strait Islander students, she has been privileged to work alongside the First Australians in a range of contexts. With colleagues, she has written related reports for government, professional articles, and sector-specific publications including Fleet & Hamilton (2018) Valuing Aboriginal Educators in Pedagogy+ (v3); Fleet, Kitson, Cassidy, Hughes (2007) University-qualified Indigenous early childhood teachers: Voices of resilience. *Australian Journal of Early Childhood* 32(3).

Leena Halttunen works at the Department of Education at the University of Jyväskylä, Finland. Before beginning her university career, she worked as a kindergarten teacher and as a day care centre director. Her current teaching focuses especially on early childhood education leadership and in-service training. In addition, she teaches research methods and works with international students. Her main research interest is in distributed leadership, within new organisational and leadership structures and especially in understanding the role of deputy directors and their leadership.

Johanna Heikka works as a senior lecturer at the School of Applied Educational Science and Teacher Education at the University of Eastern

Finland, Finland. Her current teaching focuses mainly on the research methods, thesis guidance, pedagogy and organisational and leadership issues in early childhood education. Her research interests focus on leadership and pedagogical development in early childhood education. Her publications focus on distributed pedagogical leadership and teacher leadership. She is the Editor-in-Chief of the *Journal of Early Childhood Education Research* (JECER) and the leader of the International Leadership Research Forum (ILRF).

B. Denise Hodgins is a pedagogist and researcher at University of Victoria Child Care Services, the Executive Director of the Early Childhood Pedagogy Network in British Columbia, Canada, a founding member of the Early Childhood Pedagogies Collaboratory, and a member of the Common Worlds Research Collective. Her research interests include gender and care as material-discursive phenomena, and the implications that postfoundational theories and methodologies have for early childhood research and pedagogy. She explores these in her books *Gender and care with young children: A feminist material approach to early childhood education* (to be published by Routledge in 2019) and the edited collection *Feminist research for 21st-century childhoods: Common worlds methods* (to be published by Bloomsbury in 2019), chapters in edited books on critical perspectives in ECE/CYC, and published articles in various journals.

Kathleen Kummen is both an instructor in the School of Education and Childhood Studies and the Chair of the Centre of Innovation and Inquiry in Childhood Studies at Capilano University. She is also the Co-Director of the Early Childhood Pedagogy Network in British Columbia, Canada, a founding member of the Early Childhood Pedagogies Collaboratory, and a member of the Common Worlds Research Collective. Her current research and practice explores the implications for pedagogy when learning is no longer understood as an event that occurs collectively through encounters with other humans and the more-than-human world.

Wendy Lee is the Director of the Educational Leadership Project (Ltd), a professional learning provider for the early childhood sector in New Zealand. She has been involved in the ECE field for almost 50 years as a teacher, tutor, lecturer, manager, professional learning facilitator and researcher. Wendy was Co-Director with Professor Margaret Carr of the National Early Childhood Assessment and Learning Exemplar Project that developed the Kei Tua o te Pae books on assessment for learning for the

NZ ECE sector. She is enthusiastic about the power of documentation to strengthen the learner identity. Wendy has a deep interest in leadership, curriculum and advocacy issues in ECE. She has co-authored books on both Te Whāriki and Learning Stories. She has given keynote presentations at conferences on ECE curriculum, leadership and learning stories throughout the world, including the UK, Germany, Japan, China, Belgium, the USA, the United Arab Emirates, Kazakhstan, Canada and Australia.

Professor Lasse Lipponen is an accomplished international academic voice. His research work is directed to understanding cultures of compassion, leadership in early childhood education, children's agency, and play. He has authored over 100 research articles on teaching and learning.

Sirene May-Yin Lim is currently developing a new locally awarded full-time early childhood degree programme. Prior to this, she worked as a teacher, a curriculum officer and as a teacher educator in the National Institute of Education. She continues to contribute towards building local research and strengthening the local community of early childhood professionals in Singapore.

Jackie Musgrave joined the Open University as Programme Lead for Early Childhood in October 2017. Jackie's professional background is nursing, she trained as a General Nurse and then undertook post-registration training to become a Sick Children's Nurse at Birmingham Children's Hospital, UK. Many years later, after moving into teaching early childhood in colleges of Further Education, her interest in Higher Education developed when she taught Early Years Foundation Degree students. Her doctoral research brings together her professional and personal interests in children's health and early education. Her research explores the effects chronic health conditions on young children and reports ways in which early years practitioners create inclusive environments for children with a range of health issues.

Christine Pascal OBE is Director of the Centre for Research in Early Childhood (CREC) and Director of Amber Publications and Training Ltd (APT) in the UK. She was a teacher in primary schools in Birmingham from 1976 to 1985, before moving into the university sector and specialising in early childhood research and evaluation projects. Currently she is President of the European Early Childhood Education Research Association (EECERA). She was President of the British Association for Early

Childhood Education from 1994 to 1997, and is now Vice President. She has also done extensive work at government level to support the development of early years policy, sitting on a number of national committees, has served as a ministerial advisor, and Early Years Specialist Adviser to the House of Commons Select Committee on Education. She has written extensively on early childhood development and the quality of early education services and served as an Expert Advisor to Dame Tickell's review of the EYFS in England. She was awarded an OBE in 2001 and a Nursery World Lifetime Achievement Award in 2012.

Alison Prowle began her career as a primary school teacher where she first began to see the effects of multiple disadvantage on children's outcomes. This sparked a passion for early intervention with families with young children, working within schools, children's centres, the voluntary sector and local government. As Integrated Services Manager for Children, Young People and Families for a Welsh local authority, Alison was responsible for managing a range of universal and preventative services for children and families. She is an advocate of strength- based approaches that empower families and communities. Since April 2013 Alison has been teaching, researching and writing in the area of Adverse Childhood Experiences, Integrated Working, Parenting and Families at the University of Worcester.

Michael Reed is an Honary Senior Fellow of the School of Education, University of Worcester, England. He is also a Visiting Professor at the University of Ibn Zohr, Business School, Agadir, Morocco. He has a particular interest in ways of leading effective early education practice and has produced a number of articles and book chapters on that theme, the latest of which explored leading collaborative engagement.

Lorraine Sands has worked as a teacher/researcher for the past 24 years at Greerton Early Childhood Centre. As a result of the collegial research undertaken there, Shared Leadership has become embedded in the fabric of the Learning and Teaching culture at this centre. This encourages a community of practice to develop where leadership is truly shared and fully distributed. Lorraine also works as a professional learning facilitator for Educational Leadership Project, supporting teachers to explore learning and teaching initiatives in their own settings. She is a fervent advocate of the critical nature of leadership and the ways in which it impacts on pedagogy.

Anthony Semann is an early childhood teacher who has directed an Aboriginal child and family service, and managed children's and family services for an inner city council in Sydney, Australia. Anthony developed a consultancy firm, Semann & Slattery with a colleague. As change and performance enhancement strategists, Semann & Slattery assist organisations and people who value quality, innovation and evidence based practice with an interest in transformational practices. Anthony holds a degree in education and a Masters degree in Sociology.

Andrew J. Stremmel is Professor and Department Head in Teaching, Learning and Leadership in the College of Education and Human Sciences at South Dakota State University. His research is in the area of early childhood teacher education, in particular, teacher action research and Reggio Emilia-inspired, inquiry-based approaches to early childhood teacher education and curriculum. He has published over 60 refereed journal articles and book chapters and has co-edited two books and co-authored two books. His book, *Teaching as inquiry: Rethinking curriculum in early childhood education* (2005, Allyn & Bacon) is the first comprehensive early childhood education text provoked and inspired by the Reggio Emilia Approach.

Jacqui Tapau is a descendent of the Kullilli and Kabi Kabi nations of the southwest and the sunshine coast of Queensland. She is currently the nominated supervisor of an 81 place early childhood service within her local Aboriginal community of Cherbourg, the home of the Wakka Wakka people. Working in the community has helped her with personal and academic growth. After 18 years of working in early childhood, she has completed her Bachelor of Teaching (Early Childhood Services) and is part of a Leadership Circle. She shares the belief of role modelling quality early childhood practices and training with her fellow educators and managers which can only benefit the families, children and community as a whole. She has four children, seven grandchildren and has helped raise her nephews and nieces.

Rosie Walker is a Senior Lecturer at the Department for Children and Families, School of Education, University of Worcester. She co-wrote *Success with your early years research project (2014)* and co-edited *A critical companion to early childhood (2015)* as well as writing journal articles. Professionally, she has managed two large children's centres and is a qualified social worker.

Manjula Waniganayake has been involved in the early childhood sector as a teacher, a parent, a policy analyst, a teacher educator, a researcher and a writer for over three decades. Her teaching and research interests cover childhood socialisation, family diversity, as well as educational leadership and quality assurance matters. She was awarded an Honorary Doctorate from the University of Tampere, Finland for her contribution to Early Childhood Leadership. Manjula has been working with colleagues from England, Estonia, Finland, Malaysia, Norway, Singapore, South Africa and Thailand. She believes in diversity and social justice. She values pedagogy and learning from others and considers teaching to be a noble profession.

PREFACE

Finding purpose and direction

This volume is a critical companion for those studying ways to lead early educational practice: a contemporary theme which is considered key to promoting quality experiences for children. It therefore introduces differing viewpoints, asks questions and encourages further study. Its production has involved many people, including the children, parents and professionals who allowed us to enter their worlds and capture day-to-day practice. It also involved drawing upon the expertise of experienced chapter authors, publishing editors and administrators, who worked together to make that practice visible and become much more than simply words on paper. It was a process which took a number of years to come to fruition and involved Series Editors locating people with expertise who could write about issues relevant for the advanced study of early education. It also involved the Volume Editors who have shaped and exposed issues within and between chapters in order to provoke critical thinking.

The series is therefore the product of a shared personal and professional community of practice and its ethos and design reflects the collaborative forms of leadership that you will read about in this volume. The growth and well-being of all participants in this educative process are key, particularly as the processes engage, support and extend children.

The volume itself, as with the other five volumes in this series, is divided into four interlocking sections:

- Being alongside children
- Those who educate
- Embedding families and communities
- Working with systems.

The sections represent key influences on pedagogical practice in action and should be regarded as interconnected themes which underpin pedagogical practice. They contain views intended to take the reader beyond known cultural, ethical and geographical boundaries and to explore contemporary practice in action. This is particularly important in an early educational world which appears to be struggling to find a balance in working to meet national regulatory requirements while developing local educational environments nurtured in relationships. These issues can be informed by and challenged through developing local interpretations of these larger ideas (Fleet, 2017) and considering what actually promotes professional decision-making and pedagogical leadership.

The chapters have been shaped by distinguished authors and accompanied by carefully constructed provocations from volume editors. Collectively, these provide insights and challenges for those seeking to be called pedagogical leaders and those who are already in roles incorporating this responsibility. The chapters should be seen as a professional invitation to examine existing practice, explore new philosophies and re-imagine practice.

It is a volume which therefore touches upon many facets of professional behaviour and asks questions about professional approaches to managing people and leading pedagogy. "Pedagogical leadership can involve coaching, mentoring, initiating professional conversations and modelling ethical practice in order to build the capacity of the staff team as curriculum decision-makers" (Waniganayake, Cheeseman, Fenech, Hadley, & Shepherd, 2017, p. 102).

This message underlines the need to carefully consider and understand differing and agreed professional practices and develop personal and professional questions about a wider intellectual and moral professional landscape. For example, who determines the accepted behaviour for a profession, to what extent is this a primary role for a leader? To what extent does contemporary professionalism mean the ability of a leader to understand the relationship between day-to-day pedagogical practices and meeting regulatory requirements? Where are the intersections between the cultures of the community, the lives of children and their families, and the responsibilities of pedagogical leaders?

Many of these questions are discussed and given prominence in the volume; the chapters also consider wider overlapping dimensions such as differing international professional practices and diverse institutional demands. They also interrogate the way provision varies in terms of scale and the extent to which it reaches out to local communities. They ask questions about differences in power, collaborative working, policy formation and how change has occurred and is managed. These are questions which we hope are useful not only as pointers for discussion, but potentially to prompt further study alongside professional colleagues.

Michael Reed & Alma Fleet

References

Fleet, A. 2017. The landscape of pedagogical documentation. In A. Fleet, C. Patterson, & J. Robertson (Eds.), *Pedagogical documentation in early years practice: Seeing through multiple perspectives*. London: SAGE.

Waniganayake, M., Cheeseman, S., Fenech, M., Hadley, F., & Shepherd, W. 2017. *Leadership: Contexts and complexities in early childhood education* (2nd ed.). South Melbourne: Oxford University Press.

Section 1

BEING ALONGSIDE CHILDREN

1

ENGAGING WITH DATA TO FOSTER CHILDREN'S LEARNING

From population data to local projects

Sandra Cheeseman

The last decade has seen increased attention to population data studies to inform early childhood policy and practice. Designed to capture broad trends in social, economic and education patterns, "big data", as these studies have come to be known, are increasingly cited as the "evidence base" for recommending policy approaches to early education and care. Taking a broad population view, big data studies aim to capture a macro-view of human experience. Capturing broad trends and changes in social, economic, health, and education outcomes, big data studies aggregate information and generate results, "... as a means of monitoring the status of early childhood development and then tracking progress over time" (Janus, Harrison, Goldfeld, & Guhn, 2016, p. 1). Not designed to capture the nuanced experience of the individual, or represent the complexity of lived experience, population data sets provide a helicopter view of life, a high-level overview. They require cautious and careful analysis, to avoid over-simplifying lived experience and representing life as quantifiable or measurable.

This chapter will examine the trend toward big data as it relates to early childhood policy and practice. Beginning with an international perspective and the announcement of the Organisation for Economic Coppoeration and Development's (OECD) International Early Learning Study (IELS) (OECD, 2015), I join others in problematising the status of international comparative work that is carried out through a standardised assessment of children's learning and development. I contemplate the potential of such instruments to generalise and

3

simplify the complexity of young children's lives and contribute to a narrowing focus on their early childhood experience, in order to achieve a limited range of desirable outcomes. In the second part of the chapter, I focus more specifically on the Australian context and findings from their early years population study, the Australian Early Development Census (AEDC). I conclude with a reflection on how Educational Leaders might be both challenged and inspired by their engagement with big data and contribute to meaningful understandings of early learning using their own wisdom, reflection and localised research in working alongside young children.

I come to this chapter with a background as an early childhood teacher with a more recent experience as a research academic. I draw on these two experiences to find synergies between research and practice and to advocate for the importance of the intellectual work of teachers as researchers in their daily practice. As a long-time proponent of localised qualitative studies, I have more recently recognised the need to get some "skin in the game" of big data studies. The chapter invites Educational Leaders to critically engage with the trend toward big data with a view to making informed contributions to its design and use. Moving from broad based population studies to locally contextualised practitioner inquiry projects may offer early childhood educators a way to contribute and influence big data conversations. In this way, Educational Leaders can capitalise on what big data studies offer but use them to shift conversations toward more democratic and inclusive understandings of the complexity of local contexts and the lived experience of young children.

An international trend

The world of big data in relation to young children has gained unprecedented momentum over the past decade both internationally and in Australia. In a relatively short space of time, advances in technology have enabled not only the capacity to collect and collate big data sets in ways that we have not known before, but now to also link data sets, and to correlate and compare findings from one source to others. For example, it is now possible to link population data to systems data generated through quality assurance schemes, and then later to school achievement standardised test results. Such linkages afford governments the capacity to connect the experiences of children in their early years settings with their later educational attainments. A confidence in these linkages and their assumed value appears to be an attractive option for governments attempting to design education policy based on science. The rhetoric is couched in terms of the end benefit to children, in better understanding how best to support their learning and development (OECD, 2015). Urban and Swadener (2016) note the persuasiveness of this, but question if such linkages will in fact lead to the desired aim of a more socially just and equitable future.

Confidence in big data relating to early childhood was signalled perhaps most clearly by the OECD's announcement to conduct an IELS (OECD, 2015).[1] While in the design stage, the purpose of the study was said to, "... provide countries with a common language and framework to learn from each other and, ultimately, to improve children's early learning experiences. Countries interested in this study are particularly focused on improving equity of outcomes for disadvantaged children" (OECD, 2015, p. 9).

The OECD's ambition to provide a "common language" and "framework" along with claims that such a study will improve equity outcomes, has been widely critiqued. In particular, Moss et al. (2016) warn of the potential of such a comparative work to reduce childhood to a series of desirable, narrow academic outcomes, all geared toward the production of a citizen measured by the capacity to contribute to national and global goals. Aimed at capturing information about children aged 4 to 5 years, the identified domains for assessment were determined as: self-regulation, oral language/emergent communication, mathematics/numeracy, executive function, locus of control and social skills. The domains identified draw on earlier work undertaken by University College, London, and have been affirmed by the OECD as being "... predictive of early learning skills" (OECD, 2017, p. 18). The explicit intent of the study states that

> In time, the information can also provide information on the trajectory between early learning outcomes and those at age 15, as measured by PISA. In this way, countries can have an earlier and more specific indication of how to lift the skills and other capabilities of its young people
>
> (OECD, 2015, p. 103)

While not dismissing this well-intentioned and interesting piece of work, the end point of PISA (Program for International Student

Assessment) (see OECD, 2018) – the academic performance of 15-year olds, on a selected dimension of human achievement – as the focus of determining what might shape the experiences of very young children, is somewhat concerning. The potential to reduce learning and development outcomes for ever-younger children to a handful of predictive characteristics, runs the risk of technicising early childhood programmes and promoting pedagogies that produce identifiable results on a limited range of outcomes (Moss et al., 2016; Pence, 2017; Urban & Swadener, 2016).

Vandenbroeck (as cited in European Early Childhood Education Research Association, 2017) argues that the claims of studies such as PISA reflect a myth, that "facts and objectivity... produce truth" (p. 4). Lister (2003, cited in Vandenbroeck, Roets, & Roose, 2012) warns of the propensity for governments to value measures based on predefined outcomes as the most valid form of research. "The evidence-based paradigm and the subsequent outcome-focused research, frame children as ciphers for future economic prosperity in becoming self-providing, autonomous and responsible individuals, rather than recognising them in what they are" (Vandenbroeck et al., 2012, p. 543). While considerable debate surrounds the collection, use and potential dangers of the International Early Learning and Child Well-Being Study (IEL&CWS) (see Moss et al., 2016), such population studies appear to be of increasing interest to governments seeking a scientific evidence base on which to establish policy decisions.

The rhetoric of big data is hard to contest. Seeking to overcome the impact of social and economic inequities and providing a knowledge base on which to plan for brighter futures, the promise of big data studies is indeed persuasive. Their potentials and limitations must, however, be critically examined to ensure that they do not supplant other notable research methods that provide rich understandings of human experience. Without such critical reflection, there is the risk of narrowing the focus on those dimensions that can easily be measured in a big data study while silencing or diminishing the importance of those things not so easily captured within big data methodologies.

The prominence and importance of school readiness

A further concern expressed about the focus on big data studies in early childhood is as Keating (2007) claims, their focus on young children as largely framed in terms of their "readiness for school" with a view to recommending strategies to mitigate the limitations for children who are "less ready" and help them overcome their "lack of readiness" (p. 562). Vandenbroeck et al. (2012) concur and warn that defining early childhood education and care (ECEC) as a preparation for school narrows the focus of ECEC and dismisses the views of parents, children and practitioners about other important aspects of learning and development. Secondly, they highlight that such a focus on the child being readied for school discredits and makes invisible the "... fundamentally pedagogical question: how can we make schools ready for diverse children and their parents?" (Vandenbroeck et al., 2012, p. 543).

The danger of population studies that frame the desirable end point as academic achievement in later schooling is that they have the potential to narrow the possible ways of constructing early childhood education and care programmes and direct attention to a relatively small number of desirable skills and attributes. Such assumptions have the potential to ignore the cultural, social and historical diversity that underpin children's rights and run the risk of privileging particular ways of being and knowing. My position at this point is not to suggest that there is no place for population studies, but I caution that big data studies have the potential to mislead and provide a false sense of confidence if not treated with a high level of analysis and contextualisation. Understanding the purpose and limitations of big data studies is the first step in using them wisely

An Australian example of big data – the Australian Early Development Census (AEDC)

In 2009, the Australian Government commissioned the Australian Early Development Index (AEDI). Based on a Canadian population data instrument – the Early Development Instrument (EDI) was designed to measure the developmental health and well-being of populations of young children (Australian Government, 2018a). The triennial data collection based on the AEDI is now known as the Australian Early Development Census (AEDC) (Australian Government, 2018b). Data collection is held every three years, with collection in 2009, 2012, 2015 and 2018. The census involves teachers of children in their first year of full-time school (at approximately age 5) completing a research tool that collects data relating to five key areas of early childhood development referred to as "domains". Table 1.1 shows the five development domains and descriptors that form the basis of the AEDC data collection.

Similar to the IEL&CWS, the AEDC domains have been shown to predict later health, education and social outcomes (Australian Government, 2013). Importantly and similar to the IEL&CWS, the AEDC is not a screening tool and is thus not intended for individual diagnostic purposes (Goldfeld, Sayers, Brinkman, Silburn, & Oberklaid, 2009). The AEDC data is used by communities, policy-makers and researchers "to review the status of children's development and to guide service planning to improve children's outcomes" (O'Connor et al., 2016, p. 33).

As stated, the purpose and intent of the AEDC has merit. In capturing trends, the information gained can provide a useful starting point for reflecting on how Australian children are faring and where more supports might be useful. While acknowledging that the AEDC was never designed for service level interpretation, the trends highlighted in the data can be important starting points for early childhood professionals to engage in the critical conversations that are generated by the introduction of big data studies in shaping policy and programmes for young children. The purpose of the critiques raised in this chapter are to invite conversations among early childhood Educational Leaders about the strengths and limitations of the AEDC in relation to their work and to better understand how big data can inform critical conversations about early childhood programme delivery. It is equally an opportunity to explore the potential for the results of big data to be interpreted

Table 1.1 Descriptions of the AEDC development domains

Domain	Icon	Domain description
Physical health and wellbeing		Children's physical readiness for the school day, physical independence and gross and fine motor skills.
Social competence		Children's overall social competence, responsibility ans respect, approach to learning and reading to explore new things.
Emotional maturity		Children's pro-social and helping behaviours and absence of anxious and fearful behaviour, aggressive behaviour and hyperactivity and inattention.
Language and cognitive skills (school-based)		Children's basic literacy, interest in literacy, numeracy and memory, advanced literacy and basic numeracy.
Communication skills and general knowledge		Children's communication skills and general knowledge based on broad developmental competencies and skills.

simplistically and to limit the scope and possibilities for early childhood programmes.

Any attempt to reduce the experiences of young children to five discrete domains will inevitably hide or silence other important domains of learning and experience. Less easily measured or observed characteristics of learning and development can be over-looked and ultimately eliminated from a holistic pedagogical approach, in favour of the evidence identifying the known predictive factors. No instrument that collects data on the AEDC scale will ever provide a complete picture of what we really need to know about the children we work with. It can provide some information in much the same away as a litmus test will show the presence or absence of acid or alkaline. It does little to show us what concentra-tion, the extent of the influence or the how harmful or useful the presence or absence might be across a range of contexts.

Aggregated data from the AEDC is presented in interactive tables on a public website. The tables outline national, state and territory, region and locality (to the level of postcode/zipcode). Figure 1.1 shows an example of one local area (Herston in Queensland) giving comparative results across the five domains in the 2015 census.

In this table, the vertical axis on the left shows the percentage of children across Australia that, according to the AEDC, start school with vulnerabilities in each domain. Along the horizontal axis, the results for each domain of development are shown (from left to right), for Austra-lian (national average), the state (Queensland), then the region (inner Brisbane) and finally the local area of the suburb of Herston (Australian Government, 2018b). The two categories on the far right of the table note the percentage of children who are shown to have vulnerabilities in one domain and then the percentage of children who show vulnerabil-ities on two or more domains. Of note is that the national figures (bars to the left of each domain) show that in Australia, over 20% of children in their first year of school are identified as having some form of vulnerability, with more than half of those children showing vulnerabil-ities on more than one domain.

In Inner Brisbane/Herston, more than one in five (almost one in four) children start school with one of these vulnerabilities – higher than the Australian average – and just less than the state average. In looking at this table, the areas of physical skill and emotional vulner-ability are particularly concerning where over 15% of children start school with vulnerabilities in these areas. In fact, all areas of

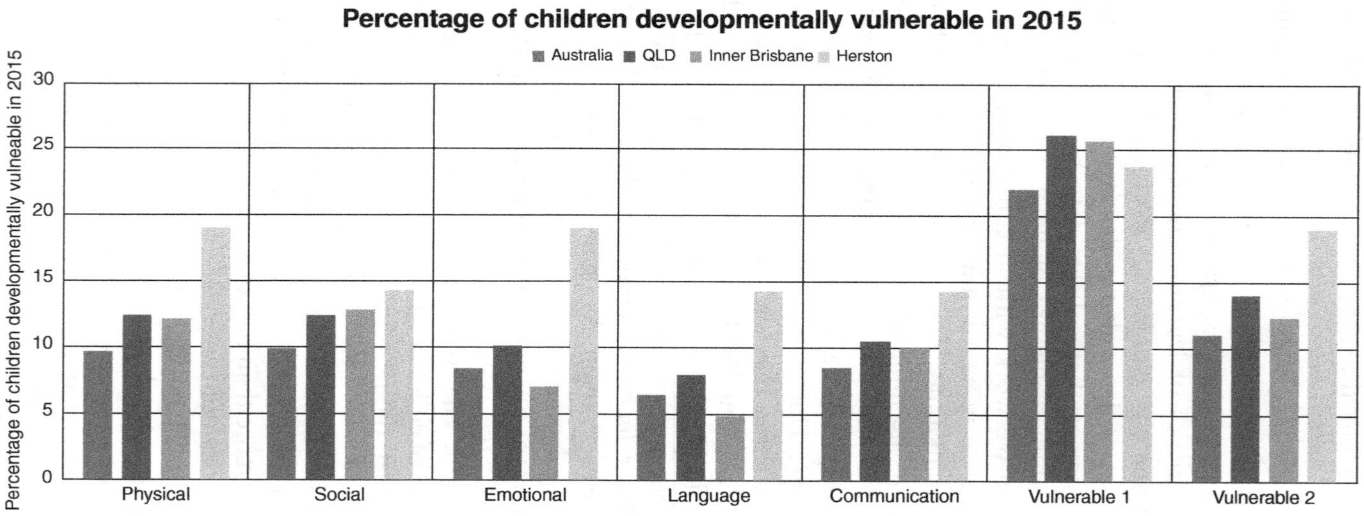

Figure 1.1 Percentage of children developmentally vulnerable in 2015

development are concerning for a number of children in these communities. What is worrying in this table are the number of children with two or more vulnerabilities.

The information provided in these tables is difficult to ignore. We can criticise the narrow focus of the measures and we can warn of the limitations of viewing children on such a limited range of dimensions. We must acknowledge as Keating (2007) attests, there are risks to this type of work. In his closing commentary to the first Special Issue on the EDI, in *Early Education & Development*, Keating outlined the challenges that were ahead, considering the methodological approach used by the EDI. He argued that the benefits of collecting population-level data with the EDI did not come without risks, and that the way to mitigate those risks was to identify them and then "carry out well-designed research studies that minimise the potential risk" (p. 565). Understanding and identifying those risks is the starting point for working wisely with such data.

Having presented a case for caution in relation to big data studies, I now wish to propose that the trend toward a confidence in big data cannot be ignored by early childhood leaders. For the immediate future at least, big data is here and present and increasingly relied on to inform policy and practice. It is after all the aim of big data studies to create certainty in approaches to early childhood education that will better equip children to be more successful in their later school years. It is difficult to argue with a strategy or approach that promises to ensure more equitable outcomes for children from their ECEC experience, but it is also naive to trust that a magic bullet, with one streamlined application, can rescue children from disadvantage and create utopian worlds for all. While most would agree that such ideals are unlikely to be realised through over-simplified solutions derived from big data sets, the issues of equality and equity of educational experience should be a concern for all educators. As Australia's pedagogic guide, the Early Years Learning Framework (EYLF) suggests, two fundamental questions should underpin the work of all educators:

- **Who is advantaged when I work in this way?**
- **Who is disadvantaged?** (Australian Government Department of Education Employment and Workplace Relations, 2009, p. 13).

As part of critical conversations, these questions offer the opportunity for Educational Leaders to work wisely with the presence of big data studies and complement their limitations with localised, contextualised and authoritative work. Early childhood educators working alongside children may feel little reason to engage with big data or its findings. It is, after all, directed at policy-makers and not directed at those working at the individual child or setting level. The results of big data studies, however, are gaining increasing exposure and are cited often as evidence underpinning policy directions. As discussed earlier in this chapter, early childhood educators should be alert to the power of big data studies to ultimately shape the experiences of children and the work of educators at the local level.

What do early childhood educators need to know about big data?

Big data does not answer questions: it provides high-level views about trends and can only provide information about the specific criteria used in the measures. Big data measures use very blunt instruments. Rating scales, yes/no options and "observed or not observed" checklists are the favoured instruments for gathering broad generalisable data. The weakness of big data is that it is not able to capture the complexity of any situation, the reasons why something was not observed or the variation in circumstances that may have influenced the event measured on a particular day or time. Used wisely, big data should encourage us to ask more questions. At its best, big data can encourage us to ask better and deeper questions.

Big data is blunt: it does not measure everything we need to know. We must add value to big data; if we don't we are missing what really matters. Big data is the starting point. Those working alongside children have the skills and knowledge to dig deeper, understand the importance of the context and most importantly, to keep an eye on individuals and variation within the limitations of what blunt instruments can measure.

Big data is dangerous if used in isolation: it is not generalisable to a smaller group. Big data shows trends among large numbers of children and is misleading if assumed that what applies to the broader population applies to all sections of the population. For example, the AEDC shows that in the suburb of Herston, Queensland (see Figure 1.1), almost 25% of children start school with one or more vulnerabilities. This does not necessarily mean that 25% of the children in any particular setting within Herston, will also have these vulnerabilities. The big data shows that there may be cause for concern across a community, but more specific, more nuanced information is needed before assuming that this trend is relevant in any particular setting. This is where Educational Leaders can use the big data available for their locality to lead conversations about the translation from the big data findings to the important questions for the children in their setting or context.

Striving for equity

What population studies such as the AEDC have revealed is the difference in young children's experiences in their first five years. The AEDC has shown that across Australia there remains an unacceptable divide in both opportunity and outcome between the poorest and wealthiest communities, between cities and very remote towns, and between children from different cultural backgrounds. Drawing on the AEDC data and assessment of children on five domains of learning, the Mitchell Institute has recently reported that more than one in five Australian children start school with vulnerabilities that can make it hard for them to take up the opportunities that schooling provides (O'Connell, Fox, Hinz, & Cole, 2016). This report also suggested that a third of Australian children do not attend preschool for the number of hours needed to make a difference and that children in poorer communities have fewer high quality services available to them.

Big data can be the starting point for recognising how significant early gaps in experience can be for children. It can help to think about ways to differentiate approaches to early childhood, not only across communities but within and among groups of children. These critical conversations can ensure a broad and contextually relevant response and ensure that simplistic and generalised solutions do not drive the programme. In choosing to be critical consumers of big data, I am proposing that big data can assist educators to find more equitable ways of working with children – where all children experience the advantages of high quality and relevant early childhood education and care.

From big data to localised projects

Drawing on Keating's (2007) advice that population studies must sit alongside other forms of research, the later part of this chapter will focus

13

on how big data studies can generate important conversations among educators, families and children and be the impetus for more localised and nuanced work that reflects local priorities and individual differences. I will use the example of a research methodology known as Practitioner Inquiry (PI), to show how teachers working with young children can respond to the findings of big data studies but extend, enrich and contextualise those findings within a localised context. For many years the academic literature has reported on this style of research which is undertaken by teachers, alongside the children and families that they work with. In their extensive work with teachers using PI, Fleet, De Gioia, and Patterson (2016, p. 5) reflect that the value of this model of inquiry, "benefits from a relationship-based context in which reflective practice positions educators alongside children".

The following is one example of a PI project that took place in a Sydney early childhood setting in 2013 as part of a funded pilot. The project explored how Educational Leaders could use PI to introduce their staff to the recently launched EYLF. In looking at the EYLF and its recommendations for rich play-based numeracy experiences for children, alongside the 2012 AEDC data for the region in which their centre was located, Karen, a centre director, led her team in a critical conversation about the AEDC which led them to a consideration of how numeracy experiences, and in particular patterning, was available to their children. Karen and her team recognised their own lack of confidence with mathematics. They were aware of the research suggesting patterning as an important foundation for both literacy and numeracy so sought to better understand what their children knew about patterns and how they might be more intentional in their provisions of opportunities for children to engage and play with patterns.

Karen and her team started with observation of how children engaged with patterning concepts in their everyday play. When patterning materials were provided they observed carefully how the children engaged and what they showed an interest in finding out more about. Importantly, they did not simply jump to the most obvious solution and provide more maths activities based on the AEDC findings for their general community. They gathered their own base-line data to inform their approach to their work with the children and based their planning on what the children already showed an interest in. Their base-line data revealed a limited use of patterning in play and quite shallow understanding of the potentials

14

of the materials that were offered to the children. The staff read widely and drew on related studies that directed them to a range of possible approaches. The staff team became more aware themselves of the importance of patterning in children's mathematical understandings and explored a range of materials that they could introduce to the children.

Starting with the resources that were readily available to them, they noticed that their intentional provisioning of the environment and support for children's play with pattern soon translated into a keen interest of many children in the group. They then expanded the range of materials offered, extending to many collections initiated by the children of gathered items – for example, natural materials such as leaves, gumnuts, twigs and pine cones. After three months, the educators gathered further data and noticed a remarkable change in the way the children engaged with patterns, talked about and explained their patterns and supported each other to create ever more complex patterns.

This small-scale localised project made a significant impact on children's engagement with important foundational knowledge about patterns. It is one example of how a dedicated team of educators, inspired by their Educational Leader, were able to smoothly incorporate an important piece of inquiry into their everyday practice. This team made a difference to both their confidence to offer meaningful patterning play and improve the children's sophistication in working with the materials as a result of those initial conversations about big data and related research. The example provides a glimpse into an approach that can assist early childhood teachers to engage with big data conversations and offer important contributions to the way that data might be interpreted and acted upon. Far from concerns about big data shaping the work of early childhood teachers, this team of educators positioned themselves as experts who could read the data, interpret it using their own localised knowledge, and shape their practice in ways that they could be confident would work meaningfully with their children.

Conclusion

Much has been written to contest the prominence of the reductionist potentials of big data as the leading source of influence in early childhood education and care policy and practice. In this chapter, I take the view that the trend toward standardised assessment of young children is limiting and requires the wisdom and intellect of those who work alongside children to become meaningful. The potential of big data studies to shape programmes and determine learning directions while being blind to important aspects of children's lives have been examined. This chapter acknowledges and supports this debate, but seeks to find ways to cross borders between opposing views of big data and its use in the early childhood context – finding a place for local practitioner inquiry to work alongside big data to enhance its limitations. This chapter suggests that Educational Leaders can – and must – be critical consumers of big data. They must understand the intents, methodologies and assumptions that big data produce and work thoughtfully to shape the findings within the framework of the local, cultural, economic and political context of their early childhood settings.

Note

1 Note that in 2017 the Project title was changed to the International Early Learning and Child Well-Being Study, (IEL&CWS).

References

Australian Government. (2013). *A snapshot of early childhood development in Australia 2012 – AEDI national report re-issue November 2013.* Canberra: Australian Government.

Australian Government. (2018a). *The Australian Early Development Census. About the AECD.* Retrieved from www.aedc.gov.au/about-the-aedc

Australian Government. (2018b). *Australian Early Development Census.* Retrieved from www.aedc.gov.au/

Australian Government Department of Education Employment and Workplace Relations. (2009). *Belonging, being and becoming. The Early Years Learning Framework for Australia.* Retrieved from http://files.acecqa.gov. au/files/National-Quality-Framework-Resources-Kit/belonging_bein g_and_becoming_the_early_years_learning_framework_for_australia.pdf

European Early Childhood Education Research Association. (2017). 27th EECERA annual conference abstract book. *Paper Presented at the Social Justice, Solidarity and Children's Rights Conference*, Bologna, Italy.

Fleet, A., De Gioia, K., & Patterson, C. (Eds.). (2016). *Engaging with educational change: Voices of practitioner inquiry.* London: Bloomsbury.

Goldfeld, S., Sayers, M., Brinkman, S., Silburn, S., & Oberklaid, F. (2009). The process and policy challenges of adapting and implementing the Early Development Instrument in Australia. *Early Education and Development*, 20(6), 978–991.

Janus, M., Harrison, L. J., Goldfeld, S., & Guhn, M. (2016). International research utilizing the Early Development Instrument (EDI) as a measure of early child development: Introduction to the special issue. *Early Childhood Research Quarterly, 35,* 1–5.

Keating, D. (2007). Formative evaluation of the Early Development Instrument: Progress and prospects. *Early Education & Development, 18*(3), 561–570.

Moss, P., Dahlberg, G., Grieshaber, S., Mantovani, S., May, H., Pence, A., & Vandenbroeck, M. (2016). The OECD's early learning study: Opening for debate and contestation. *Contemporary Issues in Early Childhood, 17*(3), 343–351.

O'Connell, M., Fox, S., Hinz, B., & Cole, H. (2016). *Quality early education for all: Fostering creative, entrepreneurial, resilient and capable learners.* Retrieved from www.mitchellinstitute.org.au/wp-content/uploads/2016/04/Quality-Early-Education-for-All-FINAL.pdf

O'Connor, M., Gray, S., Tarasuika, J., O'Connor, E., Kvalsvig, A., Incledona, E., & Goldfeld, S. (2016). Preschool attendance trends in Australia: Evidence from two sequential population cohorts. *Early Childhood Research Quarterly, 35,* 31–39.

Organisation for Economic Cooperation and Development. (2015). *Call for tenders: International.* Early Learning study 100001420. Retrieved from www.oecd.org/callsfortenders/CfT%20100001420%20International%20Early%20Learning%20Study.pdf

Organisation for Economic Cooperation and Development. (2017). *International early learning and well-being study.* Retrieved from www.oecd.org/edu/school/the-international-early-learning-and-child-well-being-study-the-study.htm

Organisation for Economic Cooperation and Development. (2018). *Programme for International Student Assessment (PISA).* Retrieved from www.oecd.org/pisa/

Pence, A. (2017). *Baby Pisa: Dangers that can arise when foundations shift: A call and commentary.* Retrieved from https://journals.uvic.ca/index.php/jcs/article/view/16549/7044

Urban, M., & Swadener, B. B. (2016). Democratic accountability and contextualised systemic evaluation. A comment on the OECD initiative to launch and international early learning study (IELS). *International Critical Childhood Policy Studies, 5*(1), 6–18.

Vandenbroeck, M., Roets, G., & Roose, R. (2012). Why the evidence-based paradigm in early childhood education and care is anything but evident. *European Early Childhood Education Research Journal, 20*(4), 537–552. doi:10.1080/1350293X.2012.737238

2

LEADING PEDAGOGICAL PRACTICE

Co-constructing Learning between educators and children

Rebecca Dalgleish

The metaphor of the mind of the infant as a blank slate has been challenged (Goswami, 2008). Young children have a willingness and capability to learn; brain structures at birth are capable of putting together theories, possible answers, analogies and metaphors. Yet genes alone cannot determine cognitive structures, rather gene expression is controlled by the environment (Goswami, 2008). These cognitive structures become active before they are fully mature and therefore activity shapes their development – the environment that we facilitate as adults is key to the cognitive development/epigenetic expression of the child.

The setting for the research reported in this chapter is a well-established, urban pre-school setting that has been graded "Outstanding" by Ofsted (Office for Standards in Education, Children's Services and Skills, 2015) for their last two inspections. Within the setting there are 17 children aged 3 and 4 years and four staff including myself, the manager. Co-constructing Learning (CCL) with children is already in practice in the setting and as the manager of that setting I engaged in praxeological research in order to determine how CCL is achieved within it. Ensuring relational ethicality to maintain my role as practitioner/manager/insider-researcher simultaneously required extra care to not take for granted that the successful day-to-day interactions, relationships and dialogues that take place normally would automatically continue through the research process. Respect for those most closely involved, reflexivity, and a heightened self-awareness of the way in which I conducted myself ensured those involved in the research were accurately represented and fairly treated (Callan, Picken, & Foster, 2011).

The selection of praxeology as the methodological approach for this research was underpinned by other carefully selected methodological tools such as ethnography and appreciative inquiry, due to the unique circumstances that being a professional practitioner brings. Ethnographic methods were used to underpin the process of this research. A narrative description of the perspective of the child and the adult's interactions with the child was captured through the use of pedagogical documentation (Rinaldi, 1998). This was generated by the interactions of staff and children and through conversations with a purpose that occurred at the beginning or end of a session where staff discussed CCL that had occurred during the previous session.

Research was organic; staff acted as they normally would during their role. The following three examples of CCL emerged over the course of a ten-week period: Firstly, a singular episode of CCL involving one child and one adult exploring the concept of electricity through construction; secondly, a series of episodes of CCL over a period of weeks involving the whole group and all adults exploring tadpoles; thirdly, an extended episode of CCL over a week involving a small group and one adult exploring dinosaurs. Documentation took the form of floor book planning, discourse, mind maps, display panels and photographs.

This chapter aims to engage others in critically examining practice to generate reflections that are real, tangible and have applicable results that make meaningful contributions to immediate work. Hopefully, others in similar situations may also be able to repeat these methods and reach their own probably different but equally applicable results. The chapter examines what is understood by the theory of CCL, how CCL can be achieved, and how it can be incorporated into the curriculum (see Figure 2.1). This will elucidate what constitutes CCL in its everyday form – the nuts and bolts of it – to empower readers to reflect on their own practice and work towards conditions that are favourable for its perpetuation. Threaded throughout the chapter are reflective questions designed for the reader to pause, reflect and discuss with colleagues.

Theory of CCL

The roots of CCL lie within socio-cultural theory. Progressive perspectives – emphasising children as individuals and the decentring of adult authority – and socio-cultural perspectives, agree that both what is

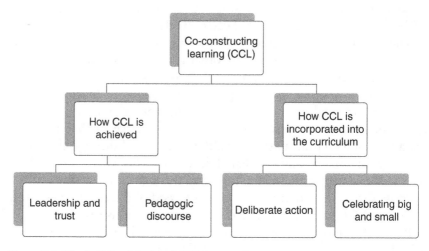

Figure 2.1 The building blocks of CCL in practice

present in the setting, and how children interact within the setting with their peers, artefacts, and adults, are important for intellectual development (Soler & Miller, 2003). Socio-cultural theory states that cognitive educational development is a cultural process; knowledge is not only possessed individually but shared amongst members of communities with people constructing knowledge and understandings jointly. Children and adults co-construct learning and meaning-making through joint interactional discourse (Vygotsky & Cole, 1978): language is used culturally to share knowledge within a community, and psychologically to process individual thought. Using language socially positively affects psychological cognition, enabling new thinking. When knowledge is viewed as socially constructed, and not as a list of skills and facts to be transmitted from adult to child, it is possible to interpret knowledge as dynamic, with multiple meanings – a construction between community members through discursive practice. It is through discursive interactions that co-construction of learning is negotiated through the sharing and consideration of multiple perspectives. The internalisation of this contributes significantly to an individual's problem-solving, knowledge construction and self-regulation skills, amongst other central psychological functions (Rojas-Drummond, Albarran, & Littleton, 2008). Socio-cultural theory espouses a process view of knowledge which is determined by the quality of educational dialogues rather than being the result of the intrinsic capability of individual children or the didacticism of adults

(Mercer & Littleton, 2007). Thus, co-construction between adults and children relies upon recognition of the importance of advancing thinking, not just replicating thinking or transmitting facts. As Rinaldi (1998, p. 118) states: "the potential of children is stunted when the endpoint of their learning is formulated in advance".

> • In what ways is thinking shared between adults and children within your setting? Are there opportunities for learning outcomes to be left unprescribed?

CCL is built upon a fundamental foundation of the child as having rights. Malaguzzi (1997) describes how children have the right to be recognised as both the "source and constructors of their own experience" and should therefore be "active participants in the organisation of their identities, abilities and autonomy" (p. 214). Such thinking mirrors the United Nations Convention on the Rights of the Child (United Nations General Assembly, 1989) articles 12 and 13 that state that children capable of forming their own views have the right to express them freely in matters concerning themselves and to seek, receive and impart information and ideas of all kinds. When children therefore are recognised as having rights, they are viewed as active citizens and contributing members of their communities. Within CCL, children have the opportunities to express their views, be listened to, and be regarded as powerful, competent protagonists able to occupy the primary active role in their learning (Mercilliott Hewett, 2001). MacNaughton, Hughes, and Smith (2007) believe children know the world in different ways to adults and sharing their insights can improve adults' understandings of children's perspectives. They therefore encourage adults to engage in "equitable, collaborative adult-child relationships" (p.168) in order to recognise the right of children's contributions and expertise.

> • In which ways are children's voices heard, deliberately sought and visibly valued within your setting?

Aligning the social-culturalism of CCL with upholding children's rights requires recognition and acceptance of multiple ways of knowing. If knowledge is actively being socially constructed, it is fluid, dynamic and ever-changing and therefore, no ultimate truth can be realised. Multiple ways of knowing borrows heavily from the work of Gardner (1995); his theory of multiple intelligences and the utilisation of these in early childhood practice is knowing and being aware of these different learning modes and the different ways of viewing children and the ways in which they exhibit intelligence. Approaching learning through co-construction facilitates a number of perspectives and because children do not all learn in the same way, more children will be reached, a term Gardner (p. 207) describes as "multiple windows leading into the same room". Understanding can also be demonstrated in more than one way; children can explain and communicate their knowledge in ways that are comfortable for them and accessible to others. The following is an example taken from documentation of a child explaining their knowledge of electricity through construction.

CHILD: I think electricity ... it floats out of the wall in the plug like this (*runs around wiggling hands. Child then runs into the outdoor classroom and comes back with some white polystyrene blocks and drops them in a pile on the grass.*)

PRACTITIONER: What is that for?

CHILD: Well that's the light for the torch ...

PRACTITIONER: Okay, can I help?

CHILD: (*Hands practitioner a building brick.*) Can you put that there? (*Points to grass and adds more bricks, making part of a rectangle shape around the "light".*)

PRACTITIONER: What is happening here?

CHILD: This is where the electricity goes through the wires to the light but I think there's other bits in there, like all colour bits to help the electricity get through the wires.

PRACTITIONER: Let me see if I can find anything... (*They look again in the outdoor classroom and decide on smaller coloured mega-blocks. Child uses them to complete the rectangle enclosure around the light.*)

PRACTITIONER: Wow...you really know about electricity! How does the electricity get into the light?

CHILD: Well that's when you plug it in and you charge it. (*Child gets several cricket bats and protrudes them from the enclosure along with some other smaller items.*)

PRACTITIONER: So that's how it works then...the electricity?

CHILD: Oh, hold on. (*Child adds a tennis racquet at the end of the line of cricket bats.*) You flip the switch here (*jumps on racquet*), and the electricity whooshes up the chargers (*runs along bats*) the coloured bits can make different coloured electricity so it looks cool and then up to the light (*stops running at the light polystyrene*).

PRACTITIONER: I've learnt so much! Can I try being the electricity? Child nods. As the practitioner sets off from the "switch" another child walks across it with a watering can and accidentally spills water on some of the bricks.

CHILD: Hey get off! You be careful!

PRACTITIONER: You can't mix water and electricity, can you?

CHILD: Why? Would it explode?

PRACTITIONER: I think that if you got water on a charger it would probably bang and stop working. What do you think?

CHILD: I think you would get lightning and it would all explode and there would be a great big massive fireball! (*Child then is quite animated by this idea and goes to get water to tip on the "light", the light "explodes" as the child scatters the pieces and makes explosion noises.*)

When the class returns to the classroom, child and adult use the internet to look at wiring and find out why you can't put water onto electricity.

This extract demonstrates what Malaguzzi (1997) terms the "hundred languages of children", a belief that children are competent citizens capable of expressing themselves in a hundred different ways, for example, through drawing, speaking, writing, creating music and movement, constructing, sculpting, and painting to name a few. Malaguzzi's work in Reggio Emilia relies on the belief that the goal of education is not to replicate thinking, but to advance thinking, a realisation achievable through co-constructing with the child to encourage the use of various forms of expression of knowledge, thus enabling the creation and development of multiple forms of knowing.

> • **In your setting consider whether children's differing intelligences are recognised and valued.**

How CCL is achieved

The significance of relationships and encounters in early years settings should not be understated as the learning environment is not just a physical one (Rinaldi, 2006), but also comprises the interrelationships between adults and children where reciprocity (Smith, 2009) is key: communication, mutual interests, respect, sharing and negotiating. Ensuring CCL is visible therefore requires certain conditions. Firstly, pedagogical discourse provides a medium that affords a gathering together of protagonists to work together in reciprocity and with agency – the "feeling you can make a difference, to your own life and to other people's" (Roberts, 2010, p. 49). Secondly, practising democratic leadership at a management-staff level and at an adult-child level offers an environment that encourages and celebrates the potential of collaborative working and the opportunity to role-model this to children.

Pedagogical discourse

Pedagogical discourse is an integral part of settings where children are viewed as active subjects with rights, knowledge as the construction of meaning, and learning as the process of construction based on relationships and listening that makes learning visible. Pedagogical documentation is a method used to capture children's learning experiences systematically and then sharing this with the children, provoking pedagogical discourse, reflection, and assessment. Dahlberg, Moss, and Pence (2006) describe the "content" of pedagogical documentation as material that records children's interactions, their work and how the pedagogue relates to the children and their work. This can take many forms such as observations, photographs, work products, discussions and so on. They also describe the "process" of documentation as using content generated as a means to promote discourse, reflection, interpretation and negotiation by all protagonists involved, including children, staff and parents. This can range from discursive action whilst engaging in CCL, such as this extract from documentation concerning work with frogs: "*We've got to do a bit each or we'll lose them…you hold the net and I'll scoop the water*", to this adult discourse from conversations with a purpose: "*it just seems so organic and natural, the unpicking and resewing of ideas, opinions and views*". This tangible negotiation between process and content is what distinguishes pedagogical documentation

(Katz & Chard, 1996) and is essential to making CCL visible within a setting.

The various adults involved with the children bring together their different perspectives and interpretations to the reflection phase of documentation enabling evaluation, searching for meaning about the children's engagements, curiosities, explorations, interpretations, and expressions, and becoming aware of the value of the learning that has taken place. For all stakeholders involved in CCL, understanding means being able to develop an interpretive "theory" (Rinaldi, 2001), a narration that gives meaning to events and objects of the world. Discourse may involve uncertainty. Looking back at pedagogical documentation often shows comments from all stakeholders such as "*I just don't know*", "*I question myself*" or "*How can we find out?*" – the uncertainty doesn't end the discourse but actually gives life to it. These theories are provisional, offering satisfactory explanations that can be continuously reworked, but are an expression of each stakeholder's point of view. For example, staff comment "*And we would say 'well why do you think it does, how can we find out?'*", and similarly one child in response to the question "*How could we find out about tadpoles?*" was confident to say: "*Well, I don't know but I've got an insect book about frogs at home but I've lost it now, but I have got a book, so we can look at books*". Staff and children knowing that exposing these vulnerabilities will not stunt further investigation and that their queries will be recognised, valued and acted upon, is pedagogic discourse in action and a key element of achieving CCL.

Democratic leadership

Democratic leadership creates scope for an environment that values each stakeholder's point of view in CCL and provides opportunities for role-modelling of and engagement in democratic learning. In order for leaders in early education settings to work democratically they "need to support others to understand the current reality, what the new reality will be, and how, collectively, they might get there" (Garvey & Lancaster, 2010, p. 73).

Therefore, a traditional form of structural "top-down" leadership (Bush, 1995), where hierarchy exists and relationships are vertical and normative would not support the stakeholders within the setting (staff, parents and children) to engage in democracy as this relies upon horizontal relationships and democratic participation to

25

respect each stakeholder's position. Furthermore, structural models tend not to recognise parents as part of the system. A distributed model of leadership (Spillane, Halverson, & Diamond, 2007) allows the move from bureaucratic practice to collaborative practice that acknowledges stakeholders' different knowledge and responsibility areas. This model moves the leader from an exclusive role to one that involves "brokering, facilitating and supporting others in leading innovation and change" (Harris, 2012, p. 8).

> • **What personal and professional qualities are required to employ democratic leadership?**

Democratic participation is essential in an early years setting where children and adults who care for and/or work with them have the right to participate in forming decisions that affect them. This is the prime environment for the development of new thinking and new practice (Moss, 2007), particularly in relation to engaging in CCL. Settings committed to engaging in CCL require using a distributed perspective lens so varying pedagogies, standpoints and expertise can be recognised, valued, developed and utilised in achieving outcomes for children. Pedagogical leadership then, from a distributed perspective, must empower stakeholders to see how the collective vision can be interpreted at a local level and how it relates to their personal values and espoused pedagogy. A genuine belief that each person has a different strength and perspective is a direct outcome from practice within a setting of distributed leadership – from management level, staff level and child level. The ability to negotiate, trust and share decision making with each other is role-modelled in a multitude of instances. Data from this study indicated that listening to others, valuing their perspective and engaging in discourse was key to successful CCL. This was illustrated by often-used phrases such as *"teamwork"* and *"learning together"* or as one child neatly put it *"[friend] is really good at it, he showed me how"*. Conversations with a purpose revealed a genuine inherent commitment to democracy amongst practitioners who are experienced and confident enough to listen and learn from others, share their thoughts and revise their understandings if necessary. This was described as *"Staff trust in children, in the creative process, in themselves and in each other"*, and *"Bouncing ideas off each other,*

26

looking for insight or just a different take". Trusting in each other at all levels of involvement may not be an innate characteristic of a setting, even though children have a strong desire to be social creatures, but something that must be nurtured and strengthened over time through role-modelling of democratic practice at every possibility. For example, instances of management role-modelling being recognised and repeated were captured in conversations with a purpose: *"I followed your lead and tried the same approach with the quieter ones on the fringes"*, and in appreciative inquiry interviews: *"It all filters along really, (you) consult and involve and discuss with us; we do the same with each other and the children, and then the children do the same with each other"*. It is clear that distributed leadership and trust are symbiotic – trust in others is required to employ a distributed model of leadership and practitioners and children must trust in distributed leadership in order to enact their roles.

> • **How are practitioners approaching the sharing of information and thoughts, and describing their interactions with children?**

How CCL learning is incorporated into the curriculum

Placing pedagogy into the curriculum requires examination of childhood education models that involve a theoretical and knowledge base (Siraj-Blatchford, 2007). Through comparison of approaches worldwide that are founded on solid, but differing, theoretical and knowledge bases – such as Reggio Emilia in Italy, and Effective Early Learning Practice in the UK – Siraj-Blatchford (2013) indicated key areas of pedagogy involved in democratic learning. These include how adults extend children's enquiries and the nature of dialogues, interactions and sustained shared thinking between adults and children. Sustained shared thinking occurs when individuals work together intellectually to solve a problem, clarify a concept, evaluate activities or extend narratives (Siraj-Blatchford, 2013); a description that could serve to underpin the notion of CCL. This was evident during the research both from staff posing reflexive questions to each other such as *"I wonder how much my preferences influence their decisions"* to a child making the statement *"when one person has an idea, everybody has to listen to them"*. Trevarthen (2006) describes how in a community of learners, children have an innate motivation and curiosity to learn. Laevers (2005) found "involvement" to be a crucial factor in quality learning, believing that satisfaction derived from involvement comes from an exploratory drive, and an intrinsic interest in how things and people are – the urge to experience and figure out. Laevers (2005) denotes curiosity, exploratory drive and flow as essential factors in deep-level-learning. Csikszentmihalyi (2002) suggests the term "flow" to describe the optimal state of total engagement in an activity, and the key to achieving flow is to pursue an activity for its own sake rather than for the rewards it brings. Achieving flow then transcends Aristotelian concepts of engaging in activity to gain rewards or avoid punishment, and instead comes from the fulfilment of absorption in an activity. Together these literature sources highlight that children's innate competencies include the motivation and capacity to explore, enquire, and to research the world around them for their own intrinsic aims. Yan (2005, p. 145) suggests that in the process of enquiry, children initially construct "naïve theories" and it is the practitioner's role not just to value these but to encourage further consideration and research alongside them. Incorporating CCL into the curriculum then requires two commitments: deliberate action and celebration of the big and small.

Deliberate action

Deliberate action from practitioners is key to ensuring the sustained shared thinking and democracy concomitant to CCL. It will not happen by chance. Time for CCL needs to deliberately be set amongst other demands of the curriculum. In the examples being shared here, staff were concerned both with CCL not being swallowed up by other activities, restraints and commitments, and children having sufficient time to engage in CCL – both of which require deliberate provision of time. Further to this, not only does CCL require allotted time but also organisation of resources, open-ended materials and preparation from staff by evaluating proposals and hypothesising on previous work. Experienced practitioners seem to be able to anticipate the paths of children's research by talking to each other and sharing ideas. This can even take the form of inaction as occasionally action from practitioners can be interfering and disruptive as conversations with a purpose revealed:

28

"Sometimes the action you choose to take is inaction" – however, inaction is not to be confused for unpreparedness. Practitioners having the forethought to supply all the aforementioned, can be thought of as deliberate action, without which CCL would not be able to be reflexive, responsive and organic in nature.

> • **How can opportunities for CCL be planned and resourced in your setting?**

Celebrating the big and small

Remembering to celebrate the big and small instances of CCL is vital to its perpetuation within a setting. CLL taking the form of projects, such as pedagogical documentation generated from inquiries that span long periods of time and seem to capture the imagination of the majority, are beautiful and inspiring to be a part of. However, much of the everyday CCL comes from respecting the smaller things that children engage in and with. For example, a member of staff described engaging in CCL that initially seemed repetitive, but upon reflection the adult concluded: *"We might not think there's anything out of it but for them, there's a good friendship forming there and they're working together, aren't they?"* There were occasions where CCL produced no huge leaps in creative ability, linguistic talent or mathematical prowess but as content analysis revealed there were intrinsic advances such as: *"increases in confidence"*, *"developed their self-esteem"* and *"a lovely friendship is forming"*. CCL is not exclusively synonymous with huge documentation panels and piles of photographic evidence, but in its purest form is simply learning together with children, something that should be an inherent part of the practitioners' and children's experiences and of the setting ethos as a whole.

> • **How can practitioners demonstrate valuing all modes of learning with children?**

Conclusion

The purpose of this chapter then was to elucidate what constitutes CCL in its everyday form – the nuts and bolts of it – to ensure that the conditions continue to be favourable for its perpetuation. Critical awareness of the importance leadership and trust play in giving children and practitioners a robust, confident framework upon which new understanding can be built and new experiences forged is essential. Without the foundation of trust and distributed leadership, CCL would be stilted, stifled and counterfeit – a mere nod to democracy that would boil "co-constructing learning" down to "working on the same thing with others". To borrow sentiment based on the work of Lewin (1951) and Force Field Analysis, pedagogic discourse and its uncertainty and distributed leadership strengthen the driving forces to keep the practice of CCL in a state of equilibrium. The converse, restraining the inhibiting factors, is addressed by making curriculum and policy changes that ensure deliberate action in the form of planned time and resources to engage in celebrating big and small instances of CCL. Maintaining this balancing act is a fundamental asset of pedagogical leadership.

References

Bush, T. (1995). *Theories of education management* (2nd ed.). London: Paul Chapman Publishing.

Callan, S., Picken, L., & Foster, S. (2011). Ethical positioning in work-based investigations. In S. Callan & M. Reed (Eds.) *Work based research in the early years* (pp. 17–31). London: Sage.

Csikszentmihalyi, M. (2002). *Flow: The classic work on how to achieve happiness*. London: Rider.

Dahlberg, G., Moss, P., & Pence, A. (2006). *Beyond quality in early childhood education and care: Postmodern perspectives*. London: Falmer.

Gardner, H. (1995). *Reflections on multiple intelligences: Myths and messages*. Phi Delta Kappan. Retrieved from https://learnweb.harvard.edu/WIDE/courses/files/Reflections.pdf

Garvey, D., & Lancaster, A. (2010). *Leadership for quality in early years and playwork. Supporting your team to achieve better outcomes for children and families*. London: NCB.

Goswami, U. (2008). *Cognitive development. The learning brain*. Hove: Psychology Press.

Harris, A. (2012). Distributed leadership: Implications for the role of the principal. *Journal of Management Development*, 31(1), 7–17. Retrieved from www.tandfonline.com/doi/abs/10.1080/0022027032000106726

Katz, L., & Chard, S. (1996). *The contribution of documentation to the quality of early childhood education*. ERIC digest. Report number: 393608. Urbana, Illinois. Retrieved from http://files.eric.ed.gov/fulltext/ ED393608.pdf

Laevers, F. (2005). *Deep level learning and the experiential approach in early childhood and primary education*. Leuven: Research Centre for Early Childhood and Primary Education. Retrieved from https://vorming.cego. be/images/downloads/BO_DP_Deep-levelLearning.pdf

Lewin, K. (1951). *Field theory in social science: Selected theoretical papers*. New York: Harper and Row.

MacNaughton, G., Hughes, P., & Smith, K. (2007). Early childhood professionals and children's rights: Tensions and possibilities around the United Nations General Comment No. 7 on children's rights. *International Journal of Early Years Education*, 15(2), 161–170.

Malaguzzi, L. (1997). A Charter of Rights. In T. Filippini & V. Vecchi (Eds.) *The hundred languages of children: Narrative of the possible*. Reggio Emilia: Reggio Children.

Mercer, N., & Littleton, K. (2007). *Dialogue and the development of children's thinking: A sociocultural approach*. London: Routledge.

Mercilliott Hewett, V. (2001). Examining the Reggio Emilia approach to early childhood education. *Early Childhood Education Journal*, 29(2), 95–100.

Moss, P. (2007). Bringing politics into the nursery: Early childhood education as a democratic practice. *European Early Childhood Education Research Journal*, 15(1), 5–20.

Office for Standards in Education, Children's Services and Skills (Ofsted). (2015). *Early years inspection handbook*. Retrieved from www.founda tionyears.org.uk/files/2015/05/Early_years_inspection_handbook.pdf

Rinaldi, C. (1998). Projected curriculum constructed through documentation – Progettazione: An interview with Leila Gandini. In C. Edwards, L. Gandini, & G. Forman (Eds.) *The hundred languages of children: The Reggio Emilia approach – Advanced reflections* (2nd ed.). Connecticut: Ablex Publishing.

Rinaldi, C. (2001). Documentation and assessment: What is the relationship? In C. Giudici, C. Rinaldi, & M. Krechevsky (Eds.) *Making learning visible: Children as individual and group learners* (pp. 78–93). Reggio Emilia: Reggio Children.

Rinaldi, C. (2006). *In dialogue with Reggio Emilia: Listening, researching and learning*. Oxon: Routledge.

Roberts, R. (2010). *Wellbeing from birth*. London: Sage.

Rojas-Drummond, S. M., Albarran, C. D., & Littleton, K. (2008). Collaboration, creativity and the co-construction of oral and written texts. *Thinking Skills and Creativity*, 3(3), 177–191. Retrieved from https://pdfs.seman ticscholar.org/4c94/3345447c3e87046e70dcadba3a192861f324.pdf

Siraj-Blatchford, I. (2007). Creativity, communication and collaboration: The identification of pedagogic progression in sustained shared thinking. *Asia-Pacific Journal of Research in Early Childhood Education*, 1(2), 3–23.

Siraj-Blatchford, I. (2013). Early childhood education. In T. Maynard & N. Thomas (Eds.) *An introduction to early childhood studies* (3rd ed.). London: Sage.

Smith, A. (2009). A case study of learning architecture and reciprocity. *International Journal of Early Childhood*, 41(1), 33–49.

Soler, J., & Miller, L. (2003). The struggle for early childhood curricula: A comparison of the English foundation stage curriculum, Te Whäriki and Reggio Emilia. *International Journal of Early Years Education*, 11(1), 57–68. Retrieved from http://dx.doi.org/10.1080/0966976032000066091

Spillane, J. P., Halverson, R., & Diamond, J. B. (2007). Towards a theory of leadership practice: A distributed perspective. *Journal of Curriculum Studies*, 36(1), 3–34.

Trevarthen, C. (2006). Doing education – To know what others know. *Early Education*, 49(2), 11–13.

United Nations General Assembly. (1989). *United Nations Convention on the Rights of the Child*. Retrieved from www.ohchr.org/EN/Professiona lInterest/Pages/CRC.aspx

Vygotsky, L., & Cole, M. (1978). *Mind in society: The development of higher psychological processes*. Cambridge: Harvard University Press. Retrieved from www.dawsonera.com/readonline/9780674076686

Yan, C. (2005). Developing a kindergarten curriculum based on children's naïve theory. *International Journal of Early Years Education*, 13(2), 145–156.

3

LEADERSHIP FOR ALL – LEARNING FOR ALL

Making this visible by writing Learning Stories that
enable children, families and teachers to have a voice

Lorraine Sands and Wendy Lee

*Leadership for all leads to learning for all. Yet what kind of leader-
ship and what kind of learning? This chapter utilises the research of
the teachers at Greerton Early Childhood Centre, supported by
their academic associates, Professor Margaret Carr and Wendy Lee
(Sands, Carr, & Lee, 2012), as they explored what happens when
teachers engage in the process of building a collaborative, leaderful
community, where the principles of Te Whāriki, New Zealand Early
Childhood curriculum (Ministry of Education, 1996, 2017) are
evident for all to see. This was a Centre of Innovation research
project (Meade, 2007) designed to examine the threads of inquiry
that underpinned a learning and teaching setting characterised by
responsiveness, reciprocity and respectfulness. The research revealed
that building a collaborative, leaderful community, within a socio-
cultural framework (Rogoff, 2003), was a dynamic, interactive
enterprise that relied on the interconnectivity of environment, relationships and context. It wove together individual interest and
passion, and shared endeavor in a social setting. It depended on
everyone helping each other to recognise and respond in ways that
enabled confident, capable leaders and learners to flourish as empathy, fair-mindedness and positive attitudes towards diversity were
valued and made visible.*

Sir Ken Robinson (2006) teaches us that creatively exploring ideas
nurtures children's capacity for innovation, for original thinking, for
diversity, and for building identities as successful learners now and into
the future. Our learning community at Greerton Early Childhood

Centre encourages everyone to follow their interests. We are a community who actively engage in the continuing process of learning that collaboration is a powerful way to work together. As we help each other, we become part of an empathic community that enables everyone to learn what is important to them, all the while making space for each of us to follow our own driving energies, passions and spirits.

This kind of learning community is invested in 'leadership'. It is a fluid one that invites each of us to play our part inside this complex notion we call learning. At Greerton, the idea of leadership as fluid, binding learners, ideas and the learning environment together, because leadership passes from one to another, has been an organic process. It evolved as teachers began to explore the way learning identities could be strengthened when responsive leaders (children, families and teachers) engage together to craft vibrant, innovative settings, designed for learners to stretch themselves to the edges of possibility, and then with flair, creativity and courage, to step beyond.

An exemplar about leadership is provided by Tanya Johnson, a teacher at Greerton Early Childhood Centre. She wrote a Learning Story (a narrative assessment) illustrating this. The story offers an example of 'expansive possibility', for as children take on a leadership mantle and develop their ideas further, they build complexity into their thinking. This is often a social response, with play uppermost in their minds. An excerpt:

> As I pulled the sewing machine out to do a repair job on our parachute, a group of curious children gathered, bursting with ideas. A piece of fur had Francesca's imagination captured and she decided to make a wolf's tail. Emma liked this idea too, but they only had one piece of fur. 'I know!' Francesca declared. 'I can cut it in two and then you can have a piece!' The smile on Emma's face said it all. What a gift to have someone make you feel so included and loved, by having them share their treasure.

Our community's definition of leadership, as a shared endeavor, sits inside a reflective vision for learning. Time is important in this view, for scheduled, time-bound routines or activities destroy creative thought processes when they cut across motivated, engaged learners in the act of 'doing'. Imagine interrupting Francesca's experience at any point along her way towards conceiving an imaginary wolf, making a theatrical prop to enhance the drama, or limiting her joyful play with Emma. Once this thread is broken, often by arbitrary decisions from the adults inside an early learning setting, the ability to practice self-managing one's life is undermined. The internal character of a burgeoning learner is interrupted, and when adults do this to children time and again, it comes at a huge cost.

Professor Sir Peter Gluckman, New Zealand's chief science advisor, links self-regulation to lifelong success (2011). Yet, self-regulation is not defined just by one's ability to be self-disciplined, to be focused, to persevere and to practice the difficult, tricky bits of a challenging goal. It is linked inextricably with the social aspect of enabling others to do this too, without interfering in their right to pursue a self-set challenge. It stretches further, as passionate learners draw others into a plan through inviting, listening and altering their ideas to accommodate multiple voices. When children get to practice all these dispositions, skills and working theories, inside a community, with people who care to learn from mistakes, take on varied ideas and act co-operatively to create new solutions, then children's identities of themselves as creative, tolerant, hardworking, diligent social beings is nurtured.

Children's working theories are complex responses to their social world. Our research has reinforced again and again that when children are offered learning environments that value struggle, effort, practice, perseverance and social competency, to name a few of the dispositions that characterise successful lifelong learners, they set themselves edgy, difficult goals, far in excess of what adults could visualise for them. Peter Gray (2015, p. 220) offers a view on how such self-initiative develops, and this too is an important precursor to thoughtfully enacted leadership:

> If freedom, personal responsibility, self-initiative, honesty, integrity and concern for others rank high in your system of values, and if they represent characteristics you would like to see in your children, then you will be a trusting parent [or teacher]. None of these dispositions can be taught by lecturing, coercion or coaxing. They are acquired (or lost) through daily life experiences that reinforce or suppress them. You can help your children build these values by living them yourself and applying them in relationships with your children. Trust promotes trustworthiness. Self-initiative and all the traits that depend on self-initiative can develop only under conditions of freedom.

Leadership can very aptly be added as one of the characteristics of self-initiative and likewise requires freedom to practice its tenets, with and alongside others who are both more and less experienced than themselves. Peter Gray (2015, p. 76) says this about free age mixed play:

> ... the presence of younger children naturally activates the nurturing instincts of older children. Older children help younger ones when they play together, and in that way they learn to lead and nurture and develop a concept of themselves as mature and caring.

A significant aspect of our community is the free association of children of all ages together, infants, toddlers and young children. Our more recent reflections have enabled us to understand the significance of everyday leadership opportunities for children as the day's rhythms and rituals unfold in surprising and relaxed ways across the whole setting.

The growth of shared leadership in relation to children's learning in the Greerton Early Childhood Centre

During the Centre of Innovation program, the team focused on an image of the child as a researcher, an explorer making sense of the people, places and things in their world (Ministry of Education, 1996, 2017). The teachers wanted to fully understand the culture of learning and teaching at Greerton, where the intention was to tilt all experiences towards a child's growing identity of themselves as a learner, with an increasing awareness that effort and practice are the key to increasing capability (Dweck, 2006). The key research question was: *How does a 'question-asking' and a 'question exploring' culture support children to develop working theories to shape and re-shape knowledge for a purpose?* As we saw children experimentally shaping and re-shaping their understandings and honing their skills, we realised that they were leading their own learning and drawing other children, teachers and families into their plans. As a consequence, teachers worked on building environments that were rich, vibrant learning settings, to support children's identities of themselves as creative, resourceful, resilient learners. One of the things we learnt during the research was that children, teachers and families were extraordinarily interested in social learning. The teachers agreed that it was this context of learning and teaching as a 'collaborative endeavor' that captivated their interest to find out more about what kinds of settings and relationships make a difference to children's learning. It was our intention to disrupt conventional thinking through writing Learning Stories that showed invested teaching including; co-construction between children and teachers, sustained shared teaching episodes extending children's thinking, valuing of children's contribution to the learning experience and making links across time by revisiting children's ideas and interests.

Because the teachers see knowledge as a process (Gilbert, 2005), a way of finding out, a way of building understanding that can occur over a long period, they created time and space for children to investigate, opening possibilities for children to be leaders of their own learning, and to be leaders who routinely invited others to join their plans. As we immersed ourselves in growing this kind of learning community, we realised we were more aware than ever before, that children ought to be designers of their own learning (Ministry of Education, 1996, 2017). Our research became more focused on childrens' and teachers' experiences as they explored the possibilities offered in an environment that embraced relationships (Ministry of Education, 1996, 2017); an environment where people listened to each other. As the research progressed, we developed 'Threads of Inquiry' detailing the aspects of a 'leaderful community' that could enable everyone to go beyond their comfort zones into more complex play and adventurous learning. Costa and Kallick's (2000, p. 34) thoughts surrounding flexibility in learning have supported our research. They write that:

> Flexible people seem to have an almost uncontrollable urge to go beyond established limits. They are uneasy about comfort; they 'live on the edge of competence'. They seem compelled to place themselves in situations where they do not know what the outcomes will be.

When children are in a community that feeds their appetites for curiosity – as well as companionship, rhythm and ritual – ideas flow, and action results. Children lead, and because we live and learn inside a socio-cultural context, teachers and families also lead, but they do so in a spirit of respect for children's burgeoning capabilities. The most salient point to make is that leadership is a shifting possibility and no one person or group has the prerogative to make all the decisions. This makes for a viscerally appealing environment as well as an intellectually exciting and socially inclusive one.

The role of Learning Stories (narrative assessment) in broadening leadership at Greerton

Over time we have continued to align our practice with the Early Childhood curriculum, Te Whāriki and its principles and strands (Lee, Carr, Soutar, & Mitchell, 2013). One of the most important reasons for deepening our understanding of these has come about through the writing of Learning Story narrative assessments. Learning Stories (Carr, 2001) offered us a practical way of connecting with the principles of Te Whāriki that had previously eluded us. We wrote in more engaged, emotionally connected ways. As families and children delighted in the stories that started with what children could do, we analysed learning pathways from a variety of perspectives, moving towards possibilities and opportunities for action. We soon realised the transforming power of these Learning Stories (Carr & Lee, 2012). Our teaching was different from before because we started to notice, recognise and respond to children's learning in ways we had never previously considered. The very act of writing our perspective of children's learning made our teaching practice visible, and the honest, often puzzling accounts about our role in supporting this learning, realigned us as researchers, learners and leaders journeying alongside children. We realised that children were equally as motivated to research their world, puzzle over things that were novel, and to lead their inquires through a growing sociability that included others (Fleet, Patterson, & Robertson, 2006). In our experience, shifts in practice result from prolonged teacher conversations around pedagogy. Team relationships are pivotal in these shifts; when Te Whāriki principles are as engaged for teachers as they are designed to be for children and families, they have a powerful impact on the way teachers, teach and learn. Terry Atkinson and Guy Claxton's (2000) writing around intuitive practitioners has had a pervasive influence on us. As teachers are freed to be comfortable about 'not knowing', not necessarily being an imparter of knowledge, they are able to throw ideas around, to be playful and to be imaginative, all inside a setting that creates space for intuition to flourish.

The teachers' Learning Stories at Greerton increasingly reflected this understanding. Many of the narrative assessments started

38

conversations with children, families and each other, valuing the idea that meaningful, collaborative, expansive learning relies on a growing sense of fair-mindedness. It also depends on care and kindness to stretch learning to the edge and beyond, with and alongside their friends. In a 21st-century world that is full of surprise and uncertainty, as change is exponentially thrust upon us, the work at Greerton is based on a view that successful learners will be those who see the world as a place full of possibility. It is the teachers' intention to foster resourceful, resilient learners who are deeply involved in their learning and who are active in leading their learning and that of others.

As the research progressed, we began to re-define our view of leadership and started making this valued view of learning more visible in the way we constructed our Learning Story narratives. Teachers were intent on ensuring our children could see themselves through these narratives, as learners and leaders, pursuing the serious fun of tackling the edgy, interesting things, as well as doing the hard graft that gets you where you want to be! The teachers began to realise that these are the kinds of 21st-century learners/ leaders the world actually needs. We write Learning Stories with wholehearted, energised intelligence, based in the view that children's play lights up every synapse in their brains (Brown, 2010) and the stories we write will make a difference, now and into the future – to children, to families and to ourselves.

Amelie is just such a learner, and the following Learning Story, written by Lorraine, offers a useful glimmer into what the Greerton community have been intent on enabling.

What about a swimming pool for dinosaurs?

It's not a usual event at Greerton, but then so much of the creative energy that explodes around here could hardly be called 'usual'. It's when friends with ideas team up that the really good 'stuff' happens! So why not add some water to a jar to create realism, put some compliant dinosaurs into the mix and create a building to contain the mayhem!

My thoughts on your learning . . .

Amelie, you know how to work with your friends and get to the 'sweet spot' which is the right level of 'skill', the right level of 'stretch' and the emotional intelligence to work creatively alongside your friends!

How might this learning stretch further?

Teachers might think they can 'plan' for learning but 'no', you do this! All we can do is plan for the environment that sits 'behind' and enables learning to happen in free spirited ways because there is time, space, interesting resources and a culture that is enthusiastic about creativity in all its mess, its logic, its unfathomable depth of creative thought and social spark! What I love to see is this all unfolding, and try to 'know' when to have fabulous conversations and when to just watch and marvel. That's a tricky thing to know because adults are very good at hijacking children's ideas and that's not fair! So Amelie, my friend, I will continue to marvel each day as your creative spirit and sheer zest for life unfolds, and be there when invited to participate or offer ideas as a contribution not as a game changer of your direction!

In the minds of each teacher at Greerton is the view that 'play'; uninterrupted complex opportunities for children to be in charge of their learning, is the key. It is in play that children are able to experience every aspect of cultural and social competency, of resilience, of social justice resourcefulness, and creativity (see Figure 3.1). Play forms the building blocks underpinning a learner's identity; David Perkins' (2009, p. 29) comments are resonant of the way we view leaderful learning.

> It's never just routine. It's about thinking about what you know and pushing further. It involves open-ended or ill-structured problems and novel, puzzling situations. It's never just problem-solving; it involves problem-finding. It's not just about right answers. It involves explanation and justification. It's not emotionally flat. It involves curiosity, discovery, creativity, camaraderie.

The 'camaraderie' notion struck a particular chord with us because it gave us another insight into what kind of leadership we wanted to grow. Many discussions ensued about the notion of what collaborative learning looked like, in particular, how we could encourage all children, each and every one, to be leaders of this kind of learning. Gavin Kerr, a teacher at Greerton, during a usual weekly trip to a local forest and farm, explored the camaraderie effect on leadership when it is

Figure 3.1 Learning is emotional

located in shared experience and common purpose. His Learning Story captured the essence of courageous, collaborative learners. The following is an excerpt focused on the way children's working theories can build surprise and uncertainty into their endeavors.

Today we discovered a number of fallen ponga trunks (NZ Tree ferns) in the forest. We hacked them out into the open field at the bottom of the farm to inspect…Using a little team work power, the children managed to carry the trunks

41

over to a stream nearby that had risen with the rain and was proving difficult to cross. It took some thinking and planning and we eventually managed to secure the trunks across the stream...The bridge held firm and a little cheer went up as Catalina (teacher) made it to the other side, still dry! After that we took turns traversing our new ponga bridge, building on the techniques we had practiced at the Quarry Park so many weeks ago.

My thoughts on this learning...
It is amazing to witness the flow of ideas being shared between the group – how they bounce thoughts and ideas off one another, triggering new ones by introducing memories of past experiences... New learning and an understanding of a range of concepts were being tangibly formed today as the children used their combined skill and understanding to re-create a practical, functioning bridge, using the resources at hand to solve a problem. What an amazing display of social learning!

No one knows when leadership will shift – and this may happen in a myriad of ways, over time or within moments. What is important here is the understanding that everyone's contribution is valued, explored, tested and deliberated on. This happens through conversation, not titled authority. All contributions are worthy of examination and each person has a right to articulate and convince others. Ideas that are offered, backed up by passion and commitment, as well as rational thought, are likely to be accepted by the group. It is in experiencing these conversations often, that children in fact become more articulate, more confident to offer ideas, even the ones that after reflection are rejected. This is called emotional stamina, empathy and collegial endeavor. Nothing creative happens unless we are prepared to be vulnerable, to be open to failure, to learn and re-think, re-make, re-conceptualise. Competition may have its place, but it is in collaboration that communities thrive.

Can early childhood education (ECE) teaching practice be effective, authentic and innovative while meeting external system demands?

Every early childhood setting and school in New Zealand is externally reviewed by the Education Review Office (ERO). The Greerton teachers value external evaluation because it offers an outsider's perspective and enables us to refine our thinking further. The latest Education Review Office (2017, p. 1) report had this to say:

> The highly-effective curriculum is implemented as a pōkeka (cloak) which embraces the whole child. The children drive the curriculum, through their interests, skills, knowledge and dispositions. Parents and whānau (wider family) have many opportunities to contribute to learning. Children benefit from a broad, rich curriculum, which offers risk and challenge in response to their interests...All areas of the holistic curriculum, including literacy, mathematics and science, are naturally incorporated into the program in meaningful contexts for children. Teachers skillfully promote oral language development. Children and teachers access information and make regular trips into the local community to support interests and investigations. A feature of the program for older children is the weekly farm visit that supports them to develop resilience and investigation skills. Children work together to plan their day and explore the natural environment. They benefit from participating in education within and outside of the center, and continue developing skills for life-long learning. The strong assessment and planning practices are credit-based and focused on dispositional learning. Teachers work in depth with the Principles and Strands of Te Whāriki (Ministry of Education, 2017) while being highly skilled at sharing educational theory, research and quality learning in early childhood with parents.

The ERO report indicates that leaderful teaching can meet the Ministry of Education's requirements. But what does it look like in practice and how are we sharing such pedagogical theory within our community? We write in ways that offer families an insight into learning theory. Our intention is to keep these ideas emotionally engaging, relevant to the family and specific to the child, by setting out the context for the learning, with photos that show aspects of progress, concentration and social connection. These stories often highlight families' contributions to our learning community. When families realise the importance of things like 'loose parts' in sparking creative thought, they are very willing, both to gather resources and offer their help. Learning Stories refrain from 'teacher talk', like the fine motor co-ordination required to manipulate the materials, and concentrates on putting forward the notion of the 'creative thinker', the power of developing a growth mindset, the role of resilience and resourcefulness in creating a self-determined learner. It illustrates to parents and families the importance of dispositions alongside skills and knowledge. It shows them the wider benefit of self-directed, open-ended play and the environments needed to nurture and promote this. Books, loose parts, freedom to move equipment and resources to the many and varied places required by children to realise their creative intent, offer provocations that bind many children together in complex play using props they have made themselves. Teachers plan for this 'environmental design' (rather than activities), and trust that children, inside a setting that offers space, and resources for curiosity unfettered by adult inter-ference, as well as unlimited time to conceive, make and share dramatic props within play scenarios, will lead their own learning.

Essential in ensuring that leadership for all leads to learning for all, is the notion that learning ought to be irresistibly engaging for all (Fullhan, 2012). Each and every one of us makes decisions about leadership and learning each and every day, and as children only get one early childhood life to build the brain they will have for life, the responsibility to build a learning community for those social/cul-tural brains to flourish is weighty indeed. That community is strengthened when everyone has the opportunity to lead their own learning, with and alongside others who care to listen to and support each other. Individually and collectively we determine what communities of learning look like, and individually and collec-tively we are responsible for the kinds of communities we build, moment by moment, idea upon idea.

References

Atkinson, T., & Claxton, G. (2000). *The intuitive practitioner: On the value of not always knowing what one is doing*. New York: Open University Press.

Brown, S. (2010). *Play, how it shapes the brain, opens the imagination and invigorates the soul*. Victoria, Australia: Scribe Publications.

Carr, M. (2001). *Assessment in early childhood settings: Learning Stories*. London: Paul Chapman Publishing.

Carr, M., & Lee, W. (2012). *Learning Stories: Constructing learner identi-ties in early education*. London: Sage Publishing.

Costa, A., & Kallick, B. (2000). *Habits of mind*. Alexandria, VA: ASCD – Association for Supervision and Curriculum Development.

Dweck, C. (2006). *Mindset: The new psychology of success*. New York: Random House.

Education Review Office. (2017). *Greerton ECC*. Retrieved from www. ero.govt.nz/review-reports/greerton-ecc-toddlers-and-young-children-30-06-2017/

Fleet, A., Patterson, C., & Robertson, J. (2006). *Insights. Behind early childhood pedagogical documentation*. New South Wales: Pademelon Press.

Fullhan, M. (2012). *Stratosphere, integrating technology, pedagogy, and change knowledge*. Canada: Pearson.

Gilbert, J. (2005). *Catching the knowledge wave: The knowledge society and the future of education*. Wellington: NZCER Press.

Gluckman, P. (2011). *Improving the transition, reducing social and psychological morbidity during adolescence*. Auckland, New Zealand: Office of the Prime Minister's Science Advisory Committee.

Gray, P. (2015). *Free to learn*. New York: Basic Books.

Lee, W., Carr, M., Soutar, B., & Mitchell, L. (2013). *Understanding the Te Whāriki approach. Early years education in practice*. London: Routledge.

Meade, A. (2007). *Riding the waves: Innovation in early childhood education*. Wellington: NZCER Press.

Ministry of Education. (1996). *Te Whāriki: He whāriki mātauranga mo nga mokopuna o Aotearoa*. Wellington: Learning Media.

Ministry of Education. (2017). *Te Whāriki: He whāriki mātauranga mo nga mokopuna o Aotearoa*. Wellington: Learning Media.

Perkins, D. (2009). *Making learning whole*. San Francisco, CA: Jossey-Bass.

Robinson, K. (2006). *Do schools kill creativity?* Retrieved from www.ted. com/talks/ken_robinson_says_schools_kill_creativity

Rogoff, B. (2003). *The cultural nature of human development*. Oxford: Oxford University Press.

Sands, L., Carr, M., & Lee, W. (2012). Question-asking and question-exploring. *European Early Childhood Education Research Journal*, 20(4), 553–564.

EDITORIAL PROVOCATIONS
Engaging readers and extending thinking

Rosie Walker

This section urges the reader to 'celebrate the big and the small' within early years practice. The chapters, from Australia, New Zealand and the UK invite you to explore how quality and equity of provision for children and families can be achieved through analysis of 'big data' in Chapter 1, then illustrated by rich examples from practice in Chapters 2 and 3.

Taken together these chapters model the effectiveness of the learning community, however big or small, in progressing good outcomes for all children. Chapter 1 explores the persuasiveness of big data in providing a 'helicopter view' of what works with children and families and providing an answer to global social and economic inequality within childhood. Understanding the purpose and limitations of big data is the first step to using it wisely as a forum for debate, and questioning what it brings to develop local communities. The subsequent two chapters illuminate quality dimensions that cannot be captured by big data – the day-to-day process features and interactions of children's learning through co-constructed learning in Chapter 2 and Learning Stories in Chapter 3. Big data cannot always portray the child's voice and the holistic experience of children and families and we are urged to be critical consumers of such data.

Within this section of the book, the authors strive to explore models of leadership which will promote response to change in a positive way for children. One certainty that we have is that changes will always be happening within the early years. Systems in place as well as communities of practice can help us to respond so that we can foster flexibility and adaptability to develop new ways of work-ing that embrace change. Within Chapter 2, one of the most important aspects of success is the ability to co-construct learning with children. Co-construction is a cultural process where knowledge is shared amongst communities. This theme is continued throughout Chapter 3 which investigates a learning community that empowers children to be designers of their own learning and where leadership shifts between children and adults. Here the importance of the need to foster resilience in learning is explored.

Having read this section you may wish to consider if the chapters are a call for change or for things to remain the same? In order for things to remain the same, you might ask: is change necessary? Fast-forward a few years and consider if the big data and examples from grass roots practice internationally enable you to envisage what the system will look like? Will it be the same, improved or different? What would be the facets of the current systems and processes in place you would like to keep and what would you change?

Section 2

THOSE WHO EDUCATE

4

PEDAGOGICAL LEADERSHIP
Interrogating self in order to lead others

Anthony Semann

This chapter is concerned with the organisational culture of leadership and why it is important for leaders to lead at a pace that is suitable to keep people engaged in the local context as well as reflecting critically on their own leadership approaches. In this context, the author interrogates the reasons why leaders should be unafraid to examine their own values and beliefs and the impact these have on those they lead. Additionally, the author provides some practical examples of how leadership of self and others may be used as a means of supporting improved pedagogical practices within an early years setting. In the context of this chapter about the role of pedagogical leaders, the terms pedagogical leader and educational leader are used. For clarity, the term pedagogical leader is used as the more internationally understood term for those who take on responsibility for curriculum and pedagogic leadership in an education setting. The term educational leader is used when referring to the role specified in Australian Law, to refer to the designated person within an early childhood setting who is responsible for overseeing the education program.

Contemporary theories and literature related to leadership have highlighted the importance of leaders undertaking a critical reading of both the intent that underpins their leadership as well as examining how leadership is embodied as a relational act between two or more individuals. Furthermore, it has been suggested that the strategies enacted as part of their leadership require further interrogation in the anticipation that leadership may produce more equitable outcomes for those who lead and those who experience the act of leadership (Sinclair, 2009). Within the Australian context, leadership has remained a cornerstone of the quality debate and has been linked to providing better outcomes for educators and children

51

(Sims, Forest, Semann, & Slattery, 2014). Research has suggested that the role of educational leader is 'fundamental in assisting others to develop a sound curriculum and to assist children to achieve identifiable outcomes' (Fleet, Soper, Semann, & Madden, 2015, p. 29). In addition, the introduction within Australian Government policy of the requirement that the role of educational leader be identified within every early childhood site, has provided further focus for both research and conversation regarding the importance of leadership and the impact leadership has within early childhood settings (Semann, Botero Lopez, Lawson, & Bennett, 2014).

In considering pedagogical leadership, it might be argued that one avenue towards enhancement is to consider and engage in a process of reflection as a strategy of improvement. In doing so, individuals might reflect on the following questions as a starting point:

- **What does it mean to interrogate one's self and how might leaders start this journey?**
- **Why should leaders begin to interrogate themselves as they enact leadership strategies and what might this interrogation deliver?**

Interestingly, leaders tend to spend a considerable amount of their time looking outwardly at their workplaces and observing and supervising those they lead, presumably to bring out the best in others and achieve determined objectives. This, in most part, is documented in organisational plans, listed as Key Performance Indicators (KPIs) and provides the basis for many a conversation amongst education staff.

The task of attending to issues 'outwardly' is often couched in a narrative of 'busyness' where leaders claim to have very little time to attend to their own work and growth as they are regularly disrupted by the goings-on around them. Such busyness can be couched as productivity and woven into a narrative of transformation for those whom leaders work alongside. However, authors including Sinclair (2009) suggest that contemplative and mindful leadership might sit opposed to such busyness. Leaders might develop greater awareness of how their leadership impacts on themselves and those they influence as they reflect on the everyday, moment to moment acts of leadership. These acts of mindful and conscious leadership might present themselves in deep reflection on oneself, exploring leader flaws, identifying the drivers that keep leaders going, and attending to more complex questions about the 'self' rather than the 'other'.

Leadership is a cultural practice; globally there are many narratives which begin to describe what makes for a great leader. Authoring such narratives of exceptional leadership seems 'too easy' these days as the stories of great leadership tend to align with each other and tend to contain many similarities: Be it the courageous leader, the leader who exudes confidence or the leader who identifies the direction the organisation must head and sets sail towards this with the team on-board. Within the role of pedagogical leader, this might present itself as a leader who has astute knowledge of pedagogy, with the role then framed around taking others to this predetermined end point of quality. Whilst such qualities are not inherently problematic, within particular systems they do tend to contain specific skills, which leaders might begin to expect from all leaders working with them, and in so doing, they may in fact lock out other forms of leadership qualities. Leaders, including pedagogical leaders, are not a homogenous group; in accepting such differences we might begin to accept the diverse ways in which leadership should and could be embodied. Furthermore, leadership is most effective when leaders themselves exercise context-specific leadership and, in doing so, understand the needs and desires of all within that context. Failing to understand the context in which individuals exercise their leadership may in fact lead to greater problems than successes.

Context-driven leadership includes developing a clear understanding of the desires and needs of all rather than focussing on how leaders prefer to exercise their leadership. More specifically, this might include understanding the cultural, social and political contexts in which leaders find themselves, and in doing so, adjusting their leadership approaches to suit the specificity of these variables. Such specificity for pedagogical leaders includes the communities their settings are located within, the needs and desires of families, the structural variabilities across sites – including staff qualifications and years of experience and employment – as well as taking into account the diversities evident amongst children. Herein lies the multiplicity of leadership. There is no one way to lead. The stories of leadership that tend to repeat themselves lack the diversity exemplified by the organisations in which followers and leaders find themselves. Pedagogical leadership should reflect a mosaic of approaches, a diversity of strategies and a resistance to the duplication of approaches which might in fact suit other sites but might not necessarily meet the needs of the sites in which pedagogical leaders find themselves.

Pedagogical leadership attends to many questions and none more importantly than 'the way in which the central task of improving teaching and learning takes place in educational settings' (Ord et al., 2013, p. 1). As such, it is leadership with a specific focus on curriculum and pedagogy, whereas leadership more generally can be seen as attending to questions of management and administration. Pedagogical leadership requires those bestowed with such responsibility to lead pedagogical improvements and in so doing, interrogate their approaches to leadership as much as they might interrogate the teaching and learning which takes place. For many, having refined the art of teaching may have been the reason for their appointment as a leader in an education site (Fleet et al., 2015); however, the skills associated with leading pedagogical improvements and working with and alongside other teaching staff are not identical skills. Good teaching acumen does not necessarily correlate with good leadership and for many, this is where the challenge may begin. Education staff might find themselves promoted into a role of pedagogical leadership without a history of leading, and subsequently this may raise some challenging yet insightful questions such as:

- **Is this a role I was suitably qualified to undertake?**
- **Do I have the necessary support around me to execute this role successfully?**
- **Have I been sufficiently mentored into this role?**

Such questions are compounded further by concerns shared in the Australian context by educational leaders. These leaders report a lack of clarity regarding their role (Fleet et al., 2015), in particular, a lack of clarity related to the measures of success they should be working towards and the level of delegated authority they have assigned to their roles. For many who have been appointed into the role of educational leader, this has meant little more than an additional line item included into their existing job description

(Semann et al., 2014). Assuming that educational leaders have clarity of purpose and clearly defined expectations to meet, it is critical to the success of the leader that the role has a high level of synchronism with the expectation and desires of other teaching staff. This means all educators understand the importance the role has in the education site as well as the interplay between the role of educational leader and the role of teaching staff, bearing in mind that the educational 'leader' is generally also a member of the teaching team, or indeed, the administrative leader as well.

If pedagogical leadership is about creating pedagogical change, then perhaps advice from Scharmer and Kaufer (2013) might be useful. These authors have argued that in times of uncertainty, there may be a tendency for leaders to misplace their change initiatives and create processes and goals which do not align to the needs and desires of those they lead. This, they argue, is a result of a culture of unpredictability and disruption. Ineffective outcomes might result from pedagogical leaders who, by flying solo, lack the skills to leverage the power of the collective when considering the focus of their work. Conversely, it might be suggested that effective pedagogical leadership is a collective journey, which includes all staff working together to identify the strategic direction they hope to work towards, clarifying the support they require as part of this role, and creating spaces of democracy where discussions are centred on developing ideas together rather than having strategies imposed onto education staff from pedagogical leaders. These ideas raise useful questions including:

- How might pedagogical leaders bring together a common understanding to the role and an articulated pathway for change?
- Furthermore, how might pedagogical leaders avoid inducing feelings of unsettlement amongst staff, which might result from unrealistic expectations being imposed onto people, or strategies which lack context or relevance in the eyes of others?

In orientating themselves towards more effective leadership, pedagogical leaders might enhance their leadership through an intentional focus on reflective practice. In doing so, reflection might bring to the surface some of the challenges faced and provide solutions. Furthermore, if reflection becomes a collective journey which includes all education staff, then pedagogical leadership can be seen as effective professional learning for all. Such questions to support reflective practices for pedagogical leaders might include:

- **Do I have understanding of my role's purpose and goals?**
- **Do other educators have an understanding of my role's purpose and goals?**
- **How might the role of pedagogical leader support improved outcomes for education staff?**
- **What might be the intersection between ideas of democracy and the enactment of pedagogical leadership?**

There is a need for both leaders and followers to be on the same page if there is a desire for pedagogical leadership to be deemed effective. Salas, Sims, and Burke (2005) suggest that the most successful teams work within a shared mental model. By this, the authors define a shared mental model as a 'knowledge structure of relationships among the task the team is engaged in and how the team members will interact' (p. 7). Lacking the ability to share in a common understanding of tasks and responsibilities, team members including those in leadership positions, will lack the necessary alignment required to achieve desirable outcomes. Relating this to pedagogical leadership may result in leaders lacking an understanding of the needs of those they aim to support and then running the ultimate risk of lacking a shared vision for pedagogical reform.

Effective pedagogical leadership rests on an understanding of the role and the acceptance that to lead pedagogy is to lead change. As such, supporting educational improvements can inevitably lead to disruption, as education staff explore the possibilities and strengths of their practice alongside the need for ongoing improvements. What is required in this case is the development of a strong working relationship amongst all. Accepting that relationships take time and effort is easier said than done, given that many pedagogical leaders still maintain a teaching responsibility within their educational sites (Fleet et al., 2015). The task of relationship-building is limited to many informal opportunities for educators and pedagogical leaders to collaborate and plan collectively for improved teaching and learning opportunities. Organisations must therefore place increased importance on the development of relationships and view this as central to the development of effective pedagogical practices.

Leader behaviour makes a difference

Examining and researching leadership brings to the surface the diversity in both understanding and enactment of leadership across educational sites (Gunter, 2001). The ways in which individuals enact leadership is diverse. There is a range of variables which might impact on the ways leadership is enacted, including individual understandings of leadership, experiences of being led, or expectations placed upon leaders. Undoubtedly the confidence of pedagogical leaders to lead people and change will also play a critical role in how they manage educational change, and additionally how they come to deal with issues as they arise. Leading people inevitably comes with its own set of challenges and the diversity in experience varies greatly from site to site. Therefore, pedagogical leaders have a range of choices available to them in how they come to respond to emerging issues. My experience as a consultant and facilitator of professional learning programs and research for over 20 years has highlighted the myriad of responses pedagogical leaders choose to mobilise when faced with challenges.

Whilst not desirable, pedagogical leaders in the face of discomfort may fall into the trappings of hopelessness and weariness. Faced with ongoing problems and a lack of support (Sims et al., 2014), many leaders find themselves isolated with little or no support available to them. Leadership and the resilience of leaders is often put to a test during times of challenge; these moments should see leaders remaining present and seeking out support from those around them, rather than viewing leadership challenges as a defining moment of failure. To give up as a leader means that all hope is lost, and can lead to individuals losing sight of their purpose. However, giving up isn't always a bad choice. From time to time, pedagogical leaders, like all leaders, need to choose carefully which battles to work with and which battles are best left alone.

Some pedagogical leaders face the inevitable challenge of trying to keep up with the abundance of change they face both within their education site but also across the sector. To try to keep up is to fail to live up to expectations imposed on oneself or by others and as such lends itself to pedagogical leaders seeing themselves as inferior when it comes to having the skills and knowledge to do their role. Generally speaking, individuals expect their leaders to have the expertise and capacity to lead people and change processes and, in doing so, there is a correlation between these expectations and the knowledge required by leaders both technically and theoretically to execute their roles effectively. Pedagogical leaders must therefore be concerned with remaining thought-leaders and staying abreast of current theories and practices related to teaching and learning. This protagonist is therefore a leader who supports deep thinking in the workplace and identifies processes which support the evolution of knowledge amongst teaching staff. Pedagogical leaders have significant responsibilities in leading change and in doing so need to see themselves as growing their own skills and knowledge just as they expect other educators to develop. Useful questions to guide this process may include:

- **What knowledge gaps do I currently have and how might I go about addressing these?**
- **What growth can I see for myself and how might I begin this journey?**

Change is inevitable; the risk to pedagogical leaders is that they find themselves constantly speeding up and perhaps 'chasing their own tail'. Always feeling like they are behind in the high stakes world of educational improvement is a risk and can lead to fatigue. Whilst pedagogical leaders must remain abreast of changes and support ongoing improvements, there is a risk of leaders attempting to create too much change with little time to embed this effectively into the workplace. Change takes time and to create sustained change requires patience and monitoring. Patience is needed in understanding that some level of resistance might be experienced and to overcome this, and opportunity for dialogue is necessary. Additionally, effective pedagogical change also requires leaders to monitor improvements and the translation of theory into practice. This does not equate to a prison-like monitoring of staff, but rather a 'work alongside' staff approach which allows pedagogical leaders to understand how staff are travelling with any change initiatives and to provide any additional support that might be required. There isn't a belief here that 'because I told people what to do, they will just get on with it and do it', but rather, pedagogical leaders value their presence in the educational space and understand the importance of serving those they aim to support.

It is wise that pedagogical leaders approach change initiatives with measured caution – that is, understanding that change takes time and that small steps towards effective outcomes are often more likely to be successful than larger steps. As such, pedagogical leaders can focus on experiencing success in a determined and measured way. They can identify the most important issue that needs addressing and take the time to methodically work through these via advice, coaching, support and mentoring of teams so that systematic changes can take place. 'One year, one project' is a useful motto to live by. Leaders might benefit by asking themselves,

---

- **What is the most pressing issue my team is facing pedagogically and how can I develop a systemic approach towards resolution?**

Standing up as a pedagogical leader is to claim power, to stand up for what matters. Teaching staff invest a considerable amount of time trying to 'get it right' and trying to 'make a difference', so it can be absolutely unsettling when they encounter a pedagogical leader who is suggesting that perhaps their practices can and should be re-considered. In doing so, leaders need to have the courage of their conviction and possess the skills to articulate the theory which underpins sound practices.

Education as a contested battleground

Education of our youngest learners is a slippery slope of truths, personal beliefs and often disagreement. Our desires and personal beliefs drive what we do; in making this claim we must be reminded of how we come to understand the practices that make up quality in our workplaces. Educators, like leaders, develop their beliefs over time. This can be through formal education, interactions with others, social media, reflection or serendipitous moments where our beliefs are challenged and we consequently change our systems of thinking and doing. But what happens when the practices we see don't fit into our system of belief on what constitutes quality? Herein lies the test of pedagogical leadership, that strange realisation that others don't think like you and that you have work to do. However, there is an assumption here that needs to be tested; that is, 'They are wrong, and I am right'. How might a pedagogical leader know if they are right or wrong? How could they come to realise that their ideas and beliefs only belong to them and no one else in the workplace? The early education sector, like other professions, holds tightly to a range of beliefs that underpin our practice. Much of these remain uncontested or challenged: for example, the belief that curriculum is best developed from an alignment to children's interests. (There are, in fact, many ways to construct curriculum.) Inevitably we all experience individuals who believe deeply in what they do, and these beliefs may not be shared by others.

It may be a useful exercise for pedagogical leaders to step away from their work and ask the following set of questions as a means of supporting their own reflections:

- **What other ways are there to understand what I have just seen?**
- **How might I understand this through a different lens?**
- **What positive opportunities might arise if I choose to step back and realise my ideas are personal to me and allow the ideas of others to take centre stage?**
- **How might we carve a new understanding of practice through the integration of diverse perspectives?**

Our thinking on quality is in a constant state of evolution – and by accepting this, pedagogical leaders become freer and more liberated leaders as they embrace the belief that all ideas are worthy of investigation and discussion. A useful exercise to highlight this state of change is for leaders to consider a belief previously held which has changed over time and to consider what allowed such changes in both thinking and practice to take place. Effective pedagogical leadership espouses and embraces the belief that tact and diplomacy are effective ingredients that support improved practices. If coercive power and a culture of fear are employed as strategies of change, the likelihood of sustained change is limited as individuals will revert back to their learned behaviour and long-held belief in the absence of such power which aims to control and manipulate others towards an outcome.

Furthermore, it is important that leaders allow others to be different and journey on a road towards self and group discovery. In doing so, there is a belief that relationship-building is central to pedagogical change, and value is therefore placed on the importance of allowing time for relationships to be built and flourish. It is imperative that leaders create an approach to leadership that focusses on and establishes an environment which values relationships and in doing so, a culture is established whereby it is acceptable to disagree and engage in robust debates about the things that matter deeply to people. Central to this task, however, is that boundaries are established that ensure safety for all staff – for example, the belief and agreement that it is okay to debate ideas, but it is never okay to debate people.

To lead others is to empower people to think both independently and collectively. It is to build a culture of accountability as much as it is to build a culture of thinking. This culture of accountability for pedagogical leaders means to be accountable to those they serve. This culture of accountability can be described as leaders having presence in their sites and making visible their aspirations and desires for change and the strategies they plan to implement. Pedagogical leaders can plan as much as they like, develop as many strategies as they wish, however in the long term, if leader 'presence' isn't felt, then they will have minimal impact. All leaders must allow their presence to be felt and not hide behind their job title or closed doors. They must understand what is going on for the people around them and how they can best support them. Leadership presence, that elusive but 'we know it when we see it' quality, is a mix of personal and interpersonal skills that signals to others 'I am here for you'. It is how leaders show up, how they make others feel, and how effectively they communicate both verbally and non-verbally. It is the combination of various factors that sets leaders up to succeed in their roles and can provide them with the boost they need to continue to succeed into the future. In supporting effective leadership, Goman (2016) offers the following advice for leaders to support their success:

1. **Power up your confidence** – A level of confidence is the personality trait most responsible for an individual being seen as

having leadership presence. It is the belief that the work ahead is worthy of time, effort and struggle and confidence is often best built over time with experience.

2. **Gain credibility** – Credibility is all about how you communicate. It is about body language that's aligned with your verbal message and it's about being truthful, diplomatic, empathetic, succinct and decisive.

3. **Connect more powerfully by changing your focus** – Capital is defined as 'accumulated wealth, especially as used to produce more wealth'. Social capital is the wealth or benefit that exists because of your social relationships. Social capital can be seen as the value created by the connection leaders have with others. There is no more valuable commodity in today's environment, and no more valuable use of leader's time than to build their professional network, within and external to their organisation.

4. **Know yourself as a leader** – It is interesting to realise that we all have some blind spots when it comes to answering the question 'who are you?' Knowing who you are takes time. However, once you know who you are you can then begin a journey in exploring what it will take to address your flaws and areas of improvement as a leader. This process of self-discovery is empowering and can often be achieved best with a mentor or critical friend who offers truthful and timely advice on how leaders are travelling in their leadership journey.

5. **Know others as people not workers** – We work with people who also are journeying through life and often share the same struggles as their leaders. The better pedagogical leaders get to know their colleagues as people, the more impactful they can become as they start to contextualise the support they offer.

6. **Develop habits that work for you not against you** – The gift of a habit is that it frees us up to focus on our performance not on habits that undermine our ability to do the work that needs to be done. Identifying both productive and unproductive habits and responding accordingly as pedagogical leaders is essential. For example, there may be a habit of over promising and under delivering. Knowing this, pedagogical leaders can set suitable expectations for themselves and communicate this with others.

Extending further on the idea of leader habits, pedagogical leaders might ask themselves 'What habits might they wish to develop?' For many leaders, taking the time out to reflect on the journey they have travelled and the impact they leave behind is seen as a luxury rather than a necessity. Mapping the impact and effectiveness of pedagogical leadership requires individuals to have a deeper understanding of effective pedagogical leadership. As such, there is always time to move away from some traditional understandings of leadership and begin to research more contemporary and collaborative approaches to leading.

Finally, pedagogical leaders must develop the skills to support ownership of issues and challenges, acceptance of what is and what needs to be done, and the responsibility to act and not shift the blame and responsibility onto others. Leadership is, and can only be successful, when individuals work alongside people in a dynamic space where thinking is seen as growth, mistakes as opportunity and change as freeing. Leadership will never be an easy role, as leaders continue to ask themselves, 'but now what do I do?'... but be assured: asking questions is liberating and marks growth. Effective pedagogical leadership can be supported by finding comfort in colleagues, reaching out in times of need and allowing individuals to say 'maybe I don't know'.

This chapter has concerned itself with pedagogical leaders developing a better understanding of themselves and those they work with. In doing so, it is anticipated that change be flagged on the agenda so leaders begin to have greater impact in their spaces. Leadership is a challenge for many, given that the context in which the leadership is taking place is often the most useful indicator of what effective leadership might look like. Within the Australian context, the identified role of educational leaders remains elusive to many as individuals continue to explore both expectations and responsibilities associated with the role. Like all other forms of leadership, however, the most effective place to start in this journey is to explore the leaders themselves and to see leadership as a space of transformation where leaders continue to practice and refine what it means to work alongside others.

References

Fleet, A., Soper, R., Semann, A., & Madden, L. (2015). The role of the educational leader: Perceptions and expectations in a period of change. *Australasian Journal of Early Childhood*, 40(3), 29–37.

Goman, C. (2016). *5 ways to instantly increase your leadership presence*. Retrieved from www.forbes.com/sites/carolkinseygoman/2016/01/18/5-ways-to-instantly-increase-your-leadership-presence/2/#4d2ae8863470

Gunter, H. (2001). Critical approaching to leadership in education. *Journal of Educational Enquiry*, 2(2), 94–108.

Ord, K., Smorti, S., Carroll-Lind, J., Robinson, L., Armstrong-Read, A., Brown-Cooper, P., Meredith, E., Rickard, D., & Jalal, J. (2013). *Te Whakapakari Kaiārahi Āhuatanga Ako Kōhungahunga: Developing pedagogical leadership in early childhood education*. Wellington: Te Tari Ora o Aotearoa. NZ Childcare Association.

Salas, E., Sims, D., & Burke, C. (2005). Is there a 'Big Five' in teamwork? *Small Group Research*, 36(5), 555–598.

Scharmer, O., & Kaufer, K. (2013). *Leading from the emerging future: From ego-system to eco system economies*. San Francisco: Berrett-Koehler Publishers.

Semann, A., Botero Lopez, V., Lawson, F., & Bennett, M. (2014). Exploring the role of the educational leader: Our journey. *Every Child*, 20(2), 4–5.

Sims, M., Forest, R., Semann, A., & Slattery, C. (2014). Conceptions of early childhood leadership: Driving new professionalism? *International Journal of Leadership in Education*. doi:10.1080/13603124.2014.962101

Sinclair, A. (2009). Seducing leadership: Stories of leadership development. *Gender, Work and Organization*, 16(2), 266–284.

5

PEDAGOGICAL LEADERSHIP
Challenges and opportunities

Gaynor Corrick and Michael Reed

Pedagogical leadership is complex and influenced by a variety of what are often called driving forces. Some are derived from policy decisions made by government, some are much more local and driven by the need to meet day-to-day regulatory and curriculum requirements, and some are located in the way those who educate think about education, share experience and communicate effectively with each other. There are also the challenges of operating within a sector where provision is far from uniform. For example, in England provision can be home-based, some represented by private daycare institutions, some as part of statutory provision. Provision may also be visible in terms of a children's centre providing a hub for the co-location of different but integrated professional services. There are also wider political constraints such as a government policy promoting a marketisation of services or a pedagogical emphasis upon preparedness for schooling. These give weight to the need to recognise issues which are less visible but nevertheless have an impact upon the complexity of developing integrated services (Walker, Reed, and Carey-Jenkins, 2017).

We are both tutors in higher education in England and often have to respond to the question: 'knowing what you know, what is the best way to lead early education?' Our answer is always the same:

> Put the child at the centre of what you do and work in tandem with those who educate, including parents. Embed what you do within local communities and try to narrow the pedagogical distance between meeting regulatory requirements and sensitively supporting the education and welfare of children.

How this is done in practice is another matter and this chapter seeks to offer some examples about leading practice in the ever-changing world of early education. In particular, we will explore a well-documented approach known as pedagogical leadership (Bolden, 2011; Halttunen, 2016; Harris, 2007; Hujala and Eskeli-nen, 2013; Siraj-Blatchford and Manni, 2007; Waniganayake, 2014). We think it is important, however, to see pedagogical leader-ship as more than describing an approach to leading practice, and rather as a means of extending critical reflection in order to trans-late pedagogical thinking into practice. This point was identified by Coughlin and Baird (2013, p. 1), who suggest that:

> Pedagogy can be defined as the understanding of how learn-ing takes place and the philosophy and practice that sup-ports that understanding of learning. Essentially it is the study of the teaching and learning process. Leadership is often defined as the act of leading or guiding individuals or groups. If we are to combine these two we are offered the notion of pedagogical leadership as leading or guiding the study of the teaching and learning process.

Sheridan (2001) extends this view and explores what is meant by pedagogical quality and how it manifests itself in various pedagogical processes in preschool. She suggests that inspection and regulatory systems and process-based approaches to working with children and families, when considered alongside self-analysis, can act as a catalyst for critical reflection. These are necessary strategies in order to deepen the discussions about what goes on in practice. They reflect a position which underpins a contemporary view of leading practice where educators collaborate in thinking about the ways children learn and how this contributes directly to deciding what is best for a child's learning and development. This is important as it is funda-mental to building professional capability amongst staff in a setting (Siraj-Blatchford and Hallet, 2014). Other commentators suggest that pedagogical leadership extends further in terms of its scope and range and encompasses features which are wider than prescribing the approach as a leadership model. They argue the need to maintain the child at the centre of all practice, but also take account of political, philosophical and educational drivers when considering a pedagogi-cal base for learning (Male and Palaiologou, 2015). Therefore, our position is that pedagogical leadership is complex, much debated and influenced by a variety of driving forces.

Context

In England, there is a requirement for every setting in the early education sector to be registered with government regulatory agencies and adhere to specific regulatory policies and the inspection framework. A central requirement of the regulatory framework is that all settings need to have in place a designated leader. This leader's role is complex as some in this position will be the only person supporting families in the community as a childminder in their own home, others may be responsible for a large multi-agency children's centre or perhaps for leading a small voluntary sector playgroup in the community. What they have in common – be they an individual or part of a group – is to engage with the teaching and learning process and develop learning opportunities which support the education and welfare of children. This is carried out under a national statutory framework of inspection whose function is to monitor provision to determine if it demonstrates quality practice (Office for Standards in Education, Children's Services and Skills [Ofsted], 2015a). The inspection follows a short period of notice and is carried out by a formally registered and experienced inspector who gathers evidence of the way both structural (regulatory features and requirements) and process (day-to-day interactions between educators, children and families) are evidenced in practice. The result is a written report, entered into the public domain, and an overall grade which indicates if the provision is performing to set criteria. The criteria include a close examination of effective leadership, the implementation of statutory legal requirements, evidence of effective curriculum planning, evidence of children's learning and the way the provision develops relationships with parents.

Inspection also involves close observations of professional interactions with children. Therefore, it is the responsibility of those who lead practice to guide and shape practice in order to maintain a focus on the child and each unique learning pattern, and at the same time have regard for a range of regulatory requirements. This is not to argue that such regulatory requirements are inappropriate, lack relevance or do not maintain a focus on learning and require reflection on practice. Indeed, a report from Ofsted (2013, p. 8) suggests it is important for those who work alongside children to engage in a process of self-evaluation to consider ways of bringing about positive change and refinement to their own practice. This is not done in isolation; Ofsted consider such reflection to be effective when staff routinely ask themselves: 'What is it like for a child here? What difference are we making, and how do we know?' The report also provides examples of when leaders created opportunities for their staff to reflect on the quality and impact of their provision and practice, and how this can become part of a self-improvement cycle of observation and reflection. This approach effectively asks educators to consider the pedagogy which underpins the children's learning and the way that learning can be evaluated in response to a development outline. A concern is that such reflection, however valuable, is set within one particular context. This can result in a somewhat insular approach without a wider platform that encourages debate via a framework of professional development opportunities, in particular, ways of carefully and co-operatively promoting quality practice. Such a framework could allow the leaders of practice to develop and share their views about effective pedagogical approaches and how each supports the individual child.

Implications for those who educate: Shared perspectives and collaboration

Faulkner and Coates (2013) provide a detailed critical appraisal of changes to the early education sector in England over past decades and argue that this has produced a range of professional requirements which have influenced a gradual professionalisation of the children's workforce. What we have now is a considerable weight of expectation placed upon leaders to promote and implement quality goals and regulations.

Leaders are required to develop a shift in thinking from a position where the leader is seen as a person who is followed and obeyed, to one where the leader involves others in questioning and critically exploring practice. Rodd (2013) emphasises this point by suggesting that the way a leader operates at a time of change is something which significantly influences the well-being of those in an organisation. This view is shared by a number of other researchers, including Siraj-Blatchford and Sum (2013) who suggest that good leaders recognise behaviours that support change and seek to encourage these. This approach involves effective communication and is dependent upon how well the leader understands and considers small details of practice whilst seeing the larger picture, often influenced by current policy and statutory requirements. Examination of the research literature by Dunlop (2008) echoes this, concluding that leaders have more influence when they work collaboratively with other leaders, sharing ideas, comparing different approaches and learning from examples of good practice. As to the impact of a leader, there is evidence that the quality of leadership in a setting has a key influence on children's learning. Note for example, the *Effective Pre-school, Primary and Secondary Education 3–14 Project* (Sylva et al., 2012). There is also evidence from the regulator in England that leadership and quality go hand in hand (Ofsted, 2015b).

The implications of such contexts are that the 'leader' must be confident in the skills, knowledge and competence of all individuals, and a positive, trusting environment must exist within the team. Bolden (2011) describes this as distributed leadership, as the result of a group or network of interacting individuals working in an organisation where there is an open approach to leadership, and expertise is spread across the many, rather than the few. Bolden reviews different types of distributed ways of working such as *collaborated distribution*, where two or more individuals work together to lead; *collective distribution*, where two or more people work separately but interdependently; and *coordinated distribution*, where people work in sequence to complete a project. Harris (2007) sees distributed leadership as part of this dynamic and encompassing a variety of shared leadership activities. We agree that the approach sits within the collaborative nature of an early years environment as suggested by Siraj-Blatchford and Manni (2007). This is because it is an approach which presents a positive approach to teamwork and is useful in developing shared practice and fostering collective responsibility. We suggest that it is this collectiveness which is the bedrock of pedagogical leadership.

We say this because pedagogical leadership is an opportunity to rethink and consider ways of encouraging people in a staff team to demonstrate the ability to be self-directed, and to take on board the concept of working as part of a team – a team which is often asked to take shared responsibility and develop a collective view of ways to support children's learning. The challenge is that this requires professional self-evaluation and reflection, and a shared commitment to improving the overall quality of practice in the provision. To an extent this is facilitated by some of the regulatory systems in place in England. Just one example, and there are many others, is when educators work collaboratively and adopt an approach which involves each person taking responsibility for monitoring the welfare of a designated number of children. This is known as the Key Person Approach and involves completing detailed observations of children and ensuring continuity of care and a 'known familiar person' for both the child and his or her parents. The key person needs to have considerable knowledge of the curriculum and the ability to consider what learning opportunities are effective to support children to learn. In effect, this requires pedagogic awareness. They are also required to pass on this information to parents and carers in a way that makes what goes on in the setting meaningful to the child's significant others. Responsibilities are also shared and distributed when educators are involved in completing a developmental check for children at the age of two or as a requirement to follow defined policies and procedures to protect and safeguard the welfare of children. These can be described as distributed actions and are required to be made visible as part of day-to-day practice. The leader is held accountable for planning and monitoring their implementation, as part of the formal inspection process.

Systems and regulatory requirements also influence pedagogical practice and offer messages about professional expectation. For example, the term 'teaching' is seen by the regulator as the ability to plan and manage the curriculum and learning in order to prepare children for the next stage in their learning. The way this is interpreted on the ground is important and now takes collaborative and distributed approaches into another wider dimension. How are the regulatory expectations interpreted on the ground? How do the leader and others decide the way this might involve child-initiated play and learning opportunities and building learning around children's dispositions to learn? Should they involve a focus on activities intended to meet goals and the outcomes expected of a child entering school? We say this not to suggest there is such a distinct binary choice between one or the other; the point we make is that systems, regulatory expectations and wider political drivers influence pedagogical approaches to learning.

Pedagogical leadership: More than teaching and learning

At the start of this chapter we suggested there were driving forces and resisting features that influence what can be described as pedagogical leadership. We have identified some of these and referred to texts that will allow the reader to follow up on some of the ongoing academic debates. In summary:

- *Changes in systems and the regulatory requirements that are influencing practice and influencing ways of leading practice*: A leader has to consider what emphasis should be given to the provision of learning opportunities for individual children and which go towards goal-driven learning activities. This involves a pedagogical and philosophical aspect which is much more than an approach to teaching and learning.
- *Accountability of the leader in terms of regulation and inspection and the reality of having to distribute responsibility and invest time to encourage and support people so they recognise that together they can shape practice*: A process which has to be done in an environment which may change and be refined without either professional development opportunities or financial support from government.
- *Developing self-directed responsibility in a team of people and (for the leader) being accountable to the team*: This is an important feature as effective early education rarely emerges from a leader working in isolation.
- *Seeing the whole picture*: An individual leader may have the desire to make things happen, but it is rare to find all the parts of an organisation coming together without active collaboration between staff, and this requires a clear direction that everyone subscribes to.

Pedagogic leadership is therefore not a simple matter of following a prescribed approach intended to promote high-quality educational practices. It requires sensitive interaction with others, caring and considerate engagement with children and parents, and a sound knowledge of the way children learn and the expectations placed upon children to learn. It is important for everyone who employs this approach to have a clear understanding of educational theory and its relationship with practice. Importantly, they should also be able to recognise effective practice and know how and why it is effective. We therefore offer a 'picture of practice', not as a whole photograph album but as a snapshot of practice. The case study, however, does illustrate the complexities of engaging in pedagogical leadership and we hope it provides the basis for further questions and discussion.

Picture of practice

This picture of practice was taken in an early education setting operating within a medium-sized rural primary school in England. It provides an example of pedagogical leadership in action, from four different perspectives: The child who is at the centre of what goes on, the key educator, the child's parents and the leader. The reason is to show different but interlocking influences on the child and to show that pedagogical leadership is to be viewed as more than an account of teaching and learning.

The setting itself is operated by an established team of five early years practitioners – an early years teacher and four early years educators. The setting provides care and education for children aged from two and a half years until entry into the main school reception class, usually the September after their fourth birthday. Although part of the school, the early years teacher leads the setting, taking the dual role of educational leader and manager of the room. In alignment with the English early education curriculum, the *Statutory Framework for the Early Years Foundation Stage* (EYFS) (Department for Education, 2017), the setting operates a key person system with all staff required to take on the responsibility for overseeing the development and progression of particular children together with maintaining strong parent/setting partnerships.

With forty children attending across the week, planning for individual children is led through key person observations which are shared at meetings, and informal chats between staff members. The team uses the children's identified interests and needs to construct a range of activities to suit both individual and group developmental requirements. Staff members each have their own skill-sets and preparation and delivery of the activities is distributed around these. Children starting at the setting are allocated an initial key person, however their attachment to staff is a major factor in selecting the right person for this role and, therefore, is subject to change.

Joe started at the setting aged three. Described as an able but quiet child by his parents, he attended another setting before moving into the local area with his family. He was already seeing a private speech and language therapist for speech delay. His mother stated she was concerned about his interactions in general, with his previous development progression reports situating him as below his developmental age group. Through meetings between the early years teacher and parents, it was decided to initially concentrate on improving Joe's social confidence within the new environment, and then consider his wider developmental progression. Joe and his family were offered a family settling-in session where Joe would be offered space to play and explore with his parents present. At the staff meeting, the teacher informed everyone of Joe's circumstances and contacted the speech and language therapist who agreed to support Joe in the setting, for six sessions.

During the settling-in session, Joe and his family were introduced to Kate, allowing them to get to know each other and provide time for Kate to gather relevant information from his parents. Kate immediately observed his communication with his parents, noting a below age ability in his language skills. It was evident that he was very under-confident. Together, Kate and Joe's parents developed a simple structure for his first few days at the setting that concentrated on his needs and interests with a settling-in plan devised for the following weeks. Recording children's development had recently changed at the setting, from learning journey books to electronic (online) journals which parents and carers received and added to online. The change was instigated in light of research at the setting, investigating approaches of effective documentation of children's learning. Joe's parents agreed to update his journal with home activities to further support Kate's understanding of his development. Looking through his journal became a regular activity between Joe and Kate who, through a sensitive and gentle approach, developed a trusting relationship with him. Kate updated both the teacher and other staff of his progression at the weekly staff meetings. The teacher also made general observations of Joe, sharing these with Kate and Joe's parents to support findings and provide another perspective to support his ongoing development.

Kate was allocated time to observe the speech and language sessions in order to continue the approaches used with Joe throughout the week. Through Kate gradually introducing other children into his play, Joe formed a friendship with one child which was relayed back to the parents who were eager to continue this outside of the setting. The parents mentioned in the online journal how Joe enjoyed helping his grandparents with their vegetable patch. After discussing this activity with him, Kate suggested to the staff team that a small vegetable patch be created in the preschool garden. The team agreed, asking Kate to take the lead in planning a topic for the whole group to grow and tend vegetables from seeds. This linked to the primary school's healthy eating initiative whilst supporting Joe's interests and skills. All the children helped to create and plan the garden with Joe's engagement and interaction being observed as high throughout. Kate recorded his interest and engagement in his online journal and, after reading it, Joe's grandparents offered to come in and help in the garden, linking Joe's experiences of home and school.

Throughout, Kate, the parents and the teacher had regular conversations about Joe's continuing development. Progression in Joe's social development was seen and there was evidence that he was gradually becoming more confident within the setting, engaging in a wider range of activities of his own accord and beginning to talk within small groups. Joe's parents reported a positive change in his speech and his general confidence. They agreed that working together, concentrating on his social engagement at a level he was comfortable with, had impacted on Joe's overall development. Kate completed a review of Joe's development against the curriculum expectations where she assessed him emerging within developmental norms for his age. At a further meeting between the teacher, the parents and Kate, it was decided that Kate would slowly reduce her interactions with Joe to develop his independence and self-confidence further. Afterwards, Kate reported feeling empowered when her ideas were respected and valued, enjoying taking responsibility in planning and driving the activities, recognising how this not only supported Joe's and the group's learning but also influencing her own professional development.

Through this case study it can be seen that, although the teacher is the leader in the room, the individual child's progression was supported and driven through interaction between his key person and parents. The teacher, seen as the 'setting leader', was involved in a supportive facilitator role with the key person and parents exchanging ideas to progress his development through his individual interests and needs. Whilst a key person approach is a requirement of the EYFS (DfE, 2017), there is not a standard procedure to follow, leaving development of interactions between setting staff, families and children at the discretion of the individuals and community. Engaging in pedagogical leadership, therefore, requires practitioners to be responsive to these individual and community requirements.

Questions that may be helpful when interrogating and looking at the points raised in the chapter and the picture of practice

- Does pedagogical leadership require honest communication between educators and is it based on the premise that staff can and will work together and look critically at practice?
- Did the picture of practice illustrate ways to make staff feel committed to a way of working?
- Did the picture of practice show that people were willing to innovate and accept change? Do you think the leader seemed to encourage the idea of staff being involved in managing change and is she therefore distributing leadership by sharing responsibility for the process of change?
- The picture of practice revealed the importance of embedding an evaluation of the child's learning within the family and listening to parents. Does this tell you that effective pedagogical leadership should be responsive to the communities a setting serves?
- A high-quality learning environment means looking, listening and carefully considering the child and it is not always about measuring content, methods and effectiveness. What do you think?
- Do you think (in the picture of practice) that the leader and the staff took a stance which met regulatory requirements and also supported the child?
- Pedagogical leadership involves reflective evaluation of practice. Is this of central importance in the way pedagogical leadership is enacted by those alongside children?
- Is pedagogical leadership a useful strategy to examine the larger picture, and the way practice is influenced by government policy and statutory system requirements?

We leave you with the views of a group of educators representing a range of settings within the early education sector. What they have in common is that they can all be called 'those who educate'. They included educational leaders, childminders, educators of children aged two to four years and some from the voluntary sector. They had responded to the question, 'What makes a good pedagogical leader?' Their response is reported here as a means of complementing the chapter content and the underlying premise that pedagogical leadership is more than developing teaching and learning strategies.

Pedagogical leadership was about having a thorough knowledge of statutory requirements and effective pedagogical practice and this was a central tenet of those who engage in pedagogical leadership. Leaders must also possess good communication skills to explain and apply such knowledge in practice. They suggested that qualities such as respect, care and consideration were an essential part of working with others, and that trust was a key element of leadership. This should include staff trusting each other and trusting the leader and also meant the leader having trust in the staff. In particular, because they were all part of making decisions that would influence children's learning. They expected leaders and managers to demonstrate the knowledge and confidence to explain why a particular approach to learning was effective, in essence championing what a team had developed together. They also thought that the ability to sensitively and professionally observe others' practice and for the leader to be observed in practice was an important part of the leadership role. They all agreed that reflection and the ability to listen to the child's voice was important and that community engagement was an essential part of adopting a pedagogical approach.

What they said could be interpreted as identifying features found within any number of textbooks about leading early education practice. On their own, none can be claimed to represent a recipe for pedagogical leadership. Taken together, however, they do identify how a leader needs to weave together a process that provides a close examination of how children learn and a sensitive engagement with people – a process that is surely more than an approach.

References

Bolden, R. (2011). Distributed leadership in organizations: A review of theory and research. *International Journal of Management Reviews*, 13, 251–269.

Coughlin, A. E., & Baird, L. (2013). *Pedagogical leadership*. Retrieved from www.edu.gov.on.ca/childcare/Baird_Coughlin.pdf

Department for Education. (2017). *Statutory framework for the Early Years Foundation Stage*. London: DfE.

Dunlop, A. W. (2008). *A literature review on leadership in the early years*. Retrieved from www.educationscotland.gov.uk/resources/a/leadershipre view.asp

Faulkner, D., & Coates, E. A. (2013). Early childhood policy and practice in England: Twenty years of change. *International Journal of Early Years Education*, 21 (2/3), 244–263.

Halttunen, L. (2016). Distributing leadership in a day care setting. *Journal of Early Childhood Education Research*, 5 (1), 2–18.

Harris, A. (2007). Distributed leadership: Conceptual confusion and empirical reticence. *International Journal of Leadership in Education*, 10 (3), 315–325.

Hujala, E., & Eskelinen, M. (2013). Leadership tasks in early childhood education, In E. Hujala, M. Waniganayake, & J. Rodd (eds.) *Researching leadership in early childhood education*. Tampere: Tampere University Press.

Male, T., & Palaiologou, I. (2015). Pedagogical leadership in the 21st century: Evidence from the field. *Educational Management, Administration and Leadership*, 43 (2), 214–231.

Office for Standards in Education. (2013). *Getting it right first time: Achieving and maintaining high-quality early years provision*. Retrieved from www.gov.uk/government/publications/achieving-and-maintaining-high-quality-early-years-provision-getting-it-right-first-time

Office for Standards in Education, Children's Services and Skills (Ofsted). (2015a). *Early years inspection handbook*. Retrieved from www.founda tionyears.org.uk/files/2015/05/Early_years_inspection_handbook.pdf

Office for Standards in Education, Children's Services and Skills (Ofsted). (2015b). *Inspection outcomes of early years providers by staff qualifications*. Retrieved from www.gov.uk/government/publications/inspection-outcomes-of-early-years-providers-by-staff-qualifications–2

Rodd, J. (2013). *Leadership in early childhood*. Maidenhead: Open University Press.

Sheridan, S. (2001). *Pedagogical quality in preschool: An issue of perspectives* (Unpublished PhD thesis). Gothenburg: Acta University.

Siraj-Blatchford, I., & Hallet, E. (2014). *Effective and caring leadership in the early years*. London: Sage.

Siraj-Blatchford, I., & Manni, L. (2007). *Effective leadership in the early years sector: The ELEYS study*. London: Institute of Education.

Siraj-Blatchford, I., & Sum, C. (2013). *Understanding and advancing system leadership in the early years*. Nottingham: NCTL.

Sylva, K., Melhuish, E., Sammons, P., Siraj-Blatchford, I., & Taggart, B. (2012). *Effective pre-school, primary and secondary education 3–14 project (EPPSE 3–14). Report from the Key Stage 3 phase: Influences on students' development from age 11–14*. London: Institute of Education/DfE.

Walker, R., Reed, M., & Carey-Jenkins, D. (2017). Educational policy and practice. In J. Musgrave, M. Saven-Baden, & N. Stobbs (eds.), *Studying early childhood education and care: A critical guide for higher education students* (pp. 82–93). Northwich: Critical Publishing.

Waniganayake, M. (2014). Being and becoming early childhood leaders: Reflections on leadership studies in early childhood education and the future leadership research agenda. *Journal of Early Childhood Education Research*, 3 (1), 65–81.

6

PEDAGOGICAL LEADERSHIP AS ETHICAL COLLABORATIVE BEHAVIOR

Andrew J. Stremmel

This chapter is concerned with leadership as ethical collaborative behavior and the importance of pedagogical leadership as a keystone of valuing children's agency. The pedagogical leader assists teachers in the process of becoming. In particular, the pedagogical leader aims to create opportunities to foster the development of teachers as human beings who are lifelong learners, researchers, and theorists, who problematise and learn from their practice, understand the dialogical relationship between teaching and research, and teacher and learner, and who continue to critically examine assumptions, beliefs, and practices in their daily encounters with children in classrooms. I accentuate the development of 'reflective' teachers, who understand the complexity of teaching, learning, identity, and positionality, as opposed to 'effective' teachers who merely implement a prescribed curriculum or follow the methodologies of others. Reflective teaching demands presence or attentiveness. This is essential to seeing teaching as an intellectual and ethical human act of caring, relationship, and inquiry.

Pedagogy is the excellence of teaching. Pedagogy refers not only to our need to act in everyday relation to (living with) the child as a learner, it suggests the need to reflect on this action (van Manen, 1991). Yet, our obsession with external curriculum mandates, accountability testing, and standardisation has minimised the true focus of pedagogy on the teacher-child relationship, moving us further away from a complex and nuanced understanding of what it means to teach and a view of learning as an inherently human activity (Hatch, 2015; Rodgers & Raider-Roth, 2006). The prevailing view of teachers

78

as inept in the United States, in particular, contributes to low teacher morale and high levels of stress that negatively impact their ability to connect to and develop meaningful relationships with children (Hatch, 2015). The effect of this pedagogical thinking is to deskill, devalue, and disempower teachers as professionals, routinising the nature of teaching and learning, and removing from teachers the process of deliberation and reflection that are vital to good pedagogy. As a result, learning as an exciting, joyful, and meaningful adventure between teacher and child is remote from the objectives of today's classrooms.

In this chapter, I suggest that pedagogical leadership is critical in helping teachers and children to engage in meaningful relationships, and in creating a view of teachers as transformative intellectuals who nurture learning through compassionate and reflective teaching. This chapter offers a counter-narrative positioned against restrictively linear conceptions of teacher education in general. Teacher education programmes should model a continuum of care for learners from early childhood through adulthood. The ideas presented in this chapter are applicable to the development of all teachers of all children of all ages. In this view, pedagogical leaders ensure that future teachers at all levels realise that their students come from somewhere and will continue on in their holistic growth as a human being. Pedagogical leadership demands that we view teacher education as the lifelong development of teachers as whole people and that we similarly view our education system, itself, more holistically.

First, I draw upon van Manen's (1991) meaning of pedagogy as an encounter of togetherness between adult and child, a relationship of practical action. I offer, as do others (Ayers, 1993; Giroux, 1985; Loughran, 2013; Rodgers & Raider-Roth, 2006) a counter-narrative of teaching as a profoundly intellectual and ethical work in which teachers, themselves, are in the best position to inquire about their work. Second, I conceptualise the role of a pedagogical leader and suggest that pedagogical leaders are in key positions to nurture a culture in which reflective thinking and collaborative inquiry are the catalysts for enabling teachers to develop awareness and understanding (Loughran, 2006). In particular, I assert that reflective teaching demands presence and offers hospitality, considering the singularity of each child and creating space for children to be received graciously. Finally, I emphasise that collaborative inquiry involving teacher research creates opportunities for teachers to engage in reflective practice, authentic conversation, and professional dialogue, and to theorise one's lived experience, which fosters and supports the development of self-awareness, self-understanding, and personal wholeness. These ideas are embedded in an education for democracy framework emphasising the need to liberate and humanise education with a pedagogy of questioning, an approach that opens the process of thinking, wondering, critically examining, and dialoguing (Dewey, 1916).

The nature of pedagogy

Pedagogy is a fascination with the growth of the other
Max van Manen

The above quote by van Manen (1991, p. 13) is at the heart of what is meant by pedagogy. Pedagogy occurs in the lived space between parent and child, teacher and student, coach and athlete, and mentor and protégé. In the literal sense, the Greek *pedagogue* (in Greek, *agogos* means to lead) was one who led the young child to school and back (van Manen, 1991). In a richer sense, then, pedagogy means to accompany, be with, and care for. Thus, the pedagogue, or one who serves in that capacity, stands in caring relation to the child and leads the child in the process of becoming.

Loughran (2013) suggests that understanding the nature of pedagogy requires the importance of two ideas. First, as I have already mentioned, is the notion that pedagogy is about the teaching-learning relationship. More specifically, it is about an orientation toward the child that centres on her [sic, throughout] process of becoming. This means that a primary ethical challenge to teachers is to see each child as a person who has hopes, dreams, aspirations, and capacities, and who brings a history and experience, as well as promise for the future (Ayers, 1993). From a perspective of an ethic of caring, it is the child before us who becomes our central concern. This does not mean a lack of concern for teaching skills; however, it does mean that skills are taught as the result of genuine concern for the child, that is, that the 'one is undertaken in light of the other' (Noddings, 1986, p. 387). This requires patience, curiosity, wonder, awe, and humility. It demands sustained focus, intelligent judgment, inquiry, and investigation. It requires what Maxine Greene (1977) terms 'wide-awakeness', because every decision a teacher makes is provisional, every view partial, and every conclusion tentative (Ayers, 1993; Rinaldi, 2006). The teacher needs to possess an attitude of research or inquiry, a disposition of

80

curiosity, and the desire to know or understand (Cochran-Smith & Lytle, 2009).

This view of pedagogy suggests that teaching is more than action and activity; thus, to Loughran's (2013) second point, it is (or must be seen as) problematic, involving reflection and speculation. That is, teachers reflect on, theorise about, and research their teaching; they make informed decisions that direct their practice and the learning that occurs. In this way, teaching is dynamic and responsive to the child and the demands of the situation. For example, the teacher must consider questions like:

- How does the situation appear from the child's perspective?
- How could I have better helped the child in this situation?
- Did my own personal needs cause me to overreact in this particular situation?

The problems teachers face are not of a technical nature; they are moral and ethical. Thus, teaching is dilemma- or problem-based not in the sense that a problem is something to be easily solved, but in the sense that teachers must continually make judgments about what is appropriate in a given situation, time, and place, for each child (Ayers, 1993; Dewey, 1916; van Manen, 1991).

Who is the pedagogical leader?

Although van Manen (1991) discussed pedagogy in terms of the adult-child relationship, pedagogy also applies to those in leadership positions who support and mentor teachers. This can be programme directors, teacher educators, or anyone who has a deep understanding of early learning and development. A vital characteristic is the ability and willingness to support teachers in their being and becoming. Pedagogical leaders promote what Ron Heifetz (1994) terms adaptive capacity. Adaptive capacity is exemplified by the ability to learn from experience, be creative in decision-making and problem solving, and be responsive to the needs of all stakeholders in the teaching-learning process. Pedagogical leaders maximise potential and performance of the teachers with whom they work. They foster the dispositions of curiosity, openness, resilience, and purposefulness to create a culture of reflective teaching and greater focus on learning for both child and adult. Pedagogical leaders assume an inquiry stance and challenge others to see themselves as researchers who study the teaching and learning process (Coughlin & Baird, 2013; Katz, 1996).

If teaching at its best depends on the implementation of certain fundamental intellectual and ethical qualities, then pedagogical leadership is the key to helping teachers develop these qualities in order to promote children's agency. These qualities include reflection, presence, hospitality, inquiry, and collaboration. The pedagogical leader's role is to establish an environment that builds trust and care and facilitates the development of reflective thinking and inquiry. Reflective inquiry supports the development of self-awareness, self-understanding, and personal wholeness and enables teachers to bring identity and integrity more fully into their experiences with children.

Pedagogical leadership is grounded in reflection

Reflective teaching belongs to the inquiry-oriented paradigm of teacher education, which holds that teachers should develop habits of inquiry, that is, to be self-monitoring, adaptive, problem-solvers, and active decision-makers (Cochran-Smith & Lytle, 2009; Zeichner, 1983). According to Dewey (1916), reflection requires the development of several dispositions and skills including introspection, open-mindedness, and willingness to accept responsibility for decisions and actions. The reflective teacher has the ability to view situations from multiple perspectives; search for alternative explanations of classroom events; and use evidence to support or evaluate a decision or position. Dewey believed that it was more important to develop an orientation toward children based on reflection on the meaning and significance of their experiences, than to acquire behavioral competencies. Rather than 'effective' teachers, we should strive to develop 'reflective' teachers who carefully and deliberately consider their experiences in the classroom.

The role of the pedagogical leader is less focused on learning procedures and strategies that lead to effectiveness in teaching, and more concerned with how to think, feel, and act in ways that allow for thoughtful analysis, creativity, and innovation. Having developed a unique self and a pedagogical orientation with the children that enables them to learn, the pedagogical leader fosters in teachers not only the goal to teach well but to create possibilities for children and themselves to learn and grow. Teaching becomes an extension of one's whole being. With an aim to transform teachers' attitudes toward teaching – to see themselves not as consumers but as producers of knowledge about children, teaching, and themselves – the pedagogical leader helps teachers to understand that they are not who they are told by others to be, by images and messages that would have them focus on self- interest and self-absorption. Rather, the aim is to help teachers to become more self-aware, more understanding, and to learn to read their own responses to their experiences with children in order to live more authentic lives (Palmer, 1999).

By thoughtfully reflecting on what they should or could have done, teachers decide how they want to be in the lives of children, what they will mean in their lives, and the role they will play in their development. The reality of teaching is more than what we see happening in the classroom between a teacher and a group of children. To understand the complexity of teaching is to be able to tune in to the thoughts, feelings, questions, and assumptions contained within the teacher and each child in the classroom and to know for each person the full range of her inner life at every moment. This nearly impossible task, when one considers the incredibly complex and intellectually challenging nature of teaching, can be achieved only through being present, receiving others, and questioning and studying one's practice.

Reflective thinking demands presence

In his marvelous story, *The Three Questions*, Leo Tolstoy (1885/2016) tells the tale of a king who wants to find the answers to what he considers the three most important questions in life: 'What is the right time for every action?', 'Who are the most necessary people?', and 'What is the most important thing to do?' (para. 2). The answers are these: 'Now is the most important time', 'The one you are with is the most important person', and 'The most important thing is to do that person good' (para. 27). This is a remarkable story about being present, that now is the only reality, and how relationships with others are our reasons for living and therefore key to teaching and learning.

Essentially, presence is about paying attention to personal experience and bringing one's whole self to full attention to what is happening in the moment (de Mello, 1990; Greene, 1977; Rodgers & Raider-

Roth, 2006). Rodgers and Raider-Roth note that presence involves not only a state of alert awareness, but receptivity and connectedness to the individual and the group in the context of their learning environments and the ability to respond with a considered and compassionate next step (p. 266). Similarly, van Manen (1991) describes presence as 'mindfulness', a kind of consciousness or intense self-awareness that leads to thoughtful action in pedagogical situations. Presence, as a critical element of pedagogy, focuses on the human quest for connectedness, purpose, meaning, and self-understanding that should be at the heart of everything we do as pedagogical leaders.

Presence or awareness is a fitting construct when describing the complex and challenging act of teaching. Without awareness, teachers become mechanical, complacent, and unresponsive to children. Without awareness, teachers become dependent on the shifting chain of events that characterises their work and leads to quick changes of mood and behavior. Teaching becomes nothing more than a series of actions and reactions that pull us away from our inner selves and the possibilities for awareness (de Mello, 1990; Nouwen, 1975).

As important as presence seems to be in the pedagogical process, however, it is not explicitly taught in teacher education programmes (Rodgers & Raider-Roth, 2006). It is a thorny challenge in an age of 24/7 connection to the world through social media and the Internet. Very little, if any, of pedagogy focuses on methods of inquiry that would help teachers to develop presence. Academic culture simply does not encourage the exploration of questions that help us to pay attention, to questions such as:

- Who am I?
- How did I get to be this way?
- What is most important in my life?
- What excites me?
- What is my passion?
- What are my gifts?
- Who am I becoming?

Nevertheless, how we make sense and meaning of our lives and everyday experiences may be among the most significant components of human development.

Paying attention to who one is in the lives of children is critical to reflective teaching practice; understanding the reasoning that underlies one's practice is critical to viewing teaching as problematic; and viewing teaching as problematic extends the understanding of pedagogy (Loughran, 2013). Pedagogical leaders, then, must have a disciplined and intentional understanding of who they are in order to make sense of what is going on inside the teachers with whom they work and to invite intentional focus on their inner landscape. They must model how to listen carefully and intuitively in order to apprehend meaning and provide a genuine response. Sharing presence is being authentic or true to ourselves, looking within ourselves to discover what authorises our choices, our decisions, and thereby our actions and who we will become. Pedagogical leaders in teacher education support the development of reflective teachers who continually examine their actions, beliefs, values, and understandings to build deeper understandings of pedagogy.

Reflective teaching involves welcoming the other

Our current educational narrative in the United States suggests that we prefer to focus on 'what the child is not', rather than on 'what the child is'. If pedagogy is a relationship, oriented toward the being and becoming of the child, then we must view the child as competent. We need to find better ways to welcome and receive children for who they are, as multi-dimensional human beings. Hospitality is about welcoming; it is about creating a space where we are open to others' ideas, their backgrounds, their ways of learning and living (Nouwen, 1975). It is about creating a welcoming space for dialogue, in which those with whom we enter a pedagogical relationship can reveal what they have to offer. It is about creating space to listen, to care, and to learn. Thus, the pedagogical leader must ponder the question: 'In what ways have I tried to welcome the ideas and views of teachers, to listen to their needs, and to honour their voices?'

To listen is to hear without imposing our commentary or judgement. For example, when children are crying or fighting during a conflict, what do we actually hear? Do we hear: 'These children can't get along?' 'They don't know how to listen?' Or, are we allowing ourselves to truly hear children's needs, intentions, and feelings; be present in that moment; and be open to what is really happening? When we are truly welcoming of the child and open to possibilities, we begin to hear not what children are saying, but what they are trying to say. We experience the situation not piecemeal but as a translucent whole. O'Reilley (1998) beautifully states that, through deep listening, we are better able to offer our most nurturing and productive response to children's questions, needs, and concerns, that may create a space into which the child may grow and more fully become.

It may sound strange to speak of the pedagogical relationship in terms of hospitality. If, however, we think about children as guests who enter our classrooms, require careful attention while they are with us, and then leave to follow their own way, our pedagogy should strive to create a sacred space that allows children to nurture their inner lives. This is pedagogy as an ethical behavior.

Pedagogical leaders foster collaborative inquiry

Learning to teach is a lifelong developmental journey, a process of becoming that involves continual inquiry and renewal. The pedagogical leader's primary role is that of assisting and supporting the development of understanding through inquiry (Loughran, 2006). Teachers must become learners in their own classrooms. They must become students of their own thinking and practice, reflecting on what they believe, the decisions they make, and the reasons underlying what they do. Hence, pedagogical leaders lead and guide the study of teaching and learning processes.

Assuming an inquiry stance, pedagogical leaders challenge teachers to see themselves as researchers who question or challenge what happens in the classroom. They foster the dispositions of curiosity, openness, resilience, and purposefulness to create a culture of reflective teaching and greater focus on learning for both child and adult. Establishing learning communities for regular conversation and collaborative inquiry helps construct the culture, convey commonality of experience, and identify problems to be resolved through teacher research.

A community of learners is a safe space for teachers and pedagogical leaders to promote feelings of hospitality, unity, and shared vision among children, teachers, and families. The pedagogical leader has the important task of establishing a caring, inclusive community in which everyone can develop and learn, and each person's strengths and interests can be woven into the fabric of the overall school's function.

In this way, each person's contribution can be celebrated and respected. In particular, I believe that one of the primary roles of the pedagogical leader is to offer the community of learners a glimpse of what it can become and to enlist teachers in the common task of learning, caring, and developing. By recognising the unique skills and strengths that they bring to the community, teachers are able to develop a sense of ownership in their professional development. They may feel more empowered to make choices about curriculum and teaching strategies; make better decisions within their classrooms; take risks and test ideas; and evaluate their established goals and constructed practices. Further, they may be better able to articulate the reasons and purposes for their actions in the classroom. In essence, the pedagogical leader's challenge to teachers is this:

> • How can you more effectively assist and support children's learning and cultivate an environment which supports both the children's and your development?
> • How can I assist and support you, as teachers, to learn through systematic inquiry and investigation of your teaching and curriculum practice?

One important aspect of being a professional means reflectively assessing all aspects of our work and constantly seeking to improve. This ongoing reflective practice is markedly enhanced when pedagogical leaders facilitate collaborative inquiry to identify areas where improvement is needed and to assess the effectiveness of changes that are made (Hatch, 2015). Instead of assuming that teachers are incapable of shaping their own professional development, teacher research, especially when done collaboratively under the guidance of a pedagogical leader, assumes that teachers are in the best position to figure out what they need to improve and have the abilities and methods common to everyday practice to make improvement happen.

Carlina Rinaldi (2006) suggests that teachers must constantly examine and reflect on their understandings, and share them with others comparing their hypotheses. Possessing an attitude of research or inquiry, a disposition of curiosity, and the desire to know or understand means moving from a position of certainty about what teachers do to a position of questioning and wondering and not necessarily knowing.

87

The pedagogical leader helps teachers to develop a more comprehensive and accurate view of what it means to be a teacher. Viewing teachers as researchers affirms their professional status and acknowledges their important responsibility to both theory *and* practice.

If done well, teacher research has the potential not only to add to the knowledge we have about teaching and classrooms, it can change the kinds of questions we ask about children and their learning and the kinds of understanding that is produced. Thus, teacher research represents a distinctive way of knowing about teaching and learning that can alter, not just add to, what we know in the field. Central to collaborative inquiry is posing, not just asking, questions; taking practice as a site for inquiry, interrogating one's own and others' practices and assumptions, and learning from and about practice by collecting and analysing the data of daily work. The pedagogical leader, then, helps teachers to work together to develop and alter their own questions and interpretive frameworks informed by thoughtful consideration of the immediate situation and the children they teach, and by making sense of the many contexts within which they work.

In summary, pedagogical leaders give the community of learners a glimpse of what it means to be a professional and empowers teachers in the common task of learning, caring, and developing. In a community of learners, people work cooperatively and share knowledge. Learning is a social and co-participatory process. There is mutual respect, democratic conversation and dialogue, and trust.

Conclusion

I have maintained that pedagogical leaders, themselves mindful and hospitable in their practice, help teachers to become intentional and aware. They create spaces for teachers to discuss and respond thoughtfully to issues and problems that concern children and teachers in the classroom. These problems are moral and ethical. Inquiry that is aimed at addressing those issues and concerns that are important to teachers (e.g., developing responsive teaching strategies, maintaining control of a classroom, feeling respected and liked, and developing a better understanding of who they are in relation to the children they teach) enables teachers to better understand themselves and children. This is the core of learning to be a teacher, and it requires a collaborative community of support.

In a collaborative community, teachers and pedagogical leaders have time to reflect together, time to dialogue about the ways they are working with children, parents, and each other. They pay attention to how they make meaning, find connections, and create relationships. The pedagogical leader's goal is to establish a community that is a safe space for teachers to show themselves fully to each other and be welcomed, enter into dialogue with one another; develop research to solving real problems; and collaborate with one another in meaningful inquiry, creative thinking, and reflection aimed at growth and development.

References

Ayers, W. (1993). *To teach: The journey of a teacher.* New York, NY: Teachers College Press.

Cochran-Smith, M. & Lytle, S. L. (2009). *Inquiry as stance, practitioner research for the next generation.* New York, NY: Teachers College Press.

Coughlin, A. M. & Baird, L. (2013). *Pedagogical leadership.* Retrieved from www.edu.gov.on.ca/childcare/Baird_Coughlin.pdf

de Mello, A. (1990). *Awareness: The perils and opportunities of reality.* New York, NY: Image Press.

Dewey, J. (1916). *Democracy and education: An introduction to the philosophy of education.* New York, NY: The Free Press.

Giroux, H. A. (1985). Teachers as transformative intellectuals. *Social Education, 49*(5), 76–79.

Greene, M. (1977). Toward wide-awakeness: An argument for the arts and humanities in education. *Teachers College Record, 9*(1), 119–125.

Hatch, J. A. (2015). *Reclaiming the teaching profession: Transforming the dialogue on public education.* Lanham, MD: Rowman & Littlefield.

Heifetz, R. (1994). *Leadership without easy answers.* Cambridge, MA: Harvard University Press.

Katz, L. (1996). Child development knowledge and teacher preparation: Confronting assumptions. *Early Childhood Research Quarterly, 11*(2), 135–146.

Loughran, J. (2006). *Developing a pedagogy of teacher education: Understanding teaching and learning about teaching.* London: Routledge.

Loughran, J. (2013). Pedagogy: Making sense of the complex relationship between teaching and learning. *Curriculum Inquiry, 43*(1), 118–141.

Noddings, N. (1986). *Caring, a feminine approach to ethics and moral education.* Berkeley, CA: University of California Press.

Nouwen, H. J. M. (1975). *Reaching out: The three movements of spiritual life.* New York, NY: Doubleday.

O'Reilley, M. R. (1998). *Radical presence: Teaching as contemplative practice.* Portsmouth, NH: Boynton/Cook Publishers.

Palmer, P. (1999). *Let your life speak: Listening to the voice of vocation.* San Francisco, CA: Jossey-Bass.

Rinaldi, C. (2006). *In dialogue with Reggio Emilia.* New York: Routledge.

Rodgers, C. R., & Raider-Roth, M. B. (2006). Presence in teaching. *Teachers and Teaching: Theory and Practice, 12*(3), 265–287.

Tolstoy, L. (1885/2016). The three questions. In *What men live by and other tales.* Irvine, CA: Xist Publishing. Retrieved from www.public-library.uk/pdfs/9/797.pdf

van Manen, M. (1991). *The tact of teaching: The meaning of pedagogical thoughtfulness.* London, Ontario, Canada: The Althouse Press.

Zeichner, K. (1983). Alternative paradigms of teacher education. *Journal of Teacher Education, 34*(3), 3–9.

EDITORIAL PROVOCATIONS
Engaging readers and extending thinking

Sandra Cheeseman

The chapters in this section provide rich insights into the lives of those who educate. We are provided with three very different and yet companionable explorations of the complex lives of those who work to prepare and support teachers and educators in their work. Spanning three continents, we see the similarities and differences that these contexts offer to the experiences of teachers and examine some of the tensions and pressures that circulate in their professional lives.

Chapter 4 posits that the central task of early childhood pedagogical leaders is to improve teaching and therefore children's learning and development outcomes. The need for leaders to be responsive to the situational context and to the children, families and education staff with whom they work illuminates the need for pedagogical leaders to start with an examination of their own leadership approach and what they both personally and professionally bring to this role. Looking closely at the situation in Australia where the role of educational leader has been defined by law and regulation, this chapter exposes some of the raw challenges for leaders to be both confident in their knowledge but speculative in their practice. Does the pressure to demonstrate professionalism inhibit a willingness to look critically at the self?

Across the oceans to the United Kingdom, Chapter 5 speaks similarly of the challenges of teaching professionalism in an era of regulatory accountability. Akin to the Australian context, attempts in the UK to professionalise the early childhood workforce have led to a focus on the demonstration of professional practice. Inspections at the setting level can place the focus on the individual leader's performance, which these authors suggest can stifle broader conversations about leadership – beyond the fence of the setting. The

91

picture of practice presented here provides alternative ways of conceptualising pedagogic leadership as shared and respectful of what each practitioner brings to their practice. We are challenged in this chapter to revision our view of leadership by looking first at what life is like for the children in our settings and what difference our leadership decisions are making in children's lives.

Chapter 6 throws out a challenge to formularised or regulated ways of interpreting the work of teachers and leaders in early childhood contexts. Orienting the teacher-child relationship as problematic and involving reflection and speculation, contests the assumption of regulated leadership and calls for teachers to be viewed as ethical and intelligent decision-makers rather than as inept individuals in need of instruction. The emphasis on accountability raises the question as to whether the focus of professional practice might be too much on the side of measured outputs rather than a critical focus on leadership inputs.

Together these chapters provide us with opportunities for rich and complex conversations about leadership. We are encouraged to look closely not only at our own contexts and requirements, but to be brave and courageous in our visions for the future. The chapters urge us to critically examine ourselves and yet we are also challenged to be open to the Other. What might appear on the surface to be contradictory ideas provide the grist for the essential conversations about the future for leadership in early childhood. It is time to pay attention to meanings, connections and relationships in the complex world of those who educate.

Section 3

EMBEDDING FAMILIES AND COMMUNITIES

7

WALKING WITH FAMILIES IN AN INDIGENOUS EARLY CHILDHOOD COMMUNITY

Jacqui Tapau and Alma Fleet

This chapter explores connections with families in the life of an early learning centre and the place of the centre in the life of a remote Australian community. Principles of respectful relationships, connectedness, patience and time are all reflected in shared conversations. The stories reflect the spirit of 'yarning' that is central to the kinds of relaxed talk that can happen in easy-going ways with people who are comfortable talking 'around' topics on the way to things that are important. Handing 'the lead' back and forth between speakers, as in the style being offered here, is reflective of the reciprocal nature of the experiences being explored. These conversations do not shy away from exposing potentially difficult situations and equally expose challenges related to the concept of reciprocity while weaving together useful pathways for walking together. Challenges related to the concept of 'partnerships' with families are also explored.

Beginning

Notions of 'family' and 'community' are culturally-bound and contextually-defined. In this case, both authors could be described as being in the same 'learning community', that of early childhood professional practice in Australia, though with primary connections to other communities. What unfolds in this chapter illustrates complexities of the concept of 'linking early childhood practice' to local communities. For context: Alma had been invited by an Aboriginal colleague to address a conference of educators working in settings with large populations of Aboriginal and/or Torres Strait Islander

95

children and families. [Note that the term 'Indigenous', although occasionally used here for convenience, is not always accepted by the people to whom it is said to refer, as people tend to identify/label themselves according to specific cultural/regional groups.] The assigned conference topic was 'Embedding families and communities'. Given the importance of the topic, the invitation was an honour, but given the context, the task was potentially impossible. It would be naïve if not insulting to expect a non-Indigenous speaker to address an audience with a large number of Aboriginal and/or Torres Strait Islanders on how to connect with their local communities and include families in their work. The nature of community-connection is differentially defined depending on situations. A resolution was to engage in the sharing of voices, the turn-taking and melding of voices reminiscent of the idea of 'yarning', the offering of thoughts and ideas around a real or imagined gathering circle, a space in which topics might emerge and drift, with more circularity and underlying currents. The opening slide from our presentations (see Figure 7.1) highlights the strengths-based approach to 'walking with families', as evidenced through the respect shown by including the Aboriginal and Torres Strait Islander flags. This code of acknowledgment is recognised in the region.

This pattern continues in this chapter. Building on the way we worked in the conference presentation, Jacqui –a strong Aboriginal pedagogical leader at the Gundoo early learning centre, and Alma – a non-Indigenous academic friend and colleague – take turns, in different voices, thinking aloud about how the concept of 'walking alongside' families resonates with intentions to embed family and community perspectives into early childhood settings. Our thoughts

Figure 7.1 Beginning the public sharing

are then placed alongside explanations of 'partnership' that may be more familiar to readers but are not prioritised over the lived experiences being shared.

Thinking together

Jacqui

Like many Aboriginal communities across Australia, the town of Cherbourg is also an Aboriginal Mission made up of many tribes. In our community motto 'Many Tribes, One Community', we acknowledge each other as family. Therefore, it is vitally important in our practices as an Aboriginal early childhood learning centre to teach and embed our cultural connections in our children.

The families, elders and the community also acknowledge and appreciate the early childhood centre embedding respect for country, family and most importantly to respect our elders and their wisdom. The aim for our centre is: *to engage and be a gathering place for parents and community agencies; these opportunities lead to referrals to vital services within the community and build trust and rapport to support families and their children's wellbeing.*

Here is how we begin:

> *Welcome to our Aboriginal early learning centre.*
>
> *We offer education for our very young and acknowledge what our families bring to the learning of our children. Our open-door policy extends an invitation for families to come back and share their skills and knowledge with our children and staff. When walking with us, you, our families will experience the connectedness of community through the shared knowledge and caregiving of educators that are known to the children. These amazing children refer to us as Uncle or Auntie. This term of endearment and respect is instilled in all children within the community of Cherbourg.*

The engagement of Aboriginal families in our service is meaningful to meeting the diverse needs of the community, and practising transparency is building strong relationships with families and community. Respectful relationships begin the moment a family walks through the door; a tour of the learning environment helps to break down any barriers a family may have to an early learning institution.

Engaging with families is walking beside them and shar-
ing their children's journey and a tour of the learning
environment will show what they want to know. Build-
ing relationships (thinking intently) *mostly verbal. I wanted*
the centre to... (hands encompassing – pause – look for
words)...

In a lot of communities, you see a lot of services just there to
do their job. I wanted the centre to be a centre of the community, of everything that happens, to bring the other services to
our place. You can't go forward or back, you have to walk
with them to share their journey...

'Partnership' is accepting that our children have extended families,
a bond that is strong amongst all members of our large extended
families – this is a focus in an Aboriginal community. Walking with
them is sharing their children's journey; the key to connecting home
is acknowledging that open conversation is the preferred method of
communication which may also involve many voices. This is essential during the first stages of the enrolment process as families share
information or fill-out forms during the transition between home
and the learning environment.

Building pathways for Aboriginal families into an early learning
environment is an ongoing process of maintaining strong connections and relationships. We can also let families know when things
are not going well. The centre knows families and their situations so
can support them in difficult circumstances. Our priority is to
engage with our families by instilling the importance of early childhood education as it begins within the first five years of their child's
life. Our Indigenous children need a heads-up prior to entering the
school system: changing community perceptions that early childhood is not a babysitting service but a learning place that offers high
quality programmes that stimulate young children's creative curiosity in their learning experience that also connects to their home
environment or their interaction in community life.

Alma

Early childhood services/settings/schools – all variously referred to
here as 'settings', are pieces of an interconnected puzzle. The adults
who work in the settings, those who bring their children to the sites,
the children who live part of their lives bounded by the walls/fences/

98

philosophies of the setting are all linked. The degrees to which those links are nurtured, neutered or harmed can be determined by professional consideration of pedagogies relevant to communities.

Let's think what we mean by 'community'. Those of us in the same professional space may consider ourselves part of a large Learning Community, or that term may only apply to a local group of teachers working together through a vehicle like Practitioner Inquiry to further knowledge and professional practice. Neither of those usages is what is usually implied when asking educators to 'embed families and communities' in their practice; in fact, the term is usually offered in the singular, a misconception at the beginning. We are all members of different communities, and any early childhood site services a broad range of communities – not only locally, but perhaps regionally – possibly different cultural groups or employees of a particular organisation, or people bound together by remoteness. Let's imagine for this purpose, that we are talking about a sense of belonging, a sense of being part of at least one group bounded by some identifiable feature. For this moment, we are sharing with a respected Aboriginal leader, what she means when she thinks about relationships with families in her remote centre, and how those values impact pedagogy.

Jacqui

Our priority to engage more families into our early childhood service meant that we also needed to change our title from 'Day Care' to 'Early Childhood Learning Centre' to break the mindset that is within the community. Family connection is strong within an Aboriginal community, which helped during our door-knocking to get community's views on our early learning centre, as this was vital to share in a two-way expectancy of the learning centre. Know that in community, face to face yarning and word of mouth is the key to filling a centre with children. 'Early Childhood Learning Centre' is the message being heard with families for under fives. We want to empower children to become future members of our community.

We are Cultural beings – older siblings are taught to look after younger siblings. Culture shouldn't be just celebrated through NAIDOC week[1] – we live it through our practices and our homes – it needs to be brought back to the centre. People forget.

99

This is a town made up of many tribes. In the past, each clan would look after their own kin; now we all need to look after each other. To be community we have to be family – responsible for every child that comes in the door.

> *We have a Welcome policy, but we are being over-booked. 'Aunty! Stop inviting people!!' It's good for the kids – we get visitors, they run over, talk to them. Families are encouraged to share their knowledge and visit as often as they like. An open door also means open to opportunities. Everybody has something to give. Trying to expand children's knowledge and vision.*

Engaging with the elders of today will give wisdom, strengthen our future leaders to become resilient. We've got an old bloke who visits every day and the children expect him – 'Hello Pop!' 'Morning Pop!' When we have elders in, the children learn to Show Respect, to acknowledge elders. The families, elders and the community also appreciate the Early Childhood Learning Centre embedding respect for our elders and community in our curriculum for our under sixes including practices that teach children of our past history.

Alma

Jacqui's ideas resonate with Stan Grant's introduction to his friend's autobiography, both men coming from a different starting place but with shared understanding. Stan writes that he and Warren have known each other since university, but that the bond is deeper than that because of shared belongings: 'We are blackfellas and all of us circle each other, our footprints soft on the land and our songs carried on the breeze' (cited in Mundine, 2017, p. xii).

In another form of language, but situated on the same land mass, these thoughts sit comfortably alongside the national pedagogical guidelines: *The Early Years Learning Framework* (EYLF) (DEEWR, 2009) which is the reference point for educators. It is part of the section concerning educational programming and planning in the Australian National Quality Standard (NQS) expectations for early childhood sites (see Australian Children's Education and Care Quality Authority, 2018b). The NQS is linked to national learning frameworks recognising that children learn from birth, including the EYLF.

The EYLF includes principles, overviews of practice, and suggested indicators of progress within each of five components/

categories of learning outcomes. Within the explanation of how educators should engage with their responsibilities, there is an expectation of 'holistic approaches'. In this section, the Framework states (DEEWR, 2009, p. 14) that

- While educators may plan or assess with a focus on a particular outcome or component of learning, they see children's learning as integrated and interconnected.
- They recognise the connections between children, families and communities and the importance of reciprocal relationships and partnerships for learning.
- They see learning as a social activity and value collaborative learning and community participation.

These guidelines relate specifically to the work that Jacqui is describing. Interestingly, when this connection is highlighted, she shrugs and says she doesn't know what the fuss is about, *I'm just doing my job*. The fuss, of course, is that there are others without her clarity of vision and purpose, who are not connecting in these ways. She muses: *Interesting word – holistic*.

> *To make sure our children are being well-cared for, we have to look after their parents. If the parents aren't being cared for – how are we going to look after their children? We work on getting services to the centre – so health checks can happen there (hearing). Specialists become available to community in a place familiar to children and families.*

In further consideration of the Australian ELYF, we find resonance in the introductory overview for Outcome number 4 – *Children are confident and involved learners*, in which it is stated that 'Children are more likely to be confident and involved learners when their family and community experiences and understandings are recognised and included in the early childhood setting' (DEEWR, 2009, p. 33). Although this outcome sits under the umbrella of Educational Program and Practice (NQS Area #1), there are clear links with Quality Area #6: Collaborative Partnerships with Families and Communities (Australian Children's Education and Care Quality Authority, 2018a). Assessment against these Standards results in a Rating and Quality Improvement Plan to move assessments of particular categories within the Standard from the mid-point ('Working towards' or

'Meeting the standard') to higher levels of achievement (e.g. 'Exceeding'). This standard expects respectful and supportive relationships with families as well as collaboration with other service providers and organisations able to offer support to families. The Standard also notes that the expertise of families should be recognised, and that by implication, deficit orientations are not appropriate. Everyday experiences can enable these goals to be met.

Jacqui

As an Aboriginal early childhood centre, we are teaching and embedding the valuing of Respect, of the importance of family. To ensure our children have connection to our elders, we have regular visits to our nursing home for morning tea or invite the residents to our centre. Every month, staff at the old people's home prepare morning tea and some of us visit. The children play while we're there and some visit together. Lets folks know they're not forgotten. These connections allow our elders to talk and play with our little ones. It is also an opportunity for the educators to talk to our elders and share the children's genealogy; with smiles on our elders' faces, they share their connections or tell stories of growing up with members of the child's families.

In another example: To acknowledge our history and encourage respect for our elders, the educators and children planned a trip to our local museum, the Ration Shed Museum, to go 'outside the fence'. The museum's significance is that, when our town was being run by the government as a Mission, this was once a place used to give out rations to our elders. As a museum, it was set up by some special ladies (elders) to teach the younger generations about our history. The children watch videos of past elders talking about growing up in Cherbourg, look at photos on display and talk to our nans who manage the Ration Shed about our community's early years. This place is important to us. One time, our early childhood centre was invited by the Queensland Performing Arts Centre to make some artwork to be displayed at the Ration Shed. The artwork involved working with clay, drawings and interviewing the children about their belonging. The artists from the city asked if they could come to the centre to work with the older children. They wanted to see how much the children knew about their belonging. For a while they came regularly.

When people ask how all these things happen ... just Be Bold! Like, we celebrate Children's Day together, and we're looking for ways to share projects with the school. Maybe we could investigate/celebrate children who have finished Year 12? Building partnership with the school is important so that education is seen as valuable for the under fives and through life. School completion is important to investigate in our area as employment issues and family histories may mean that young people do not stay in school.

Alma

These adventures 'outside the fence' and, indeed, the arrival of interesting people within the centre, often reflect decisions made in conversations with families and other community members. Perhaps ironically, given her strong pedagogical leadership, but understandable in the community context, Jacqui can be reticent about 'unpacking' the lived experiences in this centre. Nevertheless, she mused about the range of ways that family and community relationships are made visible (and thus connect with pedagogy) at the centre. She thought about important marks of cultural connection, like activities to 'remember the Mabo event' (a tribute to a leading Lands Rights activist) as well as daily practices like having a community bus to help collect and return children to families without transport, in an area with no public transportation services, and of 'ways to be useful for families', like having a BBQ to get people into the place: 'People want to eat!'

In summarising her thoughts and reflecting out loud, there are many more aspects of community than can be explored here – things which seem obvious to the people living in the area, but not so immediate for people elsewhere. For example, Jacqui mused about the relationship with the local creek and the tensions with the health and safety regulations, while wryly commenting that, 'no-one has drowned!', or trying to help me understand the importance of the seasons, not being defined by the accepted calendar, but by the coming and going of local wildlife or the bushfire season. Her decision-making is often implicit and might not be recognised by people without her strong cultural history.

There are repeated refrains, rhythms, in the ways these ideas unfold, though they are heavily, culturally contextualised. The importance of context can be seen in an Australian national conference devoted to the work of educational leaders, where a prominent (non-Indigenous) educator from the state of Victoria spoke to gathered participants about partnerships with families. Anne Kennedy started with a story of her early teaching experience that brought home to her the importance of 'both-ways' listening, of hearing the values and voices of families alongside a teacher's educational endeavours (Kennedy, 2017). Her context was very different from Jacqui's – geographically, economically and culturally. Jacqui would think of the families coming to her centre in terms of 'relationships' rather than 'partnership', but there are resonances across space and circumstances which make it helpful to include some of Anne's thinking here (with permission).

She spoke of the common slippage between the realities of working with families and the rhetoric of partnership, of the quandary she had caused in her first teaching appointment when she had accepted the offer of afternoon tea in a high rise 'housing commission' block of flats. A father had perceived that this new graduate needed much more learning in order to be positioned to teach his son, while the Principal was concerned about the crossing of an invisible line in a professional relationship. A later story told how Anne had felt diminished as a new mother when a 'baby health nurse' had tackled the issue of her young baby's weight loss in a way that lessened the new mother's sense of expertise in the caring for her own child. Professionals certainly have a right and a responsibility to 'intervene' in circumstances where the rights of a child may be being misunderstood or ignored, but the development of a trusting relationship with a family will do more to strengthen a child's wellbeing than demeaning a situation that may not be fully understood.

Anne went on to summarise the ethical, theoretical and practical reasons why the pursuit of genuine partnerships is so important. For example, there are strong research-based arguments for gaining an image of a child which is more complex and culturally informed than is possible in the absence of connections. She then considered the reasons that educators give for not involving families, ranging from 'They're too busy' to 'We've tried everything', both of which will sound familiar to others in the sector, and encouraged participants to look at the situation through another lens, to try other perspectives. She told another story of a centre that was fairly disastrous from most perspectives. Over time, there was a plan to develop short term goals with carers, to find achievable negotiated steps to manage difficult behaviour, attendance and so on – all furthered through getting to know and trust each other – resulting in visible progress in the targeted areas over time.

Amongst the considerations offered to participants, Anne drew attention to the importance of the culture of the service, the presence of a welcoming environment and an invitational ethos. Drawing on Slee (2006), she asked, 'Are the parents hard to reach or are the services hard to reach?' and presented a flip-side version of advice often written out for parents about what they should be doing. 'How can we re-imagine our first encounters?' Imagining the reverse situation, she offered a hypothetical list from families of what a school or centre might be doing to demonstrate interest and care for the child and the family, starting with the messages that might be conveyed with the beginning steps of recruitment or enrolment, and the importance of listening 'to really hear'. Her hypothetical framework for Talking to Educators included things like: 'You could support our family by...', 'I am supporting my child at home by...' and opportunities to say, 'I have noticed that you forget my name' (Kennedy, 2017).

Much of the language being used in Anne's reflections is not what would be used 'in community', that is, on the land, in areas where most of the people identify as Aboriginal and/or of Torres Strait Islander background. Connections with land are more deep-seeded, spiritual and historic than economic or even bound by paper in the Western sense. The kind of discussion unfolding here has the danger of being 'too white', coming from a dominant culture that might benefit from listening more carefully to the older voices in this land (and perhaps in other lands where invasion or other circumstances have led to First Nations people being a minority presence, a 'smaller' voice). To help redress the balance, we can remind you of the work of an Aboriginal Elder, Denise Proud, who was born on Wakka Wakka country in Queensland, and established the centre where Jacqui now works. Sharing in another place, she said that

> My community was interactive and early childhood teaching is interactive. I felt primary schools were restrictive with too much order. I preferred the early childhood setting – like our culture – observing, watching, listening, interacting, sensing, feeling, being in the moment with a child or children.
> (Semann, Proud, & Martin, 2012, p. 247)

Referred to by those in her circle of companionship in the respectful way attributed to those women with a key role in mentoring and supporting families and communities, Auntie Denise also expresses herself through her art. In sharing her perspective and passion, she tries to help us understand the feelings/positioning of a child in an early childhood setting; in doing this, Denise refers to the 'gundoo' the word for child in this one Queensland language (there are many others!). She draws a figure representing the gundoo in the middle of intersecting crossroad-like lines and explains 'The straight white lines represent non-Indigenous tracks to the early childhood setting. The white lines on top of the black lines represent imposing non-Indigenous values over Indigenous values. This painting depicts how our gundoo feels' (p. 251). In contrast, she represented,

> an Aboriginal child in a cultural setting. The sitting down shape in the middle represents the gundoo (child). The shapes around the gundoo represent parents, elders and community members. Uncles' and Aunts' roles are just as important as the parents' roles. Our gundoo is nurtured in many ways. Respect, discipline, knowledge, wisdom and spirituality come from within this Aboriginal community. Early childhood education has always been embedded within Indigenous culture...
> (Semann, Proud, & Martin, 2012, p. 250)

She then went on to portray these two images in connection, with the gundoo 'still in the centre of this enriching complex environment. Respect and protocols of the gundoo's community must always be observed' (Semann, Proud, & Martin, 2012, p. 252).

As part of our preparation for this chapter, we met up with Auntie Denise 'to yarn about' the ideas being shared. Part of the connection was the fact that Denise was instrumental in establishing the centre where Jacqui is now the director. Beyond that structural connection is the likelihood that these two 'grew together' when Denise was teaching at Gundoo and Jacqui was one of the children in her care. Knowing Jacqui's family and the particular community where this conversation evolves, Denise is able to link her international experience as well as her cultural connections to help move the conversation along. As we talked about door-knocking to get families 'in the door', we moved onto the harsh realities of needing the educators (in any site) to be equipped to then welcome and engage with the folk who do arrive with a child. There is an uncomfortable sense that in many sites, educators lack the confidence and/or experience to develop and sustain the energising interesting environments and explorations with children that will encourage families to become part of the culture of the centre. In our joint musing, Denise spoke of 'the importance of knowing who you are, your family, your people, your community'. Given this fundamental acknowledgment of the importance of self-knowledge and self-confidence in order to grow as an educator, Denise and Jacqui made plans to work together for support of both leaders and educators wanting to strengthen ties with families and their communities. It became clear that, in this environment, one of the key things bubbling to the surface was the importance of sharing history and of shared histories. Helping that happen becomes an invitation for growth and a foundation for walking on together.

Jacqui

We are trying to pull together many things here.

Children are often underestimated – what they bring to the table. Some people are uncomfortable about sharing culture. Educators are anxious about taking risks.

There are also not many people here qualified to act as relief workers – so we are trying to encourage people, help them gain confidence – walking alongside the beginners who might be interested, seeing them grow in our place. There's the importance of mentoring educators, of having an attitude of sharing – of being open to ideas, and of Reflective Practice – self-reflection.

We welcome practice teaching students/trainees and colleagues from other centres and sites. We have things you might not expect in an isolated desert community: We've had people come in to share African drumming and a church choir from Papua New Guinea! We find opportunities for getting out of the centre – role modelling to families and other services, teaching children to respect what's in the community, yarning with others on the way, strengthening connections, valuing people and local places. In the colours of the Aboriginal flag, the big painted message on the wall tells people to: *Be strong. Be smart. Be safe.*

Thinking about thinking together

So what principles are we illustrating? Fundamentally the importance of context, and often of listening to what is not being said. Spirituality [links with the churches as well as deep cultural

107

connections with land and people] should also be acknowledged as an often unrecognised, but important part of the conversation. A colleague noted that, in this context, pedagogic leadership rests on the formation and sustaining of relationships, the taking on board of shared responsibility and of developing a collective view of ways to support children's learning. 'This means accepting that professional and community expertise is spread across the many, rather than the few' (Reed, 2018, personal communication).

There is fertile ground for growth by expanding definitions of 'community' and:

- Involving families in decision-making about relevant experiences
- Valuing reciprocity
- Foregrounding communication
- Building relationships with a wide range of interesting people
- Making a commitment to take children outside the fence and bring the outside (safely) in
- Seeing the everyday links with EYLF guidelines.

Fostering authentic curriculum through community connections can even be a matter of intergenerational connections, valuing the importance of family stories/oral language/recording stories to make books. Thus, opportunities are opened for experiences that add value to children, families, educators, and the community at large. Be Bold!

Note

1 NAIDOC week – (National Aborigines and Islanders Day Observance Committee). 'Its origins can be traced to the emergence of Aboriginal groups in the 1920s which sought to increase awareness in the wider community of the status and treatment of Indigenous Australians. Predominately, NAIDOC Week is held in the first week (a Sunday to Sunday) of July that incorporates the second Friday – which historically was celebrated as "National Aboriginal Day". It is a time to celebrate Aboriginal and Torres Strait Islander history, culture and achievements and is an opportunity to recognise the contributions that Indigenous Australians make to our country and society.' (www.naidoc.org.au/)

References

Australian Children's Education and Care Quality Authority. (2018a). *Guide to the national quality framework*. Australian Children's Education and Care Quality Authority. Retrieved from www.acecqa.gov.au/sites/default/files/2018-03/Guide-to-the-NQF_0.pdf

Australian Children's Education and Care Quality Authority. (2018b). *Quality Area 1– Educational program and practice*. Retrieved from www.acecqa.gov.au/nqf/national-quality-standard/quality-area-1-educational-program-and-practice

Department of Education, Employment, and Workplace Relations (DEEWR). (2009). *Belonging, being and becoming: The Early Years Learning Framework for Australia*. Canberra, ACT: Commonwealth of Australia.

Kennedy, A. (2017). *'Of course I believe in partnerships with families': The rhetoric, reality and ethics of leading partnerships with families*. Presented at the Semann & Slattery Educational Leader Conference in Melbourne, Sydney and Brisbane.

Mundine, W. (2017). *Warren Mundine in black and white: Race, politics and changing Australia*. Neutral Bay, NSW: Pantera Press.

Ration Shed Museum. Retrieved from http://rationshed.com.au

Semann, A., Proud, D., & Martin, K. (2012). Only seeing colour? Identity, pedagogy and ways of knowing. In A. Fleet, C. Patterson, & J. Robertson (Eds.), *Conversations: Behind early childhood pedagogical documentation*. Mt. Victoria, NSW: Pademelon Press.

Slee, P. (2006). *Families at risk: Their strengths, resources, access to services, and barriers*. Adelaide, South Australia: Shannon Research Press. Retrieved from http://ehlt.flinders.edu.au/education/FamilyNeeds/families%20at%20risk%20online.pdf

8

TRANSFORMATIVE PEDAGOGICAL ENCOUNTERS

Leading and learning in/as a collective movement

B. Denise Hodgins and Kathleen Kummen

Our exploration of pedagogies for leading practice situates both leading and learning as a thinking-doing that emerges in and through relationships with others (e.g., people, places, ideas, materials), rather than simply as an individual's trait, ability, responsibility, or experience. This chapter challenges notions of quality and educator competence in early childhood education (ECE) that have grown from and been regulated through EuroWestern developmental logics, which have positioned ECE as a technical practice (service) to be delivered/mastered. Our research argues that educator competency must be grown and lived within a system that is grounded in conditions for collective thinking. We draw on our experience within a community-based 'professional development' project to examine how it has acted as a movement of resistance that has materialised ECE practice beyond its EuroWestern developmental roots. We invite you to consider what your vision of learning is for children, educators, and communities. How do you notice practices of learning rippling beyond the individual person, classroom, and professional development circle? In what ways are educators supported in your community to develop as well as enact competencies? What conditions are necessary for such development and enactment? What might an understanding of learning and leading as a relational becoming, living such learning and leading collectively, do to transform a fragmented ECE sector? How might such an approach inform systems of ECE?

This chapter explores leadership and learning within a community-based pedagogical development model that grew out of the

110

Investigating Quality (IQ) Project in British Columbia, Canada, funded by the British Columbia Ministry of Children, Family and Development (Pacini-Ketchabaw & Pence, 2011a; Pence & Pacini-Ketchabaw, 2006). In 2011, a second phase of the IQ Project was implemented to include community pedagogical facilitators to work with a local cluster of centres and support the participating early childhood educators in their practice as before, but now additionally to connect with educators in regular weekly or bi-weekly centre visits. Pedagogical facilitators play a role similar to that of pedagogistas in the centres of Reggio Emilia, Italy: immersing themselves in the centres, supporting the educators' efforts to engage with children and families in innovative, critically reflective practice, and extending the practice of the educators and the children by introducing new ideas and materials (Moss, 2014; Rinaldi, 2006).

The IQ Project research has been led through the University of Victoria, with appropriate approvals and monitoring from the university's Human Research Ethics Board. Using a participatory action research approach (MacNaughton & Hughes, 2008), researchers and pedagogical facilitators collaborate with early childhood educators to reflect on knowledge, experiences, and values embedded in their practice. 'Working relationally, pedagogies characterised by depth, meaning, purpose, engagement, discussions, and dialogue were used to explore rich and contextually meaningful understandings of practices' (Pence & Pacini-Ketchabaw, 2009, p. 8). Throughout the project's phases, a qualitative methodology that incorporated field-based observations, focus groups, interviews, and open-ended surveys with educators, community facilitators, and families has been used to evaluate the project (for the evaluation reports see Pacini-Ketchabaw & Pence, 2011b). Since 2006, the project has worked with participants in several communities in British Columbia, with the number of groups and programmes that could participate dependent on the financial resources available. The qualitative data that we draw on in this chapter is from end-of-year evaluation surveys and focus group discussions with participating educators, as well as student feedback from completed course assignments and unsolicited emails to the ECE programme coordinator and the faculty Dean.

Vandenbroeck, Peeters, Urban, and Lazzari (2016) cite four key factors for successful professional development drawn from a Eurofound (2015) report titled: *Working conditions, training of early childhood care workers and quality of services – A systematic review* (p. 4).

1. a coherent pedagogical framework or learning curriculum that builds upon research and addresses local needs;
2. the active involvement of practitioners in the process of importing education practice enacted within their settings;
3. a focus on the practice-based learning taking place in constant dialogue with colleagues, parents, and local communities; and
4. the provision of enabling working conditions, such as the availability of paid hours for non-contact time and the presence of a mentor or coach who facilitates practitioners' reflection in reference groups.

We have written elsewhere (Hodgins & Kummen, in press) about how the IQ Project's model is an example of an initiative that has aimed to facilitate all four of these factors in local communities of practices, focusing specifically on three integral aspects: inquiry-based learning, making learning visible, and pedagogical facilitation. In this chapter we continue our exploration of the project and how this model supports pedagogical leadership and learning as co-constructed becomings that are always already situated in socio-material-historical-cultural-political contexts. We lean on the CoRe research which argues that educator competency must be balanced within the establishment of a system that allows for individuals to develop as well as enact competencies (Urban, Vandenbroeck, Peeters, Lazzari, & Van Laere, 2011), a system that is grounded in conditions for collective thinking (Bown & Sumsion, 2016). Drawing on the qualitative data generated from the project's evaluations, we consider how the IQ Project has acted as a movement of resistance that has materialised alternative pedagogical actions for those committed to a vision of 'early childhood education that welcomes, values and thrives on complexity and plurality, inclusion and democracy, experimentation and creativity' (Moss, 2017, p. 12).

Leading and learning: movements of resistance

For such a vision of early childhood education to thrive, hegemonic discourses and practices that have grown from and been regulated through Western developmental logics require transformative change. Drawing on Deleuzian theoretical perspectives, Moss (2014) argues that transformative change 'begets a state of continuous movement: not the closure that comes from achieving a new and desired but static state of being, but the open-endedness of constant becoming' (p. 10). A movement can be identified as strong when its momentum is visible, engaging the participation of others, and requiring spaces where the collective can come together in order to continue the movement. We lean on Moss's provocations to explore the work of the IQ Project *as a movement*, always in a state of becoming and emerging with/in/through groups of people in communities of practice. In this section we focus on the IQ Project as a movement of resistance. Moss (2017) provides two corresponding understandings to the term resistance movement, one drawing on Deleuzian theory which "accentuates 'movement', through the creation of new thought, new projects and new practices that maintain ECE as a dynamic field" (p. 20). We turn to that understanding in the next section of the chapter, where we consider how the IQ Project as a movement has materialised alternative ECE realities. We begin with Moss's understanding that speaks of a collective of protagonists disrupting hegemonic discourses so as to create spaces for multiple possibilities, understandings, and ways of being. With this view we explore the IQ Project as a movement of resistance to hegemonic notions of (a) quality and (b) educator competence as an individual practice and trait.

Resisting narrow notions of quality

When the single focus of quality from a universal developmental growth perspective is let go of as THE best way, the world opens up for children, educators, families to constantly become within a place with an educator who works from a view of quality beyond the developmental checklist.

(Educator survey response, 2017)

The overarching intention of the original IQ Project was to broaden and deepen what quality means for/in 21st-century ECE (Pacini-Ketchabaw & Pence, 2011a; Pence & Pacini-Ketchabaw, 2006). This resistance draws on scholarship that positions quality as the result of the interaction of diverse forces and factors, including physical, pedagogical, and cultural factors (Dahlberg, Moss, & Pence, 2013; Moss, 2014). Quality, within this literature, is understood historically and across local, diverse contexts. Quality might look differently depending on the community, the children, their families, and the milieu; therefore educators' pedagogical development that addresses these diverse forces and factors is as critical as are other quality indicators.

The IQ Project has fostered resistance to narrowly defined conceptualisations of quality through the model's mechanisms (i.e., learning circles, centre visits, online spaces) that engage educators in 'practice-based learning taking place in constant dialogue with colleagues, parents and local communities' (Vandenbroeck et al., 2016, p. 4). With the support of pedagogical facilitators, educators participate in dialogue and reflection, working with pedagogical documentations, which in British Columbia we refer to as pedagogical narrations (Government of British Columbia, 2008; Pacini-Ketchabaw, Nxumalo, Kocher, Elliott, & Sanchez, 2015). It is a process that Lenz Taguchi (2000, cited in Dahlberg & Moss, 2005) refers to as a *practice of resistance*, wherein participants engage in dialogues to critically reflect, disrupt, problematise, and reimagine their practices (see also Moss, 2014, 2017). Described as an 'ongoing, cyclical process that occurs in and with a community of learners' (Government of British Columbia, 2008, p. 13), the practice of pedagogical narrations occurs *in relationship with others* (e.g., children, colleagues, ideas, materials, places).

Resisting notions of pedagogy as an individual act

The IQ Project's resistance to traditional understandings of quality includes challenging the image that quality ECE is enacted as simply an individual technical act. Bown and Sumsion (2016) assert that spaces where individuals engage in generative dialogues that involve reimaginings of collective thoughts, questions, and aspirations are spaces that produce visionary changes and policies. A review of all of the project's evaluations highlights the tremendous value that educators placed on sharing, experimenting, and learning within a community of practice. One participant described that, '*Now I think "quality" must include engaged teacher-researchers who reflect together (not just about enviro, curriculum, etc.)*' (Educator survey response, 2017). Another educator termed this understanding of quality as '*a culture of inquiry*' (Educator survey response, 2017). This culture of inquiry began by bringing groups of educators together on a regular basis (learning circles) to critically explore research, theory, and traces of practice (pedagogical narrations) together.

In each geographical site, the project's educators meet once a month during the school year for a two-hour monthly learning circle meeting. Generally, each site has four to six programmes that are part of the project, with one to five educators participating from each programme. Each site's pedagogical facilitator organises the learning circle focus based on the observations and discussions during her weekly/bi-weekly visits to each of the educators' programmes, the previous learning circle conversations, and any overarching inquiry question(s) the group is working with that year. Part of preparing for the learning circle includes reading or watching resources that have been shared with the group for that evening's focus, and are generally connected to moments of practice that one or more of the educators shares with the group through pedagogical narrations. For example, one programme had been carefully considering moments with the children in their outdoor space. Through· talking together and with their pedagogical facilitator about relationships to place, the boundaries that mark and regulate these relationships, and their hopes and assumptions about being outdoors, they developed a pedagogical narration that included documentation, stories, and questions to share at the learning circle. ⁻

In preparation for the learning circle, the group was invited to read Nelson, Coon, and Chadwick's (2015) article *Engaging with the Messiness of Place* and bring ideas from the article to the circle. The pedagogical narration shared at the circle and the article served as a provocation for discussion, which not only supported that particular programme's inquiry but also added to the considerations and questions about the ethics and politics of ECE practice that all of the site's participants had been thinking with throughout the school year. It has been this community of practice that educators consistently report as being integral to their commitment and self-perceived success in the project. One educator who participated in the project's first learning circles noted that,

> *The idea of getting together with other professionals in the field was very useful. It was very empowering and validating. That's the thing that is lacking in this field and often people are so isolated so that was very useful, helpful and just in making you feel motivated and excited and energetic about the field.*
>
> (Educator survey response, 2007)

This model of pedagogical development is ongoing (rather than a one-off style workshop or course). Groups are supported by a consistent community pedagogical facilitator who is integral to creating conditions for trust, confidence, enthusiasm, and experimentation to grow. Since 2011, participants have commented in the evaluation surveys that this model could not be done without the facilitator, which reflects the findings of CoRe's research and recommendations (Urban et al., 2011; Vandenbroeck et al., 2016), as well as Moss's (2014) vision of transformative change in ECE. Many educators pointed to the support of the pedagogical facilitator and colleagues within the learning circles as helping to grow their confidence to try new things and share ideas. Educators have described a 'ripple effect' that occurs through the project work where an educator's (renewed) enthusiasm ripples out to the parents (Site 3 focus group, June 17, 2016). As one educator wrote, '*the project gives me the support and the language I need to engage in ongoing dialogue with parents and grandparents*' (Educator survey response, 2015). We see that this movement – confidence in self, experimenting with children, sharing with colleagues, including families – has been fostered within a collective of thinking and becoming with others.

It is important to note that the collective thinking and becoming with others includes being in relationship with ideas. Since its inception, the IQ Project's model has included theories, such as resisting the narrow understandings of 'quality' ECE, as a vital part of the collective. Making space for other stories in/of ECE, beyond the dominant developmental story (Moss, 2014), is an integral part of the project, as the following quote from one of the participating educators highlights.

> *Ideas relating to postcolonialism, modernism, and postmodernism I learned from the books and articles [in the project] but [initially] I didn't pay too much attention to them. Since our discussions at the meetings, I look in the world in a very different way...I'm more aware and...concerned about these issues and ideas than I was before.*
>
> (Educator survey response, 2014)

Leading and learning: materialising alternatives

In this section we consider how (if) the IQ Project as a movement has materialised alternative ECE realities. As Moss suggests, contesting and reconceptualising is not enough. So, has the IQ Project materialised new possibilities through contesting and reconceptualising quality, for living well with children, families, and communities in pedagogical relationships? Have material (alternative) realities been actualised? We explore these questions through three subsections that look at the IQ Project as a 'resistance movement that "accentuates movement" through the creation of new thought, new projects and new practices that maintain ECE as a dynamic field' (Moss, 2017, p. 20): (a) within the project, (b) rippling out from the project, and (c) at the policy level.

Within the project

As described in the previous section, educators spoke to their shifting ideas and expectations (i.e., what they have come to expect and demand in and from their practices) around notions of quality and relational pedagogies (i.e., beyond a child-centred understanding of being in relation to a more complex and experimental understanding and practice of being in relation with colleagues, families, places, materials, ideas, and children). As one educator recently commented, being in the project has *'firmed my belief that children deserved better, and that it was possible for me to give them that, and reasonable of me to expect others to strive to do that as well'* (Educator survey response, 2017). All of the project evaluations point to shifts not only in educators' knowledge but in their pedagogical practices. Practices that include but are not limited to: engaging with pedagogical narrations; increased time in inquiry-based practice; experimenting with routines and schedules, new materials, or materials in innovative ways; and including children, families, and communities in inquiries and pedagogical discussions. The data suggests that new practices have materialised for most educators who have participated in the project. Cautious that these changes could be (become) simply techniques applied by rote, this model's commitment to ongoing engagement in the collaborative practice of critical reflections working with pedagogical narrations works to avoid replacing one dominant discourse with another (e.g., plastic toys switched out for wood ones, circle time replaced by 'free play').

Through thinking and becoming within the collective, including with pedagogical narrations and reconceptualist perspectives, the project's participants have actually been working to transform the established (dominant, narrowly defined as quality) ECE system, at the very least within their own centres, with their families and children, and with each other in the groups, to establish alternative practices for enacting dynamic and experimental pedagogies (Pacini-Ketchabaw et al., 2015). One educator explained that,

> *I have become very interested in learning more about postmodern theories and how they can apply to every aspect of my work. The image of the child and family really drive our centres, especially those things associated with policies; once we are clear about our image of children and families, we can start constructing more child and family friendly spaces. Pedagogical narrations and analysis have really made me look at how I am practicing and whose knowledge I am using.*
>
> (Educator survey response, 2008)

This educator's comment – *whose knowledge I am using* – indicates that what has materialised through the IQ Project is a different way of thinking, knowing, and becoming for many of the participating educators. They are enacting ECE with/through a story of democracy (Moss, 2014) and challenging the primacy of technical practice, when, as Moss (2017) reminds, 'education is first and foremost a political and ethical practice' (p. 19). The IQ Project has endeavoured to create conditions for democratic and experimental pedagogies to flourish, where educators grapple with political questions and seek democratic (albeit unfinished, incomplete, imperfect) answers (Moss, 2017). In recent years, some of the educators described now seeing the classroom as a political environment, where they work with/in '*the politics of the classroom*' (Site 1 focus group, June 7, 2016, 00:13:56) and recognise pedagogies as always reaching beyond the scope of a particular moment in the classroom.

> *Children are members of a society which we live in, in this Western world, in this current time, and it is bigger than that moment of that something that we have captured on film, or in our mind, or spoken about.*
>
> (Site 1 focus group, June 7, 2016, 00:06:14)

Embedding politicised critical thinking and questioning into pedagogical practices has become a new material reality for many of the participating educators in the project. As one educator described, '*I think before I speak, listen more. I'm becoming more and more comfortable with tensions. I share more about who I am and what*

I'm doing. I invite questions. I ask questions. I'm challenging normative practice daily!' (Educator survey response, 2017).

Ripples beyond the project

Moss (2014, 2017) asserts that collective movements materialise change *as well as* generate strength with/in their movement. As already described, educators have reported back a ripple effect from the project, wherein their transformed practice of experimentation and dialogue as supported (grown) through the learning collective, begins with themselves and then ripples outward, generally first to children, then colleagues (as part of the IQ Project groups and/or their centre team), and then to families, communities and beyond. A summative evaluation of the project from 2007–2009 reported that almost all of the participants indicated that they had shared their work within their child care centre, and many found that as a result of their involvement in the project they contributed more in discussions of early learning, became more involved in networks related to their field, and increased their attendance at conferences, forums and meetings. Since 2014, every evaluation of the project has some educators reporting back that not only are they attending conferences, they are presenting at them and publishing writing in educator resources and academic journals. In other words, not only were the IQ Project researchers rippling the project out to the broader community, the educators themselves were making transformative ECE pedagogies public beyond their own centres and project groups. As one programme director noted, *'we've really seen in the last year this community grow, where programmes are working with other programmes, going into the community together'* (Site 2 focus group, June 13, 2016, 00:40:36).

This rippling beyond the project has materialised new practices. For example, we (the authors) know that since the IQ Project began, some larger institutional settings in British Columbia have implemented a pedagogical facilitator role to support the pedagogical practices of the educators in their centres (i.e., University of Victoria Child Care Services, UBC Child Care Services, Capilano University's Children's Centre). Two universities in British Columbia have developed courses about the pedagogical facilitator role as part of their ECE undergraduate programmes. The force of the ripple was clearly evident in another example, when in 2016 the provincial government funding for the project was significantly reduced. This circumstance created a new project partnership with Capilano University when the university stepped in to financially support the pedagogical facilitator in one of the geographical sites for 2016–2017. The university faculty in their commitment to reconceptualising the education of student educators believed that the IQ Project offered a protocol for the education of early childhood educators in practicum that made space for students to learn and become within a community of practice. By entering into a partnership with the IQ Project, it was possible for the university to have consistent faculty in the role of pedagogical facilitator who works with educators and student educators over the course of an academic year. The participating child care society contributed to this new relationship by taking an increased number of practicum students in four or five of their centres and creating space for students to visit for curriculum, and observing and recording courses. While we have written elsewhere about how bringing ECE training programmes and ongoing professional development together within a situated collective of learning enhances the professional learning for students and educators at diverse places in their practice (Hodgins & Kummen, in press), we share the example here to highlight the project's materialising ripple effect, a ripple that has continued with the university agreeing to fund a second pedagogical facilitator in a new geographical site for 2017–2018.

Shifting policy

Moss (2017) calls for democratic experimentalism in ECE and comments that resistance discourses, 'though lively and dynamic, make little impact on policy and have but very limited influence on actual services' (p. 12). We have pointed to some of the ways that the IQ Project, as a movement of resistance and transformative change, has influenced actual 'services' for the educators, children and families (centres) within the project, as well as for services (e.g., centres, postsecondary classes) beyond the project. Importantly, we turn now to the question Moss raises regarding alternative discourses having little impact on policy. Based on the findings from the CoRe research (Urban et al., 2011), Bown and Sumsion (2016) argue that for transformative change to take hold in early childhood, individual or isolated groups need to merge into a larger collective to work together to reimagine and enact new possibilities. We agree. Within the IQ Project, bringing one educator together with other educators, one centre together with other centres, one group in the project together with other groups, and participating project groups together with other community initiatives (e.g., university training programmes), strengthened our working together to envision and materialise alternative possibilities.

In 2016–2017, with the financial support from the British Columbia Ministry of Children, Family and Development and from Capilano University, the project supported 16 programmes. This model *has* rippled out to generate other groups actively exploring how they can establish and support similar communities of practice, which we (the authors) are aware of and in different ways have tried to support (e.g., writing letters of support, providing the IQ model as an example). And while we celebrate the moves to strengthen and grow what we see as a movement of resistance that can actualise material change, the problem is that our patchwork and siloed efforts ultimately maintain a fragmented ECE sector (Bown & Sumsion, 2016). We take this caution very seriously as we turn our attention to the next academic year with the IQ Project and consider what it might mean to have 'the resistance movement actively engaging with policy, not leaving the field to the dominant discourse' (Moss, 2017, p. 23).

It's time for systems to learn and lead

For necessary as critique is, and it is very necessary, it is not enough; there must also be hope.

(Moss, 2017, p. 20)

The IQ Project, as previously noted, emerged from the reconceptualising early childhood movement that began with the critical questioning of hegemonic discourses that regulate, simplify and commodify early childhood practices. We suggest that it has been through the generative, yet at times contentious and challenging, process of questioning, disrupting and critically reflecting upon the everyday taken for granted practices, that space has been created to make visible the discursive material realities that shape our understandings of young children, families, communities, and early childhood education, as well as the opportunity to enact alternative possibilities. The IQ Project has worked to facilitate conditions for such generative dialogues to support educators' ongoing critically reflective pedagogical actions, and as a collective movement has

121

rippled beyond the early childhood classroom and the professional development circle. But can this approach ripple even further, into the fabric of an ECE system that is woven together with the knowledge, experiences, experimentations, research and support of the educators who uphold it?

We (the authors) want to feel hopeful that this is a time of possible openings for systemic change in ECE in Canada. In 2017, the Canadian Federal, Provincial and Territorial Ministers responsible for early learning and child care agreed to a Multilateral Early Learning and Child Care Framework with an aim to increase quality, accessibility, affordability, flexibility and inclusivity in early learning and child care. The federal government have committed to providing provinces and territories with $1.2 billion over three years to support early learning and child care programmes as outlined in each bilateral agreement between the federal government and the province or territory (Government of Canada, 2017a). At the time of writing, six early learning and child care bilateral agreements have been signed, though not yet for BC. In BC, the provincial government is in the midst of investing in childcare and possibly developing a 'universal system'. As the Minister of State for Child Care (a newly created position by the New Democratic Party (NDP) government) Kristina Chen noted,

> We are speeding up the creation of new child-care spaces to address years of pent-up demand for child care... Our February [2018] budget will show our long-term commitment to building a system of accessible, affordable and quality child care for families across the province.
> (Government of British Columbia, 2017)

One of the most critical questions from the field is who is there to actually work in those newly created spaces, as there are not enough qualified educators currently. Will the necessary conditions be put in place to not only attract and educate more people as early childhood educators, but to actually retain and support the profession? If governments are truly committed to a 'quality' system, with the understanding that 'early learning and child care systems are operating in increasingly complex and challenging environments' (Government of Canada, 2017b, p. 4), will they lead the way to building the infrastructure needed for educators to develop as well as to enact competencies to meet the 21st-century realties of a dynamic ECE field? If governments really believe that 'innovative practices can help develop solutions that better meet the complex needs of children and families, and can support more integrated and higher-quality early learning and child care systems' (Government of Canada, 2017b, p. 4), then they will need to foster the necessary conditions for such innovations to flourish. The time is now for creating a system that goes beyond imagining what is possible, to actually taking up the call. It is time to learn from the collectives and lead in the development of a unified ECE system where quality is understood and lived within the local community context, and where professional early childhood educators are recognised and supported as critical to its foundational backbone.

References

Bown, K., & Sumsion, J. (2016). Generating visionary policy for early childhood education and care: Politicians' and early childhood sector advocate/activists' perspectives. *Contemporary Issues in Early Childhood*, 17(2), 192–209.

Dahlberg, G., & Moss, P. (2005). *Ethics and politics in early childhood education*. New York, NY: Routledge Falmer.

Dahlberg, G., Moss, P., & Pence, A. (2013). *Beyond quality in early childhood education and care: Languages of evaluation* (3rd ed.). New York, NY: Routledge.

Eurofound. (2015). *Working conditions, training of early childhood care workers and quality of services – A systematic review*. Luxemburg: Publications Office of the European Union.

Government of British Columbia. (2008). *Understanding the British Columbia early learning framework: From theory to practice*. Victoria, BC: Crown Publications, Queen's Printer for British Columbia. Retrieved from www.bced.gov.bc.ca/early_learning/pdfs/from_theory_to_practice.pdf

Government of British Columbia. (2017). *New child-care spaces will help families around BC*. Retrieved from https://news.gov.bc.ca/releases/2017CFD0023–002011

Government of Canada. (2017a). *Federal-provincial/territorial early learning and child care agreements*. Retrieved from www.canada.ca/en/early-learning-child-care-agreement.html

Government of Canada. (2017b). *Multilateral early learning and child care framework*. Retrieved from www.canada.ca/en/employment-social-development/programs/early-learning-child-care/reports/2017-multilateral-framework.html

Hodgins, B. D., & Kummen, K. (in press). Learning collectives with/in sites of practice: Beyond training and professional development. *Journal of*

Childhood Studies Special Issue: Innovative Professional Learning in ECEC: Inspiring Hope and Action.

MacNaughton, G., & Hughes, P. (2008). *Doing action research in early childhood studies.* London: Open University Press.

Moss, P. (2014). *Transformative change and real utopias in early childhood education: A story of democracy, experimentation and potentiality.* New York, NY: Routledge.

Moss, P. (2017). Power and resistance in early childhood education: From dominant discourse to democratic experimentalism. *Journal of Pedagogy, 8*(1), 11–32.

Nelson, N., Coon, E., & Chadwick, A. (2015). Engaging with the messiness of place: Exploring animal relations, traditional hide, and drum. *Canadian Children, 40*(2), 43–56.

Pacini-Ketchabaw, V., Nxumalo, F., Kocher, L., Elliott, E., & Sanchez, A. (2015). *Journeys: Complexifying early childhood practices through pedagogical narration.* Toronto, ON: University of Toronto Press.

Pacini-Ketchabaw, V., & Pence, A. (2011a). The investigating quality project: Innovative approaches in early childhood. In N. Howe & L. Prochner (Eds.), *New directions in early childhood education and care in Canada.* Toronto, ON: University of Toronto Press.

Pacini-Ketchabaw, V., & Pence, A. (2011b). *Envisioning quality early childhood care and education in British Columbia.* Retrieved from www.veronicapaciniketchabaw.com/reports/

Pence, A., & Pacini-Ketchabaw, V. (2006). The investigating 'quality' project: Challenges and possibilities for Canada. *Interaction, 20*(3), 11–13.

Pence, A., & Pacini-Ketchabaw, V. (2009). *Investigating quality (IQ) early learning environments project: Phase II 2007–2009 final report.* Retrieved from www.veronicapaciniketchabaw.com/reports/

Rinaldi, C. (2006). *In dialogue with Reggio Emilia.* New York, NY: Routledge.

Urban, M., Vandenbroeck, M., Peeters, J., Lazzari, A., & Van Laere, K. (2011). *Competence requirements in early childhood education and care final report: A study for the European commission directorate-general for education and culture.* London and Ghent: Cass School of Education, University of East London and Department for Social Welfare Studies, University of Ghent.

Vandenbroeck, M., Peeters, J., Urban, M., & Lazzari, A. (2016). Introduction. In M. Vandenbroeck, M. Urban, & J. Peeters (Eds.), *Pathways to professionalism in early childhood education and care* (pp. 1–14). London: Routledge.

9

UTILISING STRENGTHS IN FAMILIES AND COMMUNITIES TO SUPPORT CHILDREN'S LEARNING AND WELLBEING

Alison Prowle and Jackie Musgrave

This chapter explores the importance of families and communities in enabling positive outcomes for children. Building on the work of Bronfenbrenner (1979), a bio-ecological framework is utilised to consider impacts of family and community on children's wellbeing, learning and holistic development. The chapter explores definitions and meanings associated with family and community, paying close attention to issues of culture, values and diversity. Consideration is given to the role of the practitioner in building supportive partnerships with parents and communities, using strength-based approaches to promote resilience. The chapter argues that pedagogic leaders are the glue which binds together a setting into a community of practice. It highlights that trust, respect, unconditional positive regard (Rogers, 1951), positive communication and reciprocity are at the heart of joint working with families and the wider community. Pedagogical leadership is essential in order to harness the strengths of families and communities in supporting positive child outcomes. Kagan and Bowman (1997) describe a pedagogical leader as someone who recognises that the core of early learning is to ensure quality of the day-to-day lives of the participating children and to support and enhance their growth, development and learning. Therefore, in thinking about pedagogical leadership, this chapter takes a broad perspective, arguing that pedagogical leadership is extended beyond traditional conceptions to include the way that practitioners work with families and communities, empowering them to support children's holistic development. Practice vignettes provide the reader with examples of effective practice in engaging and enabling families and communities to work in partnership with settings to support children.

Open a newspaper or turn on the television in the UK, and you are likely to encounter a myriad of messages that focus on what families are doing wrong. From disruptive behaviour in schools, to crime figures or substance misuse, the cry of 'we blame the parents' is a common response to all the ills of society. However, whilst there is no such thing as a perfect parent, in reality most parents (including many of those who may be considered 'hard to reach' or 'disadvantaged') do a lot of the 'right' things for a lot of the time. These strengths within families need to be acknowledged, supported and further developed. Moreover, parents, caregivers and communities need to be empowered to make choices that will support positive outcomes for children. Pedagogical leaders are uniquely placed to achieve this aim.

Context

The important role of families (and particularly parent/carers) in supporting children's learning and development has long been recognised. Vygotsky (1896–1934) emphasised the crucial role of parents in supporting children's development. He suggested that children learn through their interactions with what he describes as more knowledgeable partners (Brooks, 2011). For the majority of children, their first 'knowledgeable other' will be the parent with whom the child spends the majority of his/her time. Adult interaction can support the child to achieve that which they could not accomplish alone; Vygotsky described this as the *Zone of Proximal Development* (Kozulin, Gindis, Ageyev, & Miller, 2003). More recent studies have suggested that parents can positively impact on children's language development (Hart & Risley, 1995), social and emotional development (Sheffield Morris, Silk, Steinberg, & Myers, 2007) and even how children perceive their ability to learn, or mind-sets (Dweck, 2017).

A growing awareness of the importance of parents in supporting children's development has led to a recognition of parents as 'a child's first and most enduring educators' (Qualifications and Curriculum Authority (QCA), 2000, p. 17). Some parents, however, may find it easier to engage with early years services than others. Indeed, Charles Deforges's research to support the Primary Strategy (2003) suggests that parental engagement (or indeed lack of engagement) may account for up to 12% of the differences between different pupil outcomes. Hart and Risley (1995) identified that even by the age of three, some children may be falling badly behind their peers, establishing an early pattern of disadvantage that is difficult to break out of later.

So, what causes these inequalities? More importantly, what can be done to 'narrow the gap' between groups of children or indeed 'raise the bar' for all children, including those who may be deemed 'disadvantaged'? The following data uses the term 'poverty' as a form of disadvantage; however, there are many other determinants which may relate to disadvantage not covered here. In response to the first question, a number of studies have attributed differences in both parental engagement and child outcomes to child poverty. The definition of child poverty is itself hotly contested. Whilst it is commonly defined as living in a house with an income of less than 60% of median UK household income, there have been several

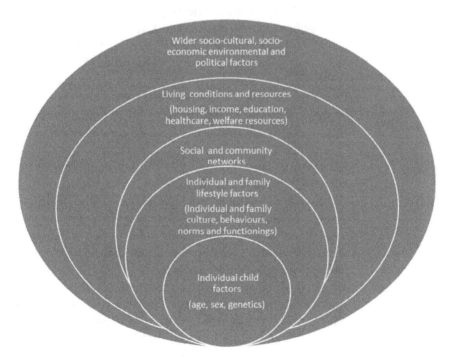

Figure 9.1 Factors contributing to parents' willingness and ability to engage with services

attempts to broaden the definition of poverty to include a wider range of indicators. These wider determinants of poverty may include parental mental health, domestic abuse, limited access to services, living in low income neighbourhoods, parental imprisonment, parents having grown up in care, poor housing, poor nutrition, and a whole host of other interrelated factors. This is perhaps best illustrated in Figure 9.1, which has been adapted from Dahlgren and Whitehead (1991):

Whilst this model was originally conceptualised to describe differences in health outcomes for individuals, it can equally be applied to explore how a range of factors can combine to affect a parent's willingness and ability to engage with services. An example of this is explored below.

Case study

A day in the life of Becky (aged 38 months)

12:30am   There is a commotion in the street outside Becky's house. Becky wakes. She is frightened and cries. The police arrive outside and there is shouting. Mum gives her some juice in a bottle to help her sleep. She finally gets back to sleep at 1:25.

7 am   Becky wakes. She has breakfast which consists of two biscuits. She cleans her teeth, with the special brush, just like the dentist showed her at nursery last week. The house is cold. Mum puts in another call to the council because the heating is broken. Becky puts on a jumper but the wool makes her eczema itch. Mum makes a note to mention it to the health visitor next time she sees her. The health visitor is pleased with Becky's development and says she is on track and doing well. Becky watches some television and plays with the cat whilst her Mum does some college work.

8:45am   Becky's Mum walks her to nursery. It is raining outside, so they almost don't go because Becky's Mum doesn't like taking her little brother out when it is wet as he has a bad chest. He has to go to the hospital for lots of check-ups. The buses only run on the hour and that would mean waiting for ages before nursery, or being late! When she gets to nursery, she has wet feet and hair. The Key Person gives Becky some spare socks and helps her dry off.

9:15am   Becky plays with the other children. She gets upset when Ben tells her that she smells funny.

11am   It is warm in the book corner. Becky falls asleep.

12:15pm   Becky's Nan picks her up as her Mum has a job interview today. There are not many jobs in her neighbourhood so Mummy is also doing some courses to improve her chances! It's stopped raining so they go to the park. The park is full of litter and dog poo. Becky falls on some glass and cuts her knee.

2pm   Becky has a sausage roll for lunch.

2:45pm   Becky goes with her Nan to a play session at the Children's Centre. As they are leaving the centre, the receptionist reminds Nan that on Friday the Credit Union will be there to give financial advice and help set up a savings account. Nan says that with all the cuts in benefits, she won't be able to save anything!

4pm   Becky's older sister, Hannah, gets in from school. Hannah has been on a school trip to the local farm park – she tells Becky all about it. Hannah makes a start on her art homework, her teacher suggested she look for inspiration on the computer, but they don't have one at home.

6pm   Becky complains of being cold. The heating isn't working... again.

7pm   Becky has a chocolate spread sandwich and a packet of crisps. She finishes her tea with some grapes which Mum picked up from the community fruit project.

8pm   Becky watches *EastEnders* with Mum. She enjoys having a cuddle. She falls asleep on the chair.

11:30pm   Becky's Mum's boyfriend arrives home. There is a lot of shouting. Becky is scared. Eventually she falls asleep.

We will re-visit Becky's story later in the chapter and discuss some of the possible responses.

- How does poverty manifest itself in the lives of Becky and her family?
- What may be the implications for the family if nothing changes?
- How does the model above help us to understand the ways in which Becky's environment impacts on her experience and ultimately her life chances?

Implications of child poverty

However we choose to define poverty, there is a strong consensus that it is likely to lead to very poor outcomes for children. The statistics presented by the Child Poverty Action Group (CPAG) (undated) are startling:

- Already at the age of three, poorer children are estimated to be, on average, nine months behind children from more wealthy backgrounds.
- Children from poorer backgrounds lag behind at all stages of education.
- By the end of primary school, pupils receiving free school meals are estimated to be almost three terms behind their more affluent peers. By 14, this gap grows to over five terms.
- By 16, children receiving free school meals achieve 1.7 grades lower at GCSE.

This disadvantage is likely to continue into adult life, with children from disadvantaged backgrounds more likely to be NEET (Not in Education, Employment and Training); more likely to be long term unemployed; more likely to have a chronic illness or mental health problem; and more likely even to die at a younger age than their peers. There is also much evidence that this disadvantage often transmits inter-generationally, creating a 'cycle of disadvantage' that is hard to break or change (Social Mobility Commission, 2017).

Approaches to addressing child poverty

The causes of poverty and disadvantage are complex and interconnected; hence there is no overall consensus as to how the issue can be addressed. There are two broad responses to tackling child poverty, both of which are visible within policy and practice. The first is to attempt to alleviate child poverty by dealing with its root causes and maximising family income. Fauth, Renton, and Solomon (2013) explore this within their report for National Children's Bureau, considering the attempts of successive governments to introduce measures to enhance family's financial resources. Such approaches would include family tax credits, minimum wage legislation and government funded schemes to enable parents from lower socio-economic backgrounds to enter employment. The levers for these approaches sit well outside the early years sector and are largely nationally rather than locally driven.

Marmot (2015) helps us to understand that 'poverty is not destiny' (p. 124), meaning that there are solutions to attempt to mitigate the effects of poverty where it arises, through compensatory approaches. Field (2010) argues that alongside measures to maximise income, a broader suite of targeted interventions are required, aimed at narrowing the outcome gaps between poor children and their more economically advantaged peers. Clearly, within this agenda, high quality early years provision has an important role to play; the early years provides a unique opportunity to make the biggest difference to children's lives, and to interrupt those inter-generational cycles of disadvantage by supporting parents when it matters most. The success of such interventions relies on practitioners having the qualities and knowledge of pedagogic leaders, as well as possessing an understanding of the rationale for interventions. It is of the utmost importance that practitioners develop the skills of diplomacy and the ability to act with sensitivity in order to engage and support parents in order to work alongside them and aim to maximise children's potential. Similarly, pedagogical leaders have a responsibility to support staff to develop their skills and dispositions in working with parents by providing effective supervision and staff development opportunities.

In his report *Early Intervention, The Next Steps*, MP Graham Allen (2011) makes a strong economic and social case for investing in parenting programmes and supporting children within the early years. He argues that early intervention will have benefits both economically and socially. However, in considering how best to work with parents, it is important to avoid stereotyping parents as 'engaged' or 'disengaged' and of making assumptions based simply on visible aspects of behaviour or interaction. Such assumptions are often based on social class norms and ignore the nuances of inequalities, personal experience, access to resources and agency. This is exemplified in some findings of the Joseph Rowntree Foundation (2012, p. 4): 'What looks like low aspirations may often be high aspirations that have been eroded by negative experience'. Similarly,

> What looks like 'parental disengagement' may actually be the result of high level of commitment to their child's education, which is not matched by the capacity to provide effective support or by the ability of the schools to work effectively with parents
>
> (Jospeh Rowntree Foundation, 2012, p. 4)

Many of the policy and practice responses aimed to counteract inequalities in children's outcomes, however, have tended to involve interventions based on a 'deficit model' of parenting (Coldron, Cripps, & Shipton, 2010), which attempts to challenge those values and behaviours that are deemed undesirable. Such approaches can result in parents feeling criticised or marginalised with the effect of making them even less likely to engage proactively in supporting their children's learning. Far more effective are attempts to identify and build upon parents' own strengths, talents and assets (along with strengths in the wider family and community) in order to build resilience and support children's learning. In other words, we need to focus not upon a family's failings but rather on how they can succeed (Walsh, 2006).

Supporting family and community

The strength-based approach described above seeks to identify those aspects of parenting and family life that are going well. It works from an assumption that all families have strengths and that by identifying and supporting these strengths, we can help families succeed. The bio-ecological model (Bronfenbrenner, 1979) provides a useful framework for thinking about the strengths that may surround a child and which can be harnessed to enable the child to meet her potential. Based around five interconnected systems from the individual and family levels through to economic and political structures, Bronfenbrenner argues that those systems closest to the child have the most direct and intense impact on the child's development and wellbeing. Moreover, the model explores the interconnections between the different systems providing a relational focus. Like Dahlgren and Whitehead's (1991) social determinants of health model (adapted above), Bronfenbrenner's model includes reference to the individual's biological features as part of the microsystem, hence in later references, the model tends to be referred to as a bio-ecological framework. The adapted version of Bronfenbrenner's model in Figure 9.2 shows how there may be both deficits (or needs) and strengths within all elements of the ecological system. Similarly intervention needs to be targeted at each of those levels too.

To explain this more clearly, we return to the example of Becky from earlier in the chapter. At the individual level, Becky is on track with her development. Although she has eczema, it is well managed. At the family level, although Becky is living in poverty, her Mum is actively trying to improve her own skills and

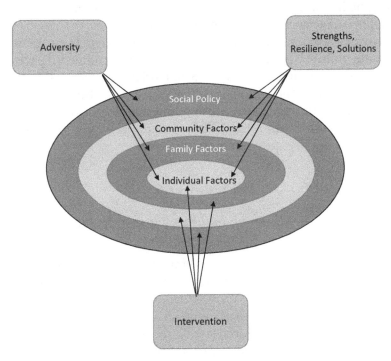

Figure 9.2 Bio-ecological model of adversity (or needs), strengths and interventions (adapted from Bronfenbrenner, 1979)

employability. Whilst the housing is inadequate, Becky's basic needs are being addressed. Her Mum and Nan are engaged with the early years setting and health services. There are undoubtedly some difficulties in the wider community, but there are also assets such as community food projects and credit unions. Ultimately, Becky lives in a country with free education and healthcare, police service and social security.

Hence, strengths and assets at individual, family, community and national levels can act as protective factors and help mitigate the effects of poverty. The concept of resilience (again operating at individual, family and community levels) provides a useful way of exploring why some children experiencing multiple adversity appear to have an ability to 'bounce up' (Hart, Blincow, & Thomas, 2008, p. 132) and move on. Indeed, Benard (2006), suggests that approximately half of all children who are challenged by poverty will manage to surmount the challenges and go on to achieve positive outcomes. This strongly suggests that experiencing poverty does not facilitate an automatic trajectory to poor outcomes, and that using strengths-based approaches and supportive interventions can help develop resilience for both the child and parents, thereby helping improve outcomes. Indeed, research has shown that programmes tackling multiple pathways such as home environment, parenting and early years practice have the potential to narrow the gap in school readiness. Indications are that these can also improve children's behaviour, support wellbeing and inspire positive changes in parents (Neville et al., 2013). The vignette below gives an example of how one organisation is doing this.

Practice vignette 1

Save the Children: building capacity to support parent partnerships

Rebecca Thomas is Programme Manager for Save the Children, Wales. Her role is to develop relationships and build capacity in order to transform the way children are supported in early years. Within Rebecca's work there is a strong focus upon improving outcomes for those children who are deemed vulnerable, and therefore most likely to fail to meet their potential. She comments:

Children spend so little of their time in an Early Years setting. The majority of their time is spent in the home environment. This is why it is so important to support and equip parents in their role as providers of care and as first educators. Our experience at Save the Children tells us that most parents really **want** to do the best for their children. However, sometimes their circumstances get in the way. For example, parents may be unemployed or working long hours to make ends meet (in-work poverty affects 60% of children). They may have other issues such as mental health difficulties or have experienced adversity in their own childhood experiences. We need to understand these issues and work **with** parents not **do to** them.

In supporting parents and children in early years, Rebecca works to three main objectives:

1. Parents are supported to create a positive home learning environment and engage in their children's early education.
2. Children in poverty have access to high quality services that boost their early childhood development.
3. Children in their early years do not experience material deprivation, supported by action to improve family incomes for the poorest families.

Rebecca explains that this is achieved by supporting children and their parents in four important areas of their lives: at home, at nursery, at school and in the wider community.

Save the Children, therefore works closely with other agencies to foster understanding of the ways in which poverty impacts children and families and how families are best engaged and supported.

Rebecca outlines some of the approaches and programmes they use to achieve this:

- *FAST programme (Families and Schools Together) – working with schools and early years settings to get parents actively involved in supporting their child's learning through guided activities. The programme brings practitioners, parents and children together, makes learning fun and helps develop parents' confidence.*

- *Families Connect* – *this focuses on supporting parents and children to learn together. It helps parents to support their children's learning in three key areas: language development, numeracy and emotional development. The eight-week programme provides a series of activities, techniques and games that parents and carers can do with their children at home. Each activity encourages parents and children to spend quality time together by talking about specific topics and reflecting on what they already do to support their children's learning.*
- *Encouraging behavioural change* – *this involves supporting parents to understand how best to help their children. The project partners with agencies and businesses to develop messaging on target products and services that parents use. For example on pre-natal scan pictures, a strapline was included which encouraged parents to talk to their unborn child.*

Rebecca summarises,

> We want to transform the lives and life-chances of children in this country – but we know we can't do this alone. We need to work in genuine partnership with policy makers, practitioners in other agencies to ensure we can give every child the best start in life – and build a better future for us all.

Rebecca recognises that pedagogical leadership goes beyond her responsibilities to her staff team and the children they work with. She defines her role broadly, recognising that transforming children's life chances requires a whole society approach. Her leadership role, therefore, extends to challenging and influencing social norms and partnering with other agencies to champion children's rights and promote their positive outcomes.

- **What does Rebecca identify as the root causes of inequalities in children's outcomes? Do you agree with her analysis?**
- **What needs to happen in order to reduce child poverty?**
- **Which of the two models presented earlier in the chapter (Bronfenbrenner or Dahlgren and Whitehead) provides the best way of thinking about how poverty impacts children's lives?**

- What does Rebecca identify as effective ways of engaging parents in early years? Do you agree?
- How does Rebecca exemplify pedagogical leadership in her role?

Implications for the practitioner

In the foregoing sections, we have considered the importance of family and community in securing positive child outcomes. Here we consider how pedagogical leaders can play an important role in supporting parents to help their children flourish and meet their potential. Research has consistently shown that individual practitioners can and really do make a difference. Trust, respect, unconditional positive regard, positive communication, and reciprocity are at the heart of joint working with families and the wider community. Pedagogical leadership is essential in order to harness the strengths of families and communities in supporting positive child outcomes. Leaders, therefore need to value and respect the contribution of parents and communities, take time to build meaningful relationships, and provide opportunities for parents to be engaged as partners and co-producers of learning with their children and not just consulted or informed in a tokenistic manner (Hart, 1992).

The personal attributes of the individual practitioner are as important as what you actually do. It is important to develop an inclusive approach to working with parents, to be empathic and compassionate, to be reflective and ethical. At times it may be necessary to be an advocate for the child. On occasions, you may need to be resilient when working with parents.

These qualities have been identified from years of experience working with parents in various contexts. They are often overlapping and interdependent. Whilst they are useful in multi- agency work or indeed other professional contexts, they are perhaps even more important when working with parents who may find services hard to access. The ability to develop rapport and engage parents from the outset is essential to establishing an effective parent/ practitioner partnership to support a child's learning and development. Leaders have a responsibility to model these qualities in their own practice and, equally, to support staff to develop their own dispositions and qualities. In the vignette below, a nursery

137

manager in an outstanding early years setting describes how she attempts to engage parents and the pedagogical approaches/tools she uses.

Practice vignette 2

Emma Davies: working with parents in an early years setting

I am the manager of a thriving preschool; one of my great passions is engaging parents in their child's learning and development. This stems from my personal values of respect and trust, concepts which are promoted in our setting ethos. It is important for the Key Person to recognise the parent or carer as the child's first educator, offering them opportunities to share information, allowing us to build a holistic picture of the child. This is advantageous for the child as we are better able to plan for their interests, celebrate achievements and work together to enable them to thrive. It is important that parents feel valued and that their contributions are worthwhile. Communication is key to this and recognising the best means of communication for individual parents is vital to ensure they are able to access and share information. The more methods we use to reach out, the greater chance we have of engaging all parents and sparking interest in their child's learning and the setting as a whole. Some parents are more likely to use Information Technology, others prefer a paper-based method of communication. It is important to be aware that some parents may not like to use written methods and others may not have English as a first language. There are time implications to consider, for example, completing a daily diary may be time-consuming for practitioners and parents.

Accepting why it is important to engage parents is an essential element of practice, beginning with the induction process of new staff. Part of my role as manager and leader is to be creative in engaging parents and motivating practitioners to value the contributions of all. Activities that go between home and the setting are popular with parents, carers and children alike. For example, we supply mark-making bags with challenges which can be completed at home. This activity offers an opportunity for us to promote learning and development at home with parents and carers who share children's creations on their online Learning Journey. This opens up lines of communication by acting as a starting point for conversation, helps us celebrate achievements and identify the best way of extending these further. Engaging in this way helps us work towards a common goal with both parties inputting and sharing information in a respectful way. It is part of the setting's ethos not to assert our professional power and knowledge about children's learning and development. We regard the relationship between setting and home as equally important.

- **Which methods of communicating with parents have you found most effective?**
- **How can leaders support staff to use these approaches?**

Conclusions and reflections

For pedagogical leaders in early years, working responsively and respectfully with parents is of paramount importance. Research suggests that whilst all children benefit from effective collaboration with parents, the benefits for disadvantaged children are particularly significant. The role of the individual practitioner is paramount; it is crucial that practitioners avoid making assumptions about families, and take the time to build open and trustful relationships. Leaders can support this by creating empowering, supportive environments and modelling effective practice. The good practice examples explored in this chapter suggest that open dialogue, a non-judgemental approach and authentic participation of parents, results in the most effective partnerships which best enable children to flourish. Strong, visionary leadership which understands and values the home contexts of children and seeks to work **with** families (instead of **doing to** them) can make a valuable contribution to supporting positive outcomes and breaking cycles of disadvantage.

References

Allen, G. (2011). *Early intervention: The next steps: An independent report to Her Majesty's Government.* January 2011. Retrieved from www.graha mallenmp.co.uk/static/pdf/early-intervention-7th.pdf

Benard, B. (2006). Using strengths-based practice to tap the resilience of families. In D. Saleebey, (Ed.) *Strengths perspective in social work practice*, pp. 197–220. Boston, MA: Allyn and Bacon.

Bronfenbrenner, U. (1979). *The ecology of human development: Experiments by nature and design.* Cambridge, MA: Harvard University Press.

Brooks, J. (2011). *The process of parenting* (8th ed.). Toronto, ON: McGraw-Hill.

Child Poverty Action Group (CPAG). (n.d.). *Child poverty facts and figures, child poverty action group*. Retrieved from www.cpag.org.uk/child-pov erty-facts-and-figures

Coldron, J., Cripps, C., & Shipton, L. (2010). Why are English secondary schools socially segregated? *Journal of Education Policy*, 25 (1), 19–35. doi: 10.1080/02680930903314285

Dahlgren, G., & Whitehead, M. (1991). *Policies and strategies to promote social equity in health. Background strategy paper for Europe*. Arbetsrap-port 2007:14. Stockholm: Institute for Futures Studies.

Deforges, C. (2003). *The impact of parental involvement, parental support and family education on pupil achievement and adjustment: A literature review, research report no 433*. Department for Education and Skills. Retrieved from www.nationalnumeracy.org.uk/sites/default/files/the_im pact_of_parental_involvement.pdf

Dweck, C. S. (2017). The journey to children's mindsets – And beyond. *Child Development Perspectives*, 11 (2), 139–144. doi: 10.1111/cdep.12225

Fauth, R., Renton, Z., & Solomon, E. (2013). *Tackling child poverty and promoting children's well-being: Lessons from abroad*. London: National Children's Bureau Report. Retrieved from www.distancelearningcentre. com/resources/tackling_child_poverty_1302013_final.pdf

Field, F. (2010). *The foundation years: Preventing poor children becoming poor adults: The report of the independent review on poverty and life chances*. Cabinet Office. December 2010. Retrieved from www.towerham lets.gov.uk/Documents/Children-and-families-services/Early-Years/The_ Foundation_Years_preventing_poor_children_becoming_poor_adults_ Frank_Field.pdf

Hart, A., Blincow, D., & Thomas, H. (2008). Resilient therapy: Strategic therapeutic engagement with children in crisis. *Child Care in Practice*, 14 (2), 131–145. doi: 10.1080/13575270701868744

Hart, B., & Risley, T. R. (1995). *Meaningful differences in the everyday experience of young American children*. Baltimore, MD: Paul H. Brookes Publishing Company.

Hart, R. (1992). *Children's participation: From tokenship to citizenship*. UNICEF. Retrieved from www.unicef-irc.org/publications/pdf/children s_participation.pdf

Joseph Rowntree Foundation. (2012). *The role of aspirations, attitudes and behaviour in closing the educational attainment gap*. Retrieved from www.jrf.org.uk

Kagan, S. L., & Bowman, B. T. (1997). *Leadership in early care and education*. Washington: NAEYC.

Kozulin, A., Gindis, B., Ageyev, V., & Miller, S. (Eds.). (2003). *Vygotsky's educational theory in cultural context (Learning in doing: Social, cognitive and computational perspectives)*. Cambridge: Cambridge University.

Marmot, M. (2015). *The health gap: The challenge of an unequal world*. London: Bloomsbury.

Neville, H. J., Stevens, C., Pakulak, E., Bell, T.A., Fanning, J., Klein, S., & Isbell, E. (2013). Family-based training program improves brain function, cognition, and behaviour in lower socioeconomic status pre-schoolers. *Proceedings of the National Academy of Sciences of the United States of America*, 110 (29), 12138–12143. doi: 10.1073/pnas.1304437110

Qualifications and Curriculum Authority (CQA). (2000). *Curriculum guidance for the foundation stage*. London: QCA.

Rogers, C. (1951). *Client-centered therapy: Its current practice, implications and theory*. Boston, MA: Houghton Mifflin.

Sheffield Morris, A., Silk, J., Steinberg, L., & Myers, S. (2007). The role of the family context in the development of emotion regulation. *Social Development*, 16 (2), 361–388. doi: 10.1111/j.1467-9507.2007.00389.x

Social Mobility Commission. (2017). *State of the nation 2017: Social mobility in Great Britain*. London. Retrieved from https://assets.publish ing.service.gov.uk/government/uploads/system/uploads/attachment_data/file/662744/State_of_the_Nation_2017_-_Social_Mobility_in_Great_Britain.pdf

Walsh, F. (2006). *Strengthening family resilience* (2nd ed.). New York: Guilford Press.

EDITORIAL PROVOCATIONS
Engaging readers and extending thinking

Rosie Walker

Having read the chapters in this section you will see how they illustrate the way the authors garner the voices of those closely involved in different communities to make visible the complexities of working alongside families and children. The contributions can be woven together to examine challenges within very different landscapes. This may be useful as a way of critically examining similarities and differences between approaches and their implications for practice which can be a useful strategy when presenting material for assignments and class discussion. For example, as a starting point: Do the approaches offer new ideas or confirm existing practices you are familiar with? In what ways does seeing things through international perspectives make a difference to your thinking?

More specifically: in Chapter 7 'yarning' was a way of 'walking alongside' families within the community encompassed by the local Gundoo or Children's Centre. In this context, the authors claim that this form of relaxed conversation between professionals, families, children and communities can assist in developing an authentic curriculum for children. Where does this view sit within your own practice? Is it familiar or completely foreign to your way of thinking and can you develop this within your own practice?

In Chapter 8, it became possible to hear the voices of early childhood educators when developing children's learning through working with pedagogical facilitators. This is a valuable example of a model of quality practice through close partnership within learning circles, centre visits and online spaces to support children in their journey towards a better future? Are there ways that you might adapt these practices to your own settings or to your future work?

Chapter 9 presents the voices of families and practitioners through a series of vignettes which together paint a picture of practice. These examples demonstrate the empowerment of practitioners and families to develop approaches which can help to alleviate the cycle of disadvantage. Consider the ways in which the vignettes convey messages about practice. This chapter may lend itself to reflection on ways in which this kind of storying might extend the work you are doing currently.

Of course we realise that reading the chapters may present more questions than answers. Each chapter shows the significant impact parents and professionals working as a community can have in shaping effective pathways for children's learning and development. Perspectives from Australia, Canada and England have been offered as provocations for considering the relationships between early childhood pedagogy and the families and communities in which children live. These present powerful considerations for you as an early years educator and we hope that you enjoy engaging with them.

Section 4

WORKING WITH SYSTEMS

10

ENACTING PEDAGOGICAL LEADERSHIP WITHIN SMALL TEAMS IN EARLY CHILDHOOD SETTINGS IN FINLAND

Reflections on system-wide considerations

Manjula Waniganayake, Johanna Heikka and Leena Halttunen

This chapter raises questions about systemic level thinking about pedagogical leadership by exploring the role of teachers leading small teams in early childhood settings in Finland. This discussion is contextualised within the Early Childhood Education (ECE) policy landscape in Finland, taking into account the recently revised national curriculum framework and quality regulation of ECE in this country. Findings from a small scale research study exploring teacher leadership within three early childhood centres in Finland are used to illustrate systemic challenges demanding attention when enacting pedagogical leadership.

ECE teachers in Finland are university graduates responsible for pedagogy in early childhood settings. Their role as pedagogical leaders comprises leading pedagogical planning, development, implementation and assessment in ensuring that the team achieves goals set in the Finnish *National Core Curriculum for Early Childhood Education and Care* (Finnish National Agency for Education, EDUFI, 2016). This work is described by the National Board of Education in the professional profile of ECE teachers, which outlines the road map for ECE in Finland. These teachers are not explicitly identified in national policy as either pedagogical leaders or called educational leaders. It is, however, taken for granted that ECE teachers are well prepared to guide children's learning and development using a child-centred play-based approach to curriculum and pedagogy (Karila, Johansson, Puroila, Hannikani-nen, & Lipponen, 2017). The role of the teacher as a competent and caring adult, with expertise to scaffold children's knowledge, under-standing and skill development, is also emphasised as this is the key to successful pedagogy in ECE settings.

Quality provisioning of ECE is closely connected with leadership, and leaders can benefit from a deep understanding of pedagogy in establishing a culture of learning within their early childhood setting (Waniganayake, Cheeseman, Fenech, Hadley, & Shepherd, 2017). Elsewhere, Heikka and Waniganayake (2011) posit that pedagogical leaders enhance children's learning outcomes in intentional ways and that this is the core business of ECE. This chapter builds on our previous publications where we have written about how teacher leadership in Finland was perceived by centre directors, teachers and childcare nurses (Heikka, Halttunen, & Waniganayake, 2016, 2018). Research reported in this chapter has shown that challenges encountered in leading pedagogical work within early childhood centres influence the planning and evaluation of pedagogy in every-day practice.

The complexity of system-wide ECE reforms being implemented in various countries, including Finland, reflects the power dynamics and layering of workplace relationships, networking, and diverse stakeholders engaged in mass education from early childhood to tertiary study. For instance, in their meta-analysis of early childhood leadership research conducted in Finland, Eskelinen and Hujala (2015, pp. 91–92) found that "pedagogical leadership is manifested as systematically planned and goal-oriented action" and that creat-ing a safe space for "open and confidential" communication was essential in building trust within early childhood settings. Establish-ing alliances between policy planners and policy implementers – especially teacher leaders, means developing trusting relationships (Fink, 2016). The seven nation study of schools including Finland, by Fink and associates (2016), illustrates how the dynamics of systemic change requires close examination of trust and distrust; this applies to education systems across the lifespan. This is the heartland of contemporary leadership theorising, and essential in achieving sustainable systemic change in practice and policy.

As indicated by Heikka and Waniganayake (2011), conceptuali-sation of leadership and pedagogy within ECE settings is relatively recent. Conceptually and in practice, the definition of pedagogical leadership continues to be shrouded in uncertainty and misinterpretations due to role ambiguity, positional authority and inadequate preparation for leadership within ECE settings (Grarock & Morrissey, 2013; Male & Palaiologou, 2015; Rodd, 2013). This chapter aims to contribute critical reflections about enacting pedagogical leadership to advance thinking and stimulate dialogue as a precursor to improving practice and policy across the sector.

Enacting pedagogical leadership

Implementation of pedagogical leadership is influenced by various contextual factors, including centre size, child and family characteristics, staff qualifications, staffing arrangements, leadership roles and responsibilities, and the level of authority teachers have in leading pedagogy within centres. Teachers motivate colleagues towards change by establishing organisational goals targeting pedagogy. Teachers are also expected to pursue pedagogical improvements by involving professionals from diverse backgrounds working with children and families at their early childhood settings (Ho, 2011; Waniganayake et al., 2017). To what extent, however, do ECE teachers have agency to lead organisational change through pedagogical practice within centres?

Practitioner voices captured in ECE leadership studies reflect the continuing need for better preparation to enact leadership decisions (Karila et al., 2017; Rodd, 2013). In their research, Hognestad and Boe (2014), for instance, found that supporting and guiding teaching practice, being a role model, and articulating pedagogically appropriate practice for team members were indicated as the most important leadership acts performed by teacher leaders in Norwegian ECE centres. Likewise, Colmer, Waniganayake and Field (2015) have also discussed how teacher leaders in Australia support the professional learning and development of the whole centre community. The value of professional conversations – both informal and formal, and including "peer group discussions enabling mutual feedback regarding the thoughts, feelings and experiences of staff" was also reinforced in the analysis of Finnish studies by Eskelinen and Hujala (2015, p. 93). Together, these findings affirm that access to continuous learning, including mentoring and management support, is therefore critical for those responsible for leading a centre's pedagogical work.

In discussing the growing interest of exploring relationships amongst centre staff, by referring to various other researchers, Kangas, Venninen, and Ojala (2015) emphasised staff "ability to create and develop a high quality pedagogical environment and practices" (p. 2). They highlighted the importance of communication processes and tools that are used "to help people to co-operate, reach agreement and work together in different forums" (p. 3). This approach comprises both individual and collective inquiry and learning based on local community knowledge and experiences within easy access to children and families at the centre. The dialogue with children, parents and others involved at the centre can include local research projects, often called practitioner inquiry as discussed by Fleet, De Gioia, and Patterson (2016).

Overall, pedagogy is as much about the relationships between the various stakeholders (Moss, 2006; Siraj-Blatchford, 2008) and the nature of supported teaching and learning that takes place during their shared encounters (Bjervas & Rosendhal, 2017; Fleet, Patterson & Robertson, 2012; Hamilton, 2009). Inherent power dynamics contained within these stakeholder relationships are also embedded in the cultural dimensions and emancipatory purposes of pedagogical practice (Freire, 1972). In keeping with this broader social imperative of pedagogical work, Fleet, Patterson, and Robertson (2006, p. 19) add that "the bigger picture matters a great deal – reflecting societal power, inequities, opportunities, curiosities, knowledges and so on, that are always present in daily events." By engaging staff in robust discussions of theory and philosophy, pedagogical leaders can foster team building and organisational cohesion within centres (Waniganayake et al., 2017).

It is difficult to find published research on how ECE teachers deal with such societal complexities encountered in their everyday work, and what long-term impact this work has had in transforming system-wide policy and practice. It is possible that demands of supporting and mentoring colleagues may mean that teacher leaders have little time and space to actively challenge the dominant discourse of compliance with government policy (Sims, Forrest, Semann, & Slattery, 2014). Resolution of local challenges through the application of national policies by aligning theory, policy and practice within settings located throughout the country, is also far from easy. Importantly, there is sufficient research-based evidence alerting us to consider how pedagogical leadership can reshape our perspectives on the quality of

hood settings (Alila
2014).

children's learning and development in early childhood settings (Alila et al., 2014; Heikka et al., 2016, 2018; Sims et al., 2014).

It follows that the potential tension that arises when leading pedagogy within a single centre or multiple centres across a municipality, may be related to the positionality, personality and relationship dynamics between teacher leaders and others including centre directors, deputy directors and municipal authorities (Heikka, 2014; Halttunen, 2009). Likewise, Boe and Hognestad (2017) also refer to the tension that is felt in the binary relationship between the single or solo leadership and distributed or collective leadership approaches enacted by the same person within one or more centres. These considerations reflect some of the challenges of communication, authority, and decision-making encountered by ECE pedagogical leaders.

Pedagogical leadership is, in effect, focused on curriculum and pedagogy. This work is not the same as being held responsible for centre administration and management traditionally perceived as key roles of ECE centre directors. Boe and Hognestad (2017, p. 147) have also warned that "external pressures increase the risk of formal teacher leaders being assigned more administrative tasks, which may result in a stronger division of labour" favouring non-pedagogical work. They also noted that "the core goal when teacher leaders engage in care is to lead by building strong collegiality within the group whilst also being fellow group members" (p. 143). Embedding pedagogical leadership as a teacher responsibility within the revised national curriculum policy framework in Finland also affirms the importance of this work.

Orientation to Finnish ECE

Under the Early Childhood Education and Care Act of 2015, Finnish children have a universal right to access 20 hours of early childhood education each per week. Since 2013, national responsibility for ECE in Finland sits within the Ministry of Education and Culture. Administration of early childhood centres however comes under municipal governance; the diversified model of systemic controls applied within each municipality is reflective of local community needs and demands for child and family services. There are 311 municipalities across Finland, giving rise to a decentralised system of governance over ECE matters. Municipal authorities are responsible for organising ECE services, including family day care, which may involve collaborating with non-government agencies and private providers. ECE administrative leaders in each municipality are also responsible for coordinating financial and human resource management functions of early childhood settings.

Within centres, as stipulated in national policy, ECE teachers have a direct role in designing centre-based pedagogy. The establishment of organisational cultures emphasising pedagogy and assessment of children's learning is also embedded in the national policy framework. This work includes preparing individual educational plans as well as optional child group plans. These educational plans serve multiple purposes in planning the pedagogy and curriculum, and include input from parents (Karila & Alasuutari, 2012). The structure and content to be included in these plans are set by each municipality, illustrating another aspect of how Finnish national ECE policy is implemented through municipal and centre-based processes. As shown in our study, the daily plans discussed in team meetings have been devised by the teachers with input from the childcare nurses, and are used by the team to guide children's learning and development over the coming weeks. Each team typically includes an ECE teacher working with two childcare nurses. In leading this work, teachers are expected to ensure that pedagogical goals are set and achieved systematically.

ECE research carried out in various municipalities illustrates innovative practice in leading pedagogy and client processes (eg, Fonsen, Akselin, & Aronen, 2015) and distributed leadership approaches adopted in service delivery (e.g. Halttunen, 2009, 2016; Heikka, 2014). Strengths of the Finnish ECE system rest on the employment of university-qualified ECE teachers who are well prepared to work with children from birth to eight years and are comfortable working with colleagues from multi-disciplinary backgrounds (Karila et al., 2017; Taguma, Litjens, & Makowiescki, 2013). That is, ECE centres in Finland have always comprised small teams of staff with professional qualifications from diverse disciplines including ECE, nursing and/or welfare. This chapter is based on the workings of these small teams in three municipalities.

The research study

Data collected and analysed from team meetings in three centres are used here to illustrate the enactment of pedagogical leadership by ECE teachers in everyday practice. At each participating centre, a team of three ECE professionals comprising one teacher working with two child care nurses was identified as a purposive sample. For this study, one weekly team meeting was observed and audio-recorded by a research team member. The teacher chaired these meetings, which each lasted about 1 to 1½ hours. Verbatim transcriptions of the meetings were analysed and used as a stimulus to provoke discussion about systemic challenges of pedagogical leadership.

Issues covered during the team meetings were analysed through the application of inductive qualitative content analysis techniques. Content analysis is a method used with verbal, symbolic or communicative data (Krippendorff, 2013). An inductive approach to data analysis was used because only limited knowledge existed about the focus area of the study and this strategy facilitated "gaining direct information from study participants without imposing preconceived categories or theoretical perspectives" (Hsieh & Shannon, 2005, pp. 1279–1280). The unit of analysis was a meaningful utterance, ranging from a couple of words up to a couple of sentences as captured in the interview transcripts. The key research question we pursued in our analysis was: How do ECE teacher leaders use observations, reflections and assessments during team discussions when planning programmes for children?

Key themes on enacting pedagogical leadership

Three key themes connected with pedagogical practice emerged through analysis of the data. Findings show that teachers utilised observations, reflections and assessments in planning programmes for children in different ways. On the one hand, teachers included childcare nurses in the discussions and were strategic in carefully planning activities for their playrooms (theme 1). On the other hand, teachers did not always inform their team members or explain the rationale for their plans (theme 2); and some teachers did not use some of the useful information from the team meetings in their planning (theme 3). Discussion of these findings is supplemented with brief data extracts reflecting the identified themes.

Theme 1: Teamwork in planning activities and pedagogy based on observations and assessments

This theme indicates how staff teams worked each week when planning activities and the pedagogy using observations and assessments of individual children engaged in various learning activities. It began with the teacher first defining the plans for a child using the information collected by the team. These plans were mainly concerned with the coming weeks and not the long-term future or the whole year, and it was very rare that the plans covered the whole group. It was important to target children's abilities, interests and needs when developing individual education plans for each child. It was possible, however, that these plans were not always focused, and the final aims of the planned activities were somewhat ambivalent. Additional data collected over a longer period is necessary to assess the full impact of these weekly meetings.

In the following extract, the teacher refers to an observation she has done with children playing a board game and it shows her concerns about Niilo's possibilities of joining the game. At the end of the extract, the teacher advises the childcare nurses on how to strengthen Niilo's moves to join the game:

> About the Alias – game. Niilo and Mikko are usually joining the game nicely. One day there was Antti playing the game and Niilo played it eagerly. However, there is always a danger that Antti or Oiva say something when Niilo tries to explain [the word]. There has to be an adult watching the game.

In this extract, the teacher brings her own observations about the children's board game into the discussion. When giving pedagogical advice to the nurses, she explains the importance of being better prepared in the future when conducting activities such as this.

Another way of leading pedagogical planning completed during team meetings was to listen to the discussion of observations made by childcare nurses and providing encouragement as indicated in the following comments made by one teacher: "*If I lead an activity, you should observe. It has been good when we are in the gym because I can't see everything.*" This example also illustrates the nature of pedagogical planning as being collaborative, although it was clear that the teacher was responsible for shaping the pedagogy in the room.

Theme 2: Pedagogical activities planned without reference to observations and assessments

This theme indicates how teachers prearranged forthcoming activities without referring to any observations, assessments and reflections during the team meeting that was recorded. The plans had been made mainly by the teacher alone without much discussion with the team. It was difficult to analyse these discussions when planning of some activities was based on long-term plans prepared at a previous meeting. For example, one teacher explained the activities in mathematics she had already done with some children and how she was going to continue these same activities with other children or how staff could continue developing the activities based on what had been completed already.

> Now when we have had mathematical activities, I could take the issue of numerical value. I mean, do the children really recognise the meaning of a number? We have gone through 1 to 10 and now we could continue from that.

This kind of planning often focused on daily practices and involved practical arrangements for the day. In these situations, teachers gave direct instructions to the team as was explained by a teacher in one centre: "*Today there are some outdoor activities at the playground. You [childcare nurses] can join in with the children.*" During the team meeting where the researcher was present, however, the teacher did not mention any observations or assessments to support her plans. The ongoing nature of these weekly team meetings meant that it was difficult for "casual outsiders" such as the researchers to keep track of matters that had been discussed at previous meetings.

Theme 3: Observations and assessments did not lead to planning

This theme describes episodes in the team meetings where observations and assessments took place, but the discussion did not move forward in planning to support children's learning. There were discussions and reflections about pedagogy and the performance of individual children during various activities. Sometimes these were based on small group activities lead by childcare nurses. In these situations, teachers usually asked questions at the meeting to understand the contexts of the children's behaviour and to find out possible reasons for children's problems. However, the teachers did not always pay sufficient attention to these reports and rushed into other topics. In the next excerpt, although the teacher herself asked about the observation done by the nurses, she also dismissed information which the nurse mentioned:

TEACHER: What did you observe when we had music?

CHILD CARE NURSE #1: I only observed. For me these are good [situations], because it strengthens to see Matti and Eero, to see how Eero takes part in tomfoolery.

TEACHER: Yes. Did you notice how difficult it is for Eero to follow instructions?

CHILD CARE NURSE #1: Yes, I wrote down that Eero and instructions and understanding. And also Jaana's concentration. Really, really difficult to focus, she just can't.

TEACHER: Yes, these we have discussed and discussed also with the parents.

CHILD CARE NURSE #1: Yes.

The continuing nature of pedagogical planning based on team discussions held during several meetings over a longer period is clearly illustrated in this extract. The teacher's comments also alerted us to consider the role played by parents in supporting their children's learning and development. Longitudinal research is necessary to examine how individual children's educational plans evolve over time through teacher leadership, and consider the impact of input from parents, children and other staff.

Overall, these three themes highlight the importance of using observations and assessments as well as reflecting on these as a team in curriculum and pedagogical planning within centres. The findings also denote the key role played by the teacher in systematically shaping these plans. Given the small scale of this study and collection of data being limited to one staff meeting at each centre, these findings are inconclusive and not generalisable even within the context of the centres participating in this study. It can nevertheless act as an alert to those in leadership roles, to promote pedagogical discussion and better understanding amongst staff in more intentional ways. These discussions can also better connect curriculum, observations and assessments in multi-modal ways. As working in small teams is common practice in ECE settings, future research should also pay attention to exploring the impact of team composition and member characteristics when considering the teacher's role in leading pedagogical planning.

Implications for improving pedagogical leadership system-wide

Stemming from the findings of this study, the challenges of enacting pedagogical leadership illustrate implications for ECE centre-based practice. These findings also raised questions for us to consider in terms of its application system-wide within municipalities and across the country.

Stakeholder perspectives

Pedagogical planning relies on documenting and discussing observations and assessments of children's learning made by a variety of stakeholders (Fleet et al., 2006, 2012, 2017). This study captured the perspectives of teachers and nurses only. Emerging empirical studies indicate that there is growing interest in looking at ECE pedagogy from the perspective of children (e.g., McInnes, Howard, Miles & Crowley, 2011) and their families (e.g., Karila & Alasuutari, 2012; Rintakorpi, Lipponen & Reunamo, 2014). Given the small scale and limited number of studies published in the English language, it is difficult to assess the extent to which the pedagogical aspects of the learning-teaching cycle incorporate children and families within a particular country such as Finland where many of these studies are located. Perhaps the time has come for an international study, so as to ascertain a better understanding of the merits of active collaboration in pedagogy involving a variety of stakeholders in more intentional ways.

When considering systemic change, as Heikka (2014) found in her doctoral research, understanding leadership for pedagogical planning at the municipal or regional level was critical; the review of national legislative frameworks also requires more in-depth inquiry. Variety in stakeholder contributions can enrich pedagogical decision-making by offering diversity in teaching-learning knowledge, with alternative approaches to satisfy the needs, interests and capabilities of children from diverse family backgrounds. It also posits creativity and innovation when asking questions about when, where and how does pedagogical planning occur? How are pedagogical decisions made at centres/municipalities/regionally and nationally? and who has the power to define who has authority for making decisions about planning and evaluating children's learning within centres?

Collaboration and continuity

The benefits of collaborative practice in leading pedagogy within centres can be seen in findings discussed in Theme 1 and Theme 2 reported here. Theme 3, however, reflects the importance of communication and coordination between teachers and nurses as well as retaining continuity over time, particularly in terms of developing partnerships with families as is expected under national ECE policy in Finland. The influx of immigrant, refugee and asylum-seeker families in recent years, are presenting new challenges in pedagogy, and requiring "new modes of culturally sensitive participation" (Karila, 2017, p. 13). Pedagogical leadership of ECE teachers can contribute to bridging the gaps in honouring diverse family and community values encountered in their everyday work.

Teamwork discussed in this chapter also reflects collective responsibility for teaching, in keeping with a distributed pedagogical leadership model as conceptualised by Heikka (2014). Bringing together our understandings from previous research, and our reflections on the current study, raises questions such as:

- How do ECE teachers promote collaboration between the multiple stakeholders, including parents, children and other professionals to create a shared, safe space for communication about pedagogy?
- To what extent is it possible to reconcile differing values, beliefs and attitudes about children's learning that exists within staff teams and between staff and families?
- Why does this matter? and how can we persuade families to get involved in pedagogical discussions?

Translating national policy into everyday practice within municipalities and ECE settings calls for trust between policy makers and policy implementers. This is described by Fink (2016, p. 1) as the "missing ingredient" in achieving school improvements. In Finland, ECE teachers have autonomy in developing children's educational plans; they are entrusted with guiding the planning, implementation and evaluation of this work with their teams and in seeking input from parents. Fink quotes preeminent education scholars such as Robinson (2011, cited in Fink 2016, p. 1) who has found "compelling evidence that the level of trust among the members of a school community makes an important difference to the way they work together and to the social and academic progress of students." Understanding the benefits of home-school collaborations in supporting children's early learning is not new. In the absence of large scale research exploring community collaborations about pedagogical matters in ECE settings, we are well advised to take heed of lessons learnt in school settings.

Intentionality of teaching and leading

Pedagogy can be described as "what a teacher does to influence learning in every day practices" (Melhuish, 2017, p. 38). As indicated in our study findings, teachers purposefully used child observations and assessments in their planning to address children's needs or areas that required strengthening. Thoughtful definition of the goals and understanding the purpose of teaching and learning can also provide strategic direction for learning outcomes to be achieved in a holistic way by a child, an organisation, a community or a nation. If the pedagogical planning and assessment at the local level occurs merely to satisfy accountabilities defined under national regulations, then all that is being achieved is compliance. This is not sufficient in nurturing either children's thinking and learning capabilities or societal expectations about educating its citizens as free and capable of independent action.

Leadership in balancing the micro-macro politics of organisational cultures, and the adoption of an optimistic stance can go a long way in sustaining the evolution of new possibilities. Transformative reforms involve understanding the structures, stakeholders, functions and their associations system-wide. Adoption of a critically reflective and action-oriented approach to systemic change is emancipatory as leaders focus on increasing professional autonomy and participative decision-making (Hopkins, 2017). The design of our study constrained the collection of data reflective of deeper levels of engagement in pedagogical planning, a precursor to systemic innovation and change.

School education scholars who are systems-thinkers such as Fullan (2005) and Hopkins (2017), refer to the concept of "intelligent accountability" as a key driver of sustainable change. Applying this concept to Finland's school education system, Sahlberg (2007, p. 152) discusses the "adoption of intelligent accountability policies and gradual building of a culture of trust within the education system that values teachers' and headmasters' professionalism in judging what is best for students and in reporting their learning progress." Application of such an approach within ECE settings calls for pedagogical leadership by ECE teachers who are critically reflective, and can rise above compliance requirements to think comprehensively across equity, quality, affordability and sustainability issues impacting the provisioning of ECE programmes within their own country and more globally.

Conclusion

Pedagogical leadership can be applied both locally and nationally. It is easy for teachers to remain focused on planning for individual children's education without regard to their collective needs as citizens of a country or their interactions as people living in the same municipality/country. In opening an international seminar focusing on pedagogy, and highlighting the important role early childhood settings play in promoting equality and social cohesion, Sanni Grahn-Laasonen (2017), Minister of Education and Culture in Finland, stated that "ECEC [early childhood education and care] must respond to social change and keep up with developments in pedagogy" (p. 8). In particular, speakers at this seminar were alluding to challenges of parent-teacher collaborations involving children from immigrant and refugee families now residing in Finland (Karila et al., 2017). ECE teachers can make use of Nordic values of democracy and equality as reflected in the Finnish National Core Curriculum for ECEC; pedagogical leadership can be applied to build partnerships with families from diverse cultural and linguistic backgrounds. This work can make a critical contribution to society as a whole as noted by Karila (2017, p. 12), who declared that "in the complicated world, social cohesion is very much needed. This is not the time to abandon the key elements of the Nordic model, but to revise and elaborate them."

This chapter is merely a provocation, to raise awareness and stimulate active dialogue towards transforming children's early learning from a systems perspective. It is by no means intended to be a comprehensive analysis or treatment of how pedagogical leadership can influence system-wide changes within ECE. We recommend that every reader leads a conversation about what Kagan and Kauerz

(2012) describe as field-defining questions that can explain the purpose, goals and responsibilities of ECE. As discussed in this chapter, this task begins with thinking and planning ECE pedagogy by aligning every day practice with national policy as well as local needs and talents to guide future directions that honour children and families from diverse backgrounds.

References

Alila, K., Eskelinen, M., Estola, E., Kahiluoto, T., Kinos, J., Pekuri, H.-M., Polvinen, M., Laaksonen, R., & Lamberg, K. (2014). *Varhaiskasvatuksen historia, nykytila ja kehittämisen suuntalinjat. Tausta-aineisto varhaiskasvatusta koskevaa lainsäädäntöä valmistelevan työryhmän tueksi* [The history, presence and the directions for the future development. The background information for the Early Childhood Education Act Working Committee]. Opetus- ja kulttuuriministeriön työryhmämuistioita ja selvityksiä, 12.

Bjervas, L., & Rosendhal, G. (2017). Pedagogical documentation and pedagogical choices. In A. Fleet, C. Patterson, & J. Robertson (Eds.). *Pedagogical documentation in early years practice* (pp. 27–39). London: Sage.

Boe, M., & Hognestad, K. (2017). Directing and facilitating distributed pedagogical leadership: Best practices in early childhood education. *International Journal of Leadership in Education, 20*(2), 133–148. doi:10.1080/13603124.2015.1059488

Colmer, K., Waniganayake, M., & Field, L. (2015). Implementing curriculum reform: Insights on how Australian early childhood directors view professional development and learning. *Professional Development in Education – Special Issue: The Professional Development of Early Years Educators, 41*(2), 203–221.

Eskelinen, M., & Hujala, E. (2015). Early childhood leadership in Finland in light of recent research. In M. Waniganayake, J. Rodd, & L. Gibbs (Eds.). *Thinking and learning about leadership: Early childhood research from Australia, Finland and Norway* (pp. 87–101). Research Monograph #2. Sydney: Community Child Care Cooperative NSW.

Fink, D. (Ed.) (2016). *Trust and Verify: The real keys to school improvement. An international examination of trust and distrust in education in seven countries.* London: UCL Institute of Education Press.

Finnish National Agency for Education (EDUFI). (2016). *National core curriculum for early childhood education and care.* Helsinki. Retrieved from www.oph.fi/english/curricula_and_qualifications/early_childhood_education_and_care

Fleet, A., De Gioia, K., & Patterson, C. (2016). *Engaging with educational change – Voices of practitioner inquiry.* London: Bloomsbury.

Fleet, A., Patterson, C., & Robertson, J. (Eds.) (2006). *Insights: Behind early childhood pedagogical documentation.* Sydney: Pademelon Press.

Fleet, A., Patterson, C., & Robertson, J. (Eds.) (2012). *Conversations: Behind early childhood pedagogical documentation.* Sydney: Pademelon Press.

Fleet, A., Patterson, C., & Robertson, J. (Eds.) (2017). *Pedagogical documentation in early years practice*. London: Sage.

Fonsen, E., Akselin, M. L., & Aronen, K. (2015). From distributed leadership towards joint leadership. In M. Waniganayake, J. Rodd, & L. Gibbs (Eds.). *Thinking and learning about leadership: Early childhood research from Australia, Finland and Norway* (pp. 116–130). Research Monograph #2. Sydney: Community Child Care Cooperative NSW.

Freire, P. (1972). *Pedagogy of the oppressed*. Harmondsworth: Penguin.

Fullan, M. (2005). *Leadership and sustainability: System thinkers in action*. Thousand Oaks, CA: Corwin Press.

Grahn-Laasonen, S. (2017). A word from the Minister of Education and Culture. In K. Karila, E. Johansson, A. M. Puroila, M. Hännikäinen, & L. Lipponen (Eds.). *Pedagogy in ECEC: Nordic challenges and solutions*. Seminar Report, Helsinki, Finland, 22 September 2016. Nordisk minsterrad. ANP, 2017:729 (pp. 7–8). doi:10.6027/ANP2017-729

Grarock, M., & Morrissey, A. M. (2013). Teachers' perceptions of their abilities to be educational leaders in Victorian childcare settings. *Australasian Journal of Early Childhood, 38*(2), 4–12.

Halttunen, L. (2009). Päivähoitotyö ja johtajuus hajautetussa organisaatiossa [Day care work and leadership in a distributed organization]. Unpublished PhD thesis, Finland: University of Jyväskylä.

Halttunen, L. (2016). Distributing leadership in a day care setting. *Journal of Early Childhood Education Research, 5*(1), 2–18.

Hamilton, D. (2009). Blurred in translation: Reflections on pedagogy in public education. *Pedagogy, Culture & Society, 17*(1), 5–16.

Heikka, J. (2014). *Distributed pedagogical leadership in early childhood education*. Acta Electronica Universitatis Tamperensis 1392. Unpublished PhD thesis, prepared under a cotutelle agreement between the University of Tampere, Australia: Finland and Macquarie University.

Heikka, J., Halttunen, L., & Waniganayake, M. (2016). Investigating teacher leadership in ECEC centres in Finland. *Journal of Early Childhood Education Research, 5*(2), 289–309.

Heikka, J., Halttunen, L., & Waniganayake, M. (2018). Perceptions of early childhood education professionals on teacher leadership in Finland. *Early Child Development and Care, 188*(2), 143–156. doi:10.1080/03004430.2016.1207066

Heikka, J., & Waniganayake, M. (2011). Pedagogical leadership from a distributed perspective within the context of early childhood education. *International Journal of Leadership in Education, 14*(4), 499–512. doi:10.1080/13603124.2011.577909

Ho, D. C. W. (2011). Identifying leadership roles for quality in early childhood education programmes. *International Journal of Leadership in Education: Theory and Practice, 14*(1), 47–57. doi:10.1080/13603120903387561

Hognestad, K., & Boe, M. (2014). Knowledge development through hybrid leadership practices. *Nordisk Barnehageforskning, 8*(6), 1–14.

Hopkins, D. (2017). *The past, present and future of school improvement and system reform*. The William Walker Oration, Monograph 56. Sydney: Australian Council for Educational Leaders.

Hsieh, H., & Shannon, S. E. (2005). Three approaches to qualitative content analysis. *Qualitative Health Research, 15*(9), 1277–1288. doi:10.1177/1049732305276687

Kagan, S. L., & Kauerz, K. (Eds.) (2012). *Early childhood systems: Transforming early learning*. New York: Teachers College Press.

Kangas, J., Venninen, T., & Ojala, M. (2015). Distributed leadership as administrative practice in Finnish early childhood education and care. *Educational Management, Administration & Leadership, 44*(4), 617–631. doi:10.1177/1741143214559226

Karila, K. (2017). ECEC pedagogy in the Nordic countries – Its roots and current challenges. In K. Karila, E. Johansson, A.-M. Puroila, M. Hännikäinen, & L. Lipponen (Eds.). *Pedagogy in ECEC: Nordic challenges and solutions*. Seminar Report, Helsinki, Finland, 22 September 2016. Nordisk minsterrad. ANP, 2017:729 (pp. 11–15). doi:10.6027/ANP2017-729

Karila, K., & Alasuutari, M. (2012). Drawing partnership on paper: How do the forms for individual educational plans frame parent-teacher relationship? *International Journal about Parents in Education, 6*(1), 14–26.

Karila, K., Johansson, E., Puroila, A.-M., Hännikäinen, M., & Lipponen, L. (2017). *Pedagogy in ECEC: Nordic challenges and solutions*. Seminar Report, Helsinki, Finland, 22 September 2016. Nordisk minsterrad. ANP, 2017:729. doi:10.6027/ANP2017-729

Krippendorff, K. (2013). *Content analysis: An introduction to its methodology* (4th ed.). Los Angeles, CA: Sage.

Male, T., & Palaiologou, I. (2015). Pedagogical leadership in the 21st century: Evidence from the field. *Educational Management, Administration and Leadership, 43*(2), 214–231. doi:10.1177/1741143213494889

McInnes, K., Howard, J., Miles, G., & Crowley, K. (2011). Differences in practitioners' understanding of play and how this influences pedagogy and children's perceptions of play. *Early Years – An International Journal of Research and Development, 31*(2), 121–133. doi:10.1080/09575146.2011.572870

Melhuish, E. (2017). Reflections from Europe on ECEC pedagogy in the Nordic countries: A critical friend's views on the way forward. In K. Karila, E. Johansson, A.-M. Puroila, M. Hännikäinen, & L. Lipponen (Eds.). *Pedagogy in ECEC: Nordic challenges and solutions*. Seminar Report, Helsinki, Finland, 22 September 2016. Nordisk minsterrad. ANP, 2017:729 (pp. 38–40). doi:10.6027/ANP2017-729

Moss, P. (2006). Structures, understanding and discourses: Possibilities for re-envisioning the early childhood worker. *Contemporary Issues in Early Childhood, 7*, 30–41.

Rintakorpi, K., Lipponen, L., & Reunamo, J. (2014). Documenting with parents and toddlers: A Finnish case study. *Early Years – An International Journal of Research and Development, 34*(2), 188–197. doi:10.1090/09575146.2014.903233

Rodd, J. (2013). *Leadership in early childhood: A pathway to professionalism* (4th ed.). Crows Nest, NSW: Allen & Unwin.

Sahlberg, P. (2007). Education policies for raising student learning: The Finnish approach. *Journal of Education Policy, 22*(2), 147–171.

Sims, M., Forrest, R., Semann, A., & Slattery, C. (2014). Conceptions of early childhood leadership: Driving new professionalism? *International Journal of Leadership in Education: Theory and Practice, 18*(2), 149–166. doi:10.1080/13603124.2014.962101

Siraj-Blatchford, I. (2008). Understanding the relationship between curriculum, pedagogy and progression in learning in early childhood. *Hong Kong Journal of Early Childhood, 7*(2), 6–13.

Taguma, M., Litjens, I., & Makowiescki, K. (2013). *Quality matters in early childhood education and care: Finland 2012.* Paris: OECD. doi:10.1787/97892617569-en

Waniganayake, M., Cheeseman, S., Fenech, M., Hadley, F., & Shepherd, W. (2017). *Leadership: Contexts and complexities in early childhood education* (2nd ed.). South Melbourne: Oxford University Press.

11

PEDAGOGICAL LEADERSHIP AND CONFLICT OF MOTIVES IN COMMERCIAL ECEC ENVIRONMENTS

Sirene May-Yin Lim and Lasse Lipponen

Singapore's early childhood education and care (ECEC) landscape is still in its nascent phases of development towards becoming a knowledge-based profession. This chapter presents initial findings from a qualitative study of 24 ECEC leaders to discuss the various ways in which pedagogical leadership could be enacted within a neoliberal, marketised ECEC system within a meritocratic culture and an academically competitive education system (Lim, 2017b).

A marketised ECEC industry has the tendency to focus on market competitiveness, profit generation, business expansion, and shaping consumer choice through entrepreneurial innovations (Lloyd, 2012; Sumsion, 2006). In this study, we were interested in how such marketised environments, coupled with Singaporean families' general concern around children's academic achievement, would shape early childhood leaders' work. While literature has shown that pedagogical concerns should be central to an educational leader's work, oftentimes leaders are entangled in time-sensitive managerial and administrative tasks. There appears to be a struggle between two conflicting motives in ECEC leaders' work: conflict between the motives of engaging in child-centric pedagogical work or performing administrative and business-related tasks that serve a neoliberal market agenda. Applying Cultural-Historical Activity Theory (CHAT), we explore the complexities of pedagogical leadership within Singapore's commercialised ECEC environment. This chapter concentrates on ECEC leaders who manage child care centres or kindergartens, the two main types of ECEC provisions that are regulated and licensed in Singapore.

Understanding leadership in ECEC

Leadership is, at present, not yet clearly defined within and across the global early childhood education and care (ECEC) sector (Rodd, 2013). There has been a traditional view of leadership that is associated with individual skills, characteristics, behaviours, and personal qualities in the leader (Nivala & Hujala, 2002). According to Rodd (2013), ECEC leadership is not reducible to a checklist of qualities and skills due to its multi-dimensionality and complexity in practice involving staff, families and local communities with varying and diverse needs and expectations. In reality, a contextualised model of leadership (Hujala, 2013; Waniga-nayake, 2014) is needed so that leaders continually clarify and co-construct with their team a common vision for the centre's work. To achieve this, leaders are to create ample learning opportunities for members of the organisation to produce positive results – that is, focused on the quality of children's learning and development, as well as the professional development and collaborative learning among teachers (Goffin & Janke, 2013; Hujala, 2013; Siraj-Blatchford & Manni, 2007; Waniganayake, Cheeseman, Fenech, Hadley, & Shepherd, 2012).

There are rapidly changing expectations of ECEC leaders due to contesting views of ECEC's purpose in societies (Goffin & Janke, 2013; Hujala, 2013). These 'change challenges' suggest a real impera-tive for the field to develop new and robust frameworks for leadership that can support people who are faced with challenges and have to initiate and facilitate change in more proactive ways (Fasoli, Scrivens, & Woodrow, 2007). As such, investigations into ECEC leadership must be carefully contextualised to take into account the leader's position and autonomy accorded in decision-making, and the place and setting in which each leader operates (Waniganayake et al., 2012).

The Singapore ECEC landscape and leadership

In Singapore, the care and education of young children is provided by about 1800 licensed child care centres and kindergartens (Lim, 2017a). Child care centres provide the option of full-day programmes (children from 18 months) whereas kindergartens only offer half-day programmes (4-to-6-year-olds). All of these services are licensed but are largely operated by private commercial entities or not-for-profit social or reli-gious organisations, except for less than 20 kindergartens run by the Ministry of Education (Goy, 2017). Before a child enters Primary One (the year of her/his seventh birthday), many families can choose between

166

a few options to meet their young child's care and educational needs even though centre-based care is increasingly preferred as Singaporean families are more nuclear and grandparent care has become less available. In the last two years, the Early Childhood Development Agency (ECDA) has worked on increasing the number of child care places (i.e., full-day and flexible care and education for children from 18 months to 6 years) to meet families' demands, creating grants to support the larger child care operators to meet this goal. This has created a shortage of EC educators to staff the newly created centres (Lim, 2017b) and become an issue for EC leaders to contend with.

Despite its growth in number, Singapore's ECEC landscape is still in its nascent phases of development towards becoming a knowledge-based profession to replace its babysitters' image. Government policies in Singapore only started focusing on improving the professional quality of ECEC around the year 2000 (Lim, 2017a). Efforts started with an incremental raise in the minimum teacher and leader requirements, a recommended kindergarten curriculum framework, and more recently, the Singapore Preschool Accreditation Framework (SPARK) for programmes catering to 4-to-6-year-olds (Lim, 2017a). The SPARK Framework requires both child care centres and kindergartens with 4-to-6-year-olds to conduct annual self-appraisal using its Quality Rating Scale and volunteer for external accreditation when the centre is ready for external feedback. By October 2017, 40 per cent of pre-schools had received the SPARK certification (Early Childhood Development Agency, 2017a).

In Singapore, an ECEC leader is commonly called 'principal', 'supervisor' or 'centre director'. Before 2016, leaders were required to have a minimum of a professional Diploma in Early Childhood Care and Education – Teaching (typically 1200 hours part-time) and a Diploma in Early Childhood Care and Education – Leadership (typically 850 hours part-time). As part of the nation's strategy to incrementally raise quality in the ECEC sector, a new Advanced Diploma in Early Childhood Leadership (also 850 hours) has replaced the previous leadership diploma (Early Childhood Development Agency, 2016). Apart from these part-time professional diplomas, some principals would have completed their academic and professional teaching-cum-leadership preparation in a three-year full-time polytechnic diploma programme before turning 20 years old. This combined teaching and leadership programme has ceased to be available (Early Childhood Development Agency, 2016).

Qualifications and training aside, many principals may have been handpicked for the role based largely on their teaching competencies and not because they were potentially good administrators and managers with strategic vision. So it is possible that inexperienced leaders struggle with their new role when given little mentoring or learning opportunities. Yet global literature tells us of the importance of competent leaders, because quality provision of ECEC for young children spending long hours in centre-based services is dependent on quality leadership (Muijs, Aubrey, Harris, & Briggs, 2004; Siraj-Blatchford & Manni, 2007).

Within Singapore's commercialised ECEC environment, ECEC leaders are potentially faced with managing different expectations and have to be accountable to a broad range of stakeholders: children and their families, teachers and staff, government agencies, external agencies and funders. They work within an industry that is not only short of teachers but is situated within a multifaceted context of a) increased quality demands by the licensing government agency; b) profit-driven expectations of their organisations, c) the academically competitive expectations of families, and d) the pedagogically child-centric intents of their teachers.

Principal matters: a professional development programme

In Singapore, ECEC teachers are reluctant to take on leadership roles due to reasons such as the lack of support and clarity of role as well as barriers within organisational cultures towards new ideas (Ebbeck, Saidon, Soh, & Goh, 2014). ECEC leaders and their leadership practices have not been investigated sufficiently to be understood. We do not yet know enough about how they were selected, how well they are managing, what kinds of support they need to become better leaders, and about the challenges they face in their workplaces. Singapore has limited experience of how best to support ECEC leaders' continued learning within a largely private, and often commercial, sector.

Our study was funded by the Lien Foundation, a Singapore-based philanthropic organisation which created Principal Matters – a six-month part-time professional development course designed to meet the learning needs of early childhood leaders with at least three years of leadership experience (commenced in 2016 with two cohorts annually). The Foundation aimed to fund six cohorts of about 25 principals each, all to be interviewed for selection into the unique programme. This study invited the first two cohorts of principals to participate in individual interviews and observations.

In this chapter, we describe how a group of Singaporean ECEC leaders have experienced their work, and especially the kinds of tensions and conflicts they faced as leaders. Our data are composed of 24 face-to-face interviews with ECEC principals whose ages ranged from 29 to 61. The 24 participants had a range of 0 to 14 years of teaching experience and a range of 3 to 14 years of leadership experience. All the principals were females. These leaders worked in different kinds of settings with a range of 7 to 32 staff members. We learned that every setting had teachers who qualified outside of Singapore and a few centres were staffed by a majority of non-Singaporean teachers from China, Taiwan, Vietnam, Myanmar and the Philippines. There has been a significant shortage of teachers in the early childhood sector since the government encouraged more child care centres to be set up in recent years. Many ECEC centres have, therefore, hired teachers from overseas due to the shortage of teachers in Singapore. This phenomenon requires leaders to spend time familiarising foreign-trained teachers with local culture and expectations.

Our participants also worked within a range of environments and types of organisations. Seven of the centres were registered as not-for-profit kindergartens (mostly affiliated with churches) which provided half-day programmes and catered mainly to children from ages 4 to 6; one centre was undergoing a transition to offer both half-day 'kindergarten' and full-day 'child care' services within the same premises; 13 were for-profit providers and the remaining were not-for-profit; six of the centres were not part of a group or chain of centres managed by a single owner or organisation. The settings also varied by the type of neighbourhood in which they were situated – public housing estates, church compounds, houses with private gardens, and commercial office buildings. Different neighbourhoods cater to different social classes and communities and would require the leader to be able to relate to the specific clientele, speak their lingo and understand their needs.

Leadership in Singapore ECEC: critical conflicts

Given its largely privatised nature, varied settings and organisational structures, and diverse clientele and staff, EC leadership practice in Singapore is complex and involves everyday decision-making and problem-solving (Ang, 2012). This study uncovers the conflictual nature of leaders' everyday work and experience. All of these leaders experienced time-deprivation in juggling administrative, managerial, and pedagogical roles. A few talked about wanting to spend more time mentoring teachers but found themselves unable to do so because they are called to 'serve' their organisation by supporting other centres in the group.

Acting as an EC leader, doing and being a leader, is continuously filled with experiences and conditions resulting from external and internal forces acting in opposition to each other. To understand the multi-dimensional nature and experiences of our participants' work, we apply Vasilyuk's (1988) concept of critical conflicts. Working from within Cultural-Historical Activity Theory, Vasilyuk (1988; see also Engeström & Sannino, 2011; Sannino, 2010) refers to critical conflicts as situations in which individuals face inner doubts when faced with contradictory motives. Critical conflicts are by their very nature personal, and they are expressed by means of emotionally and morally charged accounts. Feeling guilty and violated are common ways of experiencing critical conflicts (Engeström & Sannino, 2011).

The act of experiencing involves both cognitive and socio-emotional aspects, and it can be manifested as interpreting, perceiving, or living through conflicts. How and what individuals experience emerges as an interaction between them and their social situation and culture. In other words, a given culture is not experienced the same way by different individuals or even by the same individuals at different times. While culture influences an individual's experiences, humans always contribute towards culture-creation as well, by exercising agency in shaping their own experience.

Critical conflicts are part of experiencing and struggling against the impossible.

According to Vasilyuk (1988, p. 32),

> If one had to use one word only to define the nature of such situations one would have to say that they are situations of impossibility. Impossibility of what? Impossibility of living, of realising the internal necessities of life. The struggle against impossibility, the struggle to realise internal necessities – that is experiencing.

In Vasilyuk's (1988) theory of experiencing, struggles refer to conflicts between motives of a single person (see also Sannino, 2010). In many cases, critical conflicts are unsolvable by the subject alone. As stated by Sannino (2013, p. 48), 'Commonly, an individual without external support surrenders in front of the conflict and searches for easy ways out'. The following sections present four thematic strands that illustrate the kinds of conflicts faced by the leaders in this study.

Managing a web of internal and external expectations

The first vignette describes a principal experiencing the struggle of working within a large child care chain with a network of stakeholders with different expectations and competences. This principal had described herself as an octopus as she juggled with the multiple needs of the administration, teachers, children, and parents. Vignette 1 illustrates this.

Vignette 1

[I am] an octopus. Juggling administration, teachers and each teacher with their different sets of challenges, children [...] parents as well. My novice teachers are always very apprehensive about talking to parents. They always fear upsetting parents [...] because of that they didn't build a relationship with the parents... they didn't build a stable relationship. [When] anything happens, it is very hard for the parents... for me to gain back the trust. One forte I have, it seems to be so far across the year and it has been affirmed is that, I do have a good relationship with parents.

This leader experienced different role expectations when she interacted with the organisation's 'Headquarters' (HQ) staff and management. For many of our participants working in large organisations that manage more than 30 or 100 centres, their work involves working with different departments in the HQ, managing different due dates for paperwork, facing fixed boundaries and guidelines. Such demands also place the principal in a 'sandwich', between the HQ's expectations and the expectations among his/her staff as well as the children and families served by the centre (Vignette 2).

Building on Vignette 1, Vignette 2 demonstrates how this same principal experiences a variety of forces that act in opposition to each other – the needs and interests of the organisation's various

171

departments such as finance, human resources, marketing, curriculum specialists as well as those of the centre's novice teachers, more experienced teachers, non-teaching staff, the children their parents.

Vignette 2

I also feel that, it will be a bit of what we call a 'sandwich position' when [the] management rolls things out, we are the ones to deliver at ground level. Relationship with the team is very critical to see if the team can buy in the changes. But, so far, I would say is 50-50 for me. The biggest challenge I have is, because I have a [HQ], anything I do may not just affect me, myself but it also affects the management [of the centre]. When I have a system in place to manage my teachers [and these are] preventive measures [because] if my teachers are not happy, they complain. And when they complain to the Ministry of Manpower, for example, [HQ] will definitely come after me because I am the representation. This is something that I feel very sandwiched in because (short pause) how do you expect me to run a centre when I don't have [control or] a preventive measure?

This situation is conflictual, as described by Vasilyuk (1988), and there seems to be no way that the leader can be disentangled from this web of interactions and varied responsibilities. This principal's experience is common among participants who work with a corporate HQ office.

Asserting one's professional autonomy

Over the past two decades, the primary and secondary schools in Singapore have replaced traditional school inspection with an external validation, with the aim of encouraging schools to be more reflexive (Ng, 2010). SPARK is the equivalent for ECEC programmes catering to 4-to-6-year-olds. To receive the SPARK certification, centres volunteer when they are ready for a thorough and careful assessment by external assessors from the ECDA. The assessors would use the Quality Rating Scale, interview and observe teachers, and produce a report detailing if the processes and systems

172

need improvement. Recently, more pre-schools are recognising the value of going through SPARK even if it were for marketing purposes; while some of the not-for-profit operators receiving government funding have to complete the assessment within a stipulated timeframe (ECDA, 2017a). We learned that preparing for SPARK can sometimes be quite stressful for the principals and could generate conflicts within teams of ECEC educators.

Vignette 3 offers an illustration of how a principal had experienced the HQ management's distrust of her readiness in preparing for SPARK certification. The principal felt very upset and insulted when she recounted the experience. All she needed was to be recognised as a competent, autonomous and agentic subject who was an expert in her work.

Vignette 3

While preparing for SPARK, my [boss] did something which I really don't like. She called all [my peer principals in my area] to come down to my centre without informing me and they went into the classroom[s]. At that time, [lessons were still ongoing] but they tried to revamp all my learning centres. I really felt very upset [...] They said, 'Because [HQ's staff] said your centre will not get through [SPARK]. I know you are very busy. So, we [sent] the whole team down to help you'. [I felt] I was not being respected [as a principal] because when they came, all my teachers were stunned. [They would be] teaching [and the HQ staff would be] moving shelves and tables [...]. But I can't do anything because she was my direct superior and she sat in my centre for continuously three days to [supervise]. So, I could not say anything. I really felt upset on those three days. I am sorry to say[...]

Vignette 3 is a clear example of what Vasilyuk (1988) referred to as critical conflict. 'I can't do anything because she is my direct superior...' represents a situation in which the principal faced doubts that paralysed her in face of contradictory motives: wanting to be autonomous in her work, yet not being able to do so. She experienced injustice but did not have the courage or any possibility of defending herself, so she could not extricate herself from the unfair and conflicting situation. In the principals' lives, such contradictory motives could appear to be so strong that they cannot be solved by the principals themselves. As stated by Vasilyuk (1988), the situation appeared to be a struggle against impossibility.

Facing parents' woes and protecting one's staff

Singapore's competitive academic landscape, its overall meritocratic ideology, high stakes testing for 12-year-olds, and an emphasis on global competitiveness, is partially responsible for a thriving commercial after-school tuition industry for school-going children (Gee, 2012; Lim, 2017b; Tan, 2017; Teng, 2015). It is well known that Singapore's education system is among the most highly regarded in the world because of its performance in the Trends in International Mathematics and Science Study (TIMSS) and the Programme for International Student Assessment (PISA). What is less discussed is the rising incidence of mental and emotional stress for children and teachers as well (Teng, 2015). Singapore parents may pay a significant sum for preschool and expect a return on their investment, nothing less than having their demands met. In a free market, parents who are not satisfied with a centre could enrol their child in another that may be more aligned with their needs. The following Vignette 4 demonstrates the motive arising from the conflict between defending and protecting the teachers against parents' demands and negative behaviours, and at the same time wanting to keep up the good relationship with parents because the centre is dependent on child enrolment.

Vignette 4

[Ways to get into the principal role] that's why I put a mirror there [on my desk]. You know when you're stressed, you can see the mirror. [To remind myself] when the parents are coming I will [...] especially when you know they are coming in means serious issues. [....] My role is to protect the teachers. I do have parents who come in and want to scream and shout [demanding to see my teachers] and I would say, 'I am sorry [my teacher is not available], what's happened?' It is always minor things.

Such conflicts often arise because ECEC educators have to negotiate between their own more child-centric educational beliefs and individual families' academic aspirations for their children.

Supporting teachers' autonomy

The following Vignette 5 is an example of the motive of conflict between controlling the pedagogical implementation of curriculum ('how do I keep track of the progress of each and every single class and how the teachers are doing') and supporting teachers' autonomy and agency in their work ('I am not here to police you, to catch you doing wrong. [Rather,] I am here to journey with you and enrich the curriculum together').

Vignette 5

The challenge as a principal, I feel, is not just about tracking [progress] but helping [...] each teacher to understand and interpret what the (curriculum) framework actually means in their execution. Because we have zero [pre-created] lesson plans, which is a good thing. We have [a framework]. This means the teachers who come in need to work with frames of thinking and beginning teachers go 'What does that mean? What is a framework? [...]' So, I think my biggest challenge is that, in a very fluid way of planning, how do I keep track of the progress of each and every single class and how the teachers are doing. Yah, that would be my greatest struggle and challenge. I give a lot of autonomy to the teachers[...] My role will be going in and taking a look at what the classes are doing, [conducting] classroom observations. [...] (A lot of the observations are informal) because I want the teachers to see that I am not here to police you, to catch you doing wrong. [Rather,] I am here to journey with you and enrich the curriculum together. So, I cover [teachers'] shifts as well. I go in and [work with] the children as well.

While not common in our interview data, there were a few leaders working in organisations without prescriptive curricula who were confident about their role as curriculum leaders supporting their teachers' growth as curriculum designers.

Ensuring profit and being innovative

Singapore's ECEC system is a marketised system in which profit generation plays an important role. The need for profit may lead into a situation where centres and teachers, and the management are pitted against each other, favouring competition instead of collaboration. The following Vignette 6 shows that a critical conflict does not always lead to a dead end. Breaking away from the critical conflict opens up and expands a new horizon for enacting leadership.

In the vignette, the principal talks about wanting to do things differently and focus on delivering something that other centres cannot deliver. Simultaneously, she experiences that she is expected (she has) to take care of enrolment numbers and make a profit. There appears to be a critical conflict between these two goals – doing things differently and making profit. This seems to be unsolvable by the principal alone. At first, the situation almost crippled her, but with external help and emotional support from her management, she was able to solve the conflict: in the words of Vasilyuk (1988) '...she falls and rises again to continue the journey' (p. 32).

According to Engeström and Sannino (2011), critical conflicts may prevent individuals from engaging in a collective redesign of their material circumstances if collective resources are not mobilised for conflict resolution. Resolving critical conflicts requires one to find a new personal sense and to negotiate a new meaning for the initial situation. Such a resolution often takes the shape of personal liberation or emancipation.

Vignette 6

I have a lot of ideas. The thing is, [...] I already [reached] one of my goals, [... as] the youngest [centre in the group] but I want to be known for our curriculum delivery. I want to be known as the centre that does things differently. So, we have achieved one or two of that [...] I give credit to my teachers [...] Because we are so young as compared to all the other established [centres]. My [group supervisor] said, 'Don't worry about enrolment. Take care of your teachers, parents and all

---

that. Enrolment will come.' Initially, I had so much pressure to meet the numbers, right? So, the focus was wrong. Then she said, 'You focus on the operations, focus on your people. Then, your [enrolment] numbers will come. Don't worry about it. [...] Numbers will come. Don't worry about this kind of thing'. So, I focused on that one as well. My teachers, like I said, it's not their job to meet the enrolment. It's their job to teach well.

It is encouraging to see EC leaders aspire to innovate as curriculum leaders and have an entrepreneurial mindset while being able to manage the centre like a business (Moloney & Pettersen, 2017). While some may frown upon treating ECEC as a profit-making endeavor, this is perhaps a necessary skill that leaders need in Singapore's commercialised ECEC industry. The harsh reality is that centres can only continue to exist if they maintain healthy enrolment. Within such a marketised ECEC context, not only must leaders manage child enrolment numbers by building good relations with parents, work within the confines, constraints and expectations of their organisations and business owners, they must continue to improve the quality of the programmes. To do so, leaders must motivate their staff and must themselves be creative and innovative.

Discussion

Leadership is a dynamic process that is constructed relationally through multiple interactions within a cultural context, involving ongoing transformations of both the community and the self. Furthermore, it is through interactions that leadership is constructed, contested, negotiated and re-negotiated. It is constructed in relation to others, including teachers, children, parents, other professionals, and the wider community.

In this chapter, we have described how Singaporean ECEC leaders have talked about their work, the kinds of conflicts they have experienced, and the various ways in which they enact pedagogical leadership within a commercial ECEC system. Acting as a principal and doing and being a leader is continuously filled with conditions created by oppositional forces. To understand this leadership phenomenon, we applied Vasilyuk's (1988) idea of critical conflicts.

177

The critical conflicts that we found among these principals were determined by their working upwards, downwards, outwards and inwards, with different stakeholders and their different expectations. All the participants in the study admittedly felt that they had to be someone to everyone because everyone that the leader came into contact with wanted something from her. Our study demonstrates that Singaporean ECEC leaders have to be aware of the expectations of multiple stakeholders such as parents, teachers, operators, and the government. ECEC leaders have to manage daily operations within the given confines of their organisation and setting. And they had to constantly (re)construct a vision for their programme's curriculum and pedagogy in response to external expectations (i.e., SPARK), or to the needs of the population that they served, as well as to broader societal views of children and families. As a consequence of working in this complex field of opposing forces, every leader experiences motives arising from conflicts.

In most cases, critical conflicts are something that cannot be solved by an individual subject (Vasilyuk, 1988); they easily lead to dead ends instead of positive transformation of unworkable practices, norms or rules. This is because conflicts are strongly intertwined with contradictions in collective activities within activity systems. Contradictions are not the same as problems or conflicts (Engeström, 1987); they are historically accumulating structural tensions within and among activity systems. Contradictions generate disturbances and conflicts, but also innovations that attempt to change the activity. As a result, to solve critical conflicts requires a collective redesign of activities. Vignette 6 represents such an attempt.

While not without methodological limitations, this study's in-depth interview approach enabled the participants to reflect on their personal and professional lives, in so far as their leadership role was concerned. And in so doing, our participants simultaneously articulated their experiences to themselves. Leaders do not often have the opportunity to talk about their work and their professional challenges to many people, at least not to fellow-educators who would understand their contextual situations. Many of these leaders spoke about walking the journey alone and how the 'Principal Matters' professional development programme was valuable for their sanity and professional growth. Within the programme, they found like-minded educators who reaffirmed their mission and provided some level of assurance that they were not alone in face of similar issues. At its best, discussing one's experiences with a researcher provides social and material support for the re-articulation and revision of these experiences, and making critical conflicts visible. Having significant conversations with other leaders can create the expansive potential of transforming the way in which these principals experience their lives as leaders.

Concluding remarks

Traditional views of leadership celebrate the anointing of a single person who can play the heroine or hero role in an organisation – this model of leadership continues to dominate many early childhood settings and even in the larger Singapore education profession (Lambert, Zimmerman, & Gardner, 2016). In this small-scale examination of the work of 24 ECEC leaders, we have provided a glimpse of the kinds of intricate webs or activity systems in which each of these leaders have had to navigate in order to learn to survive or thrive. Their daily decision-making and interactions shape their professional learning and in turn, they influence the nature of ECEC leadership within their particular cultural contexts and organisational settings.

Acknowledgements

This study reported here was funded by the Lien Foundation; and we are also grateful to the leaders who were willing to speak with us, without whom this study would have been impossible.

References

Ang, L. (2012). *Vital voices for vital years: A study of leaders' perspectives on improving the early childhood sector in Singapore*. Singapore: Lien Foundation.

Early Childhood Development Agency. (2016). Press release: Enhanced support for aspiring early childhood leaders through skillsfuture study awards. Retrieved from www.ecda.gov.sg/PressReleases/Pages/ENHANCED-SUPPORT-FOR-ASPIRING-EARLY-CHILDHOOD-LEA DERS-THROUGH-SKILLSFUTURE-STUDY-AWARDS.aspx

Early Childhood Development Agency. (2017a). Press release: 40% of pre-schools now certified under Singapore preschool accreditation framework (SPARK). Retrieved from www.ecda.gov.sg/pressreleases/pages/40-per cent-of-preschools-now-certified-under-singapore-preschool-accredita tion-framework-(spark).aspx?controlmode=edit&displaymode=design

Ebbeck, M., Saidon, S., Soh, S., & Goh, M. (2014). Readiness of early childhood professionals in Singapore to take on a leadership role. *Asia-Pacific Journal of Research in Early Childhood Education, 8*(1), 79–98.

Engeström, Y. (1987). *Learning by expanding: An activity-theoretical approach to developmental research.* Helsinki: Orienta-Konsultit.

Engeström, Y., & Sannino, A. (2011). Studies of expansive learning: Foundations, findings and future challenges. *Educational Research Review, 5* (1), 1–24. doi:10.1016/j.edurev.2009.12.002

Fasoli, L., Scrivens, C., & Woodrow, C. (2007). Challenges for leadership in Aotearoa/New Zealand and Australian early childhood contexts. In L. Keesing-Styles & H. Hedges (Eds.), *Theorising early childhood practice: Emerging dialogues.* Sydney, NSW: Pademelon Press.

Gee, C. (2012). *The educational "arms race": All for one, loss for all.* Working paper 20. Singapore: Institute of Policy Studies.

Goffin, S., & Janke, M. (2013). *Early childhood education leadership development compendium: A view of the current landscape* (2nd ed.). Retrieved from https://goo.gl/LT14HB

Goy, P. (2017, August 21). Big increase in child care places, MOE kindergartens: Teaching standards to be raised, spending to go up. *The Straits Times Singapore.* Retrieved from www.straitstimes.com/singapore/big-increase-in-childcare-places-moe-kindergartens

Hujala, E. (2013). Contextually defined leadership. In E. Hujala, M. Waniganayake & J. Rodd (Eds.), *Researching leadership in early childhood education* (pp. 47–60). Tampere: Tampere University Press.

Lambert, L., Zimmerman, D. P., & Gardner, M. E. (2016). *Liberating leadership capacity: Pathways to educational wisdom.* New York: Teachers College Press.

Lim, S. (2017a). Early childhood care and education in Singapore: Context and prevailing issues. In M. Fleer & B. van Oers (Eds.), *International handbook of early childhood education, Volume 1.* Amsterdam: Springer.

Lim, S. (2017b). Marketization and corporatization of early childhood care and education in Singapore. In M. Li, J. Fox & S. Grieshaber (Eds.), *Contemporary issues and challenge in early childhood education in the Asia-Pacific region* (pp. 17–32). Singapore: Springer.

Lloyd, E. (2012). The marketisation of early years education and child care in England. In L. Miller & D. Hevey (Eds.), *Policy issues in the early years.* London: Sage Publications.

Moloney, M., & Pettersen, J. (2017). *Early childhood education management: Insights into business practice and leadership.* Abingdon, Oxon: Routledge.

Muijs, D., Aubrey, C., Harris, A., & Briggs, M. (2004). How do they manage? A review of the research on leadership in early childhood. *Journal of Early Childhood Research, 2*(2), 157–169.

Ng, P. T. (2010). The evolution and nature of school accountability in the Singapore education system. *Educational Assessment, Evaluation and Accountability, 22*(4), 275–292.

Nivala, V., & Hujala, E. (Eds.). (2002). *Leadership in early childhood education, cross cultural perspectives*. Oulu: Department of Educational Sciences and Teacher Education, Early Childhood Education, University of Oulu.

Rodd, J. (2013). *Leadership in early childhood: The pathway to professionalism* (4th ed.). Sydney, NSW: Allen & Unwin.

Sannino, A. (2013). Critical transitions in the pursuit of a professional object: Simone de Beauvoir's expansive journey to become a writer. In A. Sannio & V. Ellis (Eds.), *Learning and collective creativity: Activity-theoretical and sociocultural studies*. New York: Routledge.

Sannino, A.-L. (2010). Teachers' talk of experiencing: Conflict, resistance and agency. *Teaching and Teacher Education, 26*, 838–844.

Siraj-Blatchford, I., & Manni, L. (2007). *Effective leadership in the early years sector: The ELEYS study*. London: Institute of Education, University of London.

Sumsion, J. (2006). The corporatisation of Australian childcare: Towards an ethical audit and research agenda. *Journal of Early Childhood Research, 4*(2), 99–120. doi:10.1177/1476718X06063531

Tan, C. T. (2017). Enhancing the quality of kindergarten education in Singapore: Policies and strategies in the 21st century. *International Journal of Child Care and Education Policy, 11*, 7. doi:10.1186/s40723-017-0033-y

Teng, A. (2015, July 4). Starting from pre-school, parents sending kids for classes in race to keep up with peers. *The Straits Times Singapore*. Retrieved from www.straitstimes.com/singapore/education/starting-from-pre-school-parents-sending-kids-for-classes-in-race-to-keep-upon

Vasilyuk, F. (1988). *The psychology of experiencing*. Moscow: Progress.

Waniganayake, M. (2014). Being and becoming early childhood leaders: Reflections on leadership studies in early childhood education and the future leadership research agenda. *Journal of Early Childhood Education Research, 3*(1), 65–81.

Waniganayake, M., Cheeseman, S., Fenech, M., Hadley, F., & Shepherd, W. (2012). *Leadership: Contexts and complexities in early childhood education*. South Melbourne: Oxford University Press.

12

PEDAGOGIC SYSTEM LEADERSHIP WITHIN COMPLEX AND CHANGING ECEC SYSTEMS

Christine Pascal, Tony Bertram with Delia Goodman, Ali Irvine and Judith Parr

This chapter is concerned with the way pedagogic leadership in early childhood education and care (ECEC) operates and is influenced by factors shaped by the changes in the wider ECEC system in which early years programmes and services are placed; structural factors related to the nature, scope and capacity of early years programmes: and process factors which determine how early years programmes are experienced by those involved in the community. The chapter will first set out evidence of ECEC system changes and challenges, drawn primarily from a recent IEA cross-national study of eight countries (Pascal and Bertram, 2016) and supported by a raft of other cross-national studies of ECEC, including studies by Pascal, Bertram, Delaney, and Nelson (2012);Pascal and Bertram (2012a);OECD (2012); Economics Intelligence Unit (EIU, 2012) and Eurydice (2014). We will then critically review definitions and concepts of system leadership during a time of change. Finally, as exemplification of the challenges faced by ECEC system leaders, we offer a set of case studies focusing on the lived experiences of three ECEC service leaders based in Ireland and England who are working with us on a system leadership programme,[1] and who are at the front line in developing and enhancing their early childhood provision in response to these system changes. The case studies document the leaders' attempts to develop their own system leadership capacity during a time of rapid and substantial system change and how they use their new system leadership skills to develop and sustain high quality, accessible ECEC services which can address social inequality, enhance participation and close the gap in educational achievement on entry to compulsory schooling.

Introduction

Early childhood policy and provision is going through a time of transformation across the world as policy makers respond to the compelling and developing evidence base which indicates its potential to achieve social, economic, political and educational progress. This increased attention from government policy makers in many countries is leading to significant shifts in the way early childhood services and programmes are perceived as a vital part of national social systems and structures (EIU, 2012; OECD, 2012; Pascal et al., 2012; Eurydice, 2014; Pascal and Bertram, 2016). The key issue in the quality and effectiveness of early childhood settings, the evidence suggests, is the quality of interaction between the significant adults in a child's life (parents, carers and early years practitioners) and children, including peer relationships. Within these relationships, the quality of leadership of settings is crucial in enabling learning, pedagogy, participation, distributed power, voice, challenge, stimulation, social equity, democracy, community and achievement to flourish in a positive and purposeful climate.

Changing early childhood systems and challenges

The International Association for the Evaluation of Educational Achievement (IEA) International Early Childhood Education Study (ECES) was a comparative research programme of the IEA. The purpose of the study was to explore, describe and critically analyse ECEC provision and its role in preparing children for the learning and social demands of school and wider society. The participating countries in the study were: Chile, the Czech Republic, Denmark, Estonia, Italy, Poland, the Russian Federation and the United States. The analysis within and between the eight study countries in the IEA study highlighted major systemic shifts in ECEC which are underway across the world and to which those involved in leading and delivering early childhood services are currently having to respond. Six of these major ECEC system shifts and their consequences for local system leaders are explored below.

System shift 1: ECEC is undergoing a period of rapid and significant development and is receiving continuing policy attention and investment

It is now widely acknowledged that public policy should support the development of an ECEC system which ensures access and entitlement to high quality services for all children from birth to the start of primary schooling (Pascal and Bertram, 2016). To ensure a certain length of participation in ECEC programmes, countries often provide legal entitlements to secure access to affordable, high quality ECEC. The countries in the ECES study reflected this shift in policy but were each at a different stage in the development of their ECEC system, with some countries having well developed systems with legal entitlements from an early age and others in the process of putting in place statutory entitlements in the year or two before primary schooling. Development and change in ECEC public policy is underway in most countries. Most of the participating countries in the study had recently undergone, or had planned for the near future, significant structural and systemic changes in their ECEC policy. The findings illustrated the dynamic nature of ECEC policy and reflect the growing visibility and importance attached to the development of ECEC as a fundamental and formative part of the educational and social systems within the study countries.

However, in many countries, the continued complexity of the sector and the diversity of providers and funding mechanisms compared with that found at primary and secondary stages in the education system, make the policy challenges during this phase very different and the change agenda very complex. Leaders of ECEC services are therefore generally required to see themselves as part of a complex and interconnecting system of provision for children and families, some home-based, some centre-based, some located in private paid-for settings, others in voluntary, NGO or charitable settings, and some under the auspices of Education, Health or Social Services/Welfare or other local or national government departments when many of these agencies are themselves going through a period of change. Within a system leadership model, leaders are managing these change processes through greater partnership working and joint action at a local or regional level.

Linked to this system dynamic there has been a significant increase in expenditure on ECEC services in many countries to support the development of ECEC infrastructure, services and the development of quality. However, in some countries we found the opposite to be the case. The global banking crash of 2008 has seen many countries facing austerity policies with public expenditure on public services, including ECEC, being reined in and in some cases severe cuts to service provision being made. This financial crisis has also, sometimes, been exacerbated by embracing an ideological position developed from Milton Friedman's (1962) economic liberalism. This means that some system leaders are challenged with the task of managing a rapid expansion of service demand and delivery which is supported with increased funding. In other contexts, system leaders are being required to manage the shrinking of service delivery with significant cuts to their funding despite increased need and demand and along with this, an increasing marketisation of services, replacing collaboration with competition.

System shift 2: Multiple policy aims for ECEC are increasingly common and expected outcomes from investment are wide-ranging

Government policies often promote ECEC as critical to smart and sustainable growth, the development of stable and equitable societies, and to long term economic prosperity. The ECES study confirmed that governments across the world are recognising the value of ECEC as a key social, educational, economic and civic lever, and are investing in its development to secure benefits in all these domains. The study countries indicated a wide range of policy aims for ECEC which included aims to support parental employment and training, aims to support a child's development and learning, aims that address wider social and civic issues, and aims which support early intervention for language needs or special needs. This suggests that ECEC policy is being used to meet a spectrum of social, economic, educational and political demands which give it visibility and status. It does however mean that at times these different policy aims can compete and clash, and system leaders can be faced with conflicting and excessive demands for the outcomes they and their services are expected to deliver.

System shift 3: There is a persisting structural and organisational split between care and education which means that systemic coherence within ECEC and between ECEC and primary schooling is lacking

Cross-national studies have shown that in most countries, ECEC is split into two separate phases according to age (Pascal and Bertram, 2016). UNESCO (2012) for example, uses the International Standard

185

Classification of Education (ISCED) to define early years as ISCED Level Zero, which is further divided between Birth to 2 years, called Early Childhood Educational Development (ECED) and 3 years to the start of schooling (when ISCED Level 1 begins), called Pre-primary Education (PPE). The split system is the most usual form of ECEC structure, with provision delivered in separate settings for younger and older children. The age break is usually around 3 years old. The responsibilities for governance, regulation and funding are also divided between different authorities. In contrast, in a unitary system, ECEC provision for all children is organised in a single phase and delivered in settings catering for whole age phase. There is no break or transfer between institutions until children start primary schooling. In the ECES study countries we found both split and unitary systems, but split systems predominated. This means that ECEC system leaders in split systems are supporting children who have multiple transitions in their early years, and sometimes these transitions can occur across a single day as they move between care and education services. Leading effective cross-sector and multi-disciplinary working for staff teams within split systems to ensure coherence of experience for children and families is a major challenge for system leaders, particularly if these various sector providers straddle the public/private/voluntary divide.

System shift 4: Regulation and quality assurance of ECEC services to secure, promote and develop quality are increasing

The cross-national studies reveal that countries across the world are concerned about assuring the quality of ECEC and are moving to regulate ECEC and put in place stronger systems of accountability, usually through quality accreditation and inspection. Countries are at various stages in the development of quality assurance procedures with some countries actively resisting too much regulation, while others see it as a key priority to safeguard children's well-being and development and/or to measure effectiveness and efficiency of value for money. Pressures on system leaders to ensure they are accountable, transparent and their services deliver positive outcomes for children and families are increasing and performativity considerations are an increasing element in their professional lives. The requirement on system leaders to be fully accountable, to implement robust performance management approaches, respond to externally set targets and take responsibility for the quality and impact of their services can put enormous pressure on leaders at the front line of service provision and delivery.

System shift 5: Expectations of the role, level of professionalism and qualifications of the ECEC workforce is increasing

Research has consistently demonstrated that enriched, stimulating environments and high quality pedagogy are fostered by better qualified practitioners, and that better quality pedagogies facilitate better, longer lasting, learning outcomes (Sylva et al., 2008; OECD, 2012; Pascal and Bertram, 2012a). Qualifications are one of the strongest predictors of staff quality. It is important to note, however, that it is not the qualification level per se; it is related to how much specialised and practical training is included in initial staff education, what types of professional development and education are available to and taken up by staff, and how many years of experience staff have accumulated.

The ECES study countries reveal that the staff who work in ECEC are characterised by their diversity of qualification, role and status. Many countries do not require graduates (those who have achieved ISCED Level 5 qualification or above) to work in ECEC, even for those at a senior level. The qualification requirement for leaders, and those who work with older children, though, is usually higher than their staff. Continuing professional development is usually an optional requirement for ECEC staff and leaders. Specific training in leadership and management is rare. Salary levels also vary considerably within the sector, depending on the type of setting, role and type of delivery contract offered. However, relative low pay rates for some practitioners, particularly those working with younger children, reflect the lack of professional status and qualification level in some parts of the workforce. Changing this to ensure the early years workforce is professionalised, qualified and well remunerated is a major system challenge which countries are beginning to tackle but will take time. Meanwhile, system leaders have the challenge of recruiting and retaining well qualified staff to their services and ensuring high quality continuing professional development is available to all in the workforce.

System shift 6: ECEC curriculum guidelines are increasingly common and include provision for the under threes

Evidence from the cross-national studies reveals that many countries set learning objectives and have pedagogic guidelines related to children's progress and development and issue official curriculum guidelines to help settings improve their provision. These curriculum guidelines are increasingly being extended to include children under 3 years old, where the emphasis has often been on the care and welfare of children rather than their education and development. The curriculum guidelines tend to include personal, social and emotional development, as well as language and communication skills, physical development and health. Literacy and numeracy development tends to apply only for older children. There are also countries that have a non-subject based approach, with an emphasis on children's holistic development, including such aspects as citizenship, creativity, well-being and social competence. Some countries also recommend the type of teaching approach, and generally promote a balance between adult and child led activities and the promotion of the importance of free play. For system leaders this shift in focus to include educational as well as care objectives for the youngest children brings with it a demand for both training and a professional culture shift within their organisation to see their educational role as a primary concern.

To summarise, the evidence from the cross-national studies reveals that many countries are engaged in radical ECEC system change which is bringing real challenges to those involved at the front line of system delivery. The evidence reveals that there is no one way to secure ECEC system development and no 'one-size-fits-all' approach. Countries have a range of different options open to them to achieve the overall goal of securing high quality ECEC for all children. Depending on each country's context, there are different system opportunities to be considered. However, the identification of the nine commonly observed system shifts in ECEC set out above identifies some of the key challenges facing ECEC system leaders in many countries and the consequences of their actions for service quality, service delivery and children's participation. These leadership challenges will now be explored and exemplified in more detail through an exploration of system leadership in action.

What is Pedagogic System Leadership?

In a rapidly changing world, where system change and innovation has become the new norm, we believe that, as systems transform, old models of ECEC leadership are lacking in their capacity to meet the current practice challenges facing leaders, particularly in delivering the socially just outcomes that we know to be possible for all children. Old leadership models are often structural rather than systemic, static rather than dynamic, rigid rather than flexible, efficient rather than ethical, and logical rather than emotional. In the complex, often chaotic, human and unpredictable world of current ECEC service delivery, there is a need for new leadership approaches and models that are adaptable, responsive, localised, emotionally intelligent and socially engaged. They also need to fully understand the ethical and moral world of child-rearing in societies, and how, within this world, cultural values and social power dynamics work. Such awareness and the advocacy that flows from it, means that leaders must engage fully in an ethical and action-oriented approach to their service leadership, and have a clear orientation towards transformation. In this sense leadership is strongly **praxeological** (Formosinho and Oliveira Formosinho, 2012; Pascal and Bertram, 2012b). Leaders also need to be less managerial and so more capable of being change agents, transforming old practices into new ones, encouraging their teams to unlearn old ways of being and learn to operate in new ways. Their role therefore is strongly **pedagogic**, as they work to create learning organisations whose role is to maximise human capacity and capabilities for all, including staff, children and families. Finally, leaders need to be fully aware of their role and function as **systemic**, operating to reform and reconfigure existing services and create new ones within an open, collaborative and complex system of ECEC. We are therefore offering a new, blended approach to ECEC leadership, one which has at its roots a moral and ethical agenda, is developmental and rights based, and which acknowledges that power and responsibility must be shared within an open and flexible system of locally responsive, but nationally supported, services. This praxeological approach we are calling 'Pedagogic System Leadership'.

This approach to leadership is demanding and requires leaders to enter a process of deep and critical reflection on their professional identity, purpose and their guiding values (Argyris, 1993; Argyris and Schon, 1996). While doing so leaders often experience the discomfort of *'conscientisation'* (Freire, 1972) through which they develop a more critical awareness of their leadership reality through reflection and action. Action is fundamental to this process because it is the process of changing the reality. Through this deep reflective process of re-sculpting their leadership behaviours and actions, system leaders are asked to let go of old organisational ties and interests, so they can cross organisational boundaries and lead collegially in partnership with other service leaders within a local system of ECEC provision. They become in essence, part of a system of fellow leaders, where power is shared, and flattened hierarchies operate. This approach means that leaders are asked to develop their role and contribution to a collective, locality-wide system of ECEC, involving shared objectives, joint planning, shared resources and collective accountability for service impact. To achieve this, Pedagogic System Leadership demands a new sense of leadership identity that goes beyond institutional and organisational boundaries to stretch a leader's vision and actions across services that inter-relate laterally rather than hierarchically. In this way, Pedagogic System Leaders realise their strength, not from position but through collective agreement, influence and the brokerage of relationships and alliances. A central aspect of realising this form of leadership is the capacity to lead with emotional intelligence (EI) (Goleman, 1998). Goleman's first requirement for an EI leader is that they should know themselves.

So, what characterises Pedagogical System Leadership? Craig and Bentley (2005) set out a useful list of system leader characteristics which we have extended to embrace some key characteristics of Pedagogic System Leadership.

1. It is values and ethics driven.
2. It embodies a commitment to social justice and equality.
3. It is committed to rights based, participatory and inclusive practice.
4. It is child and family focused in its goals and actions, emphasising coherence of action.
5. It models a commitment to the learning and development of every child, parent and practitioner.
6. It involves a shift in mindset for leaders, emphasising what they share with others over how they differ.
7. It eschews 'us and them' relationships.
8. It is emotionally intelligent, understanding and utilising inter- and intra-personal skills.
9. It maximises the influence and effect of leadership across a system.
10. It represents a shift in the practice of leaders to ensure wider influence through joint advocacy within the system itself to realise positive goals for children and families.
11. It requires a capacity for 'system thinking' over 'organisational thinking'.

In summary, Pedagogic System Leaders see, and act on, the system as a whole, recognising the interdependence of local ECEC organisations as a means of achieving shared moral and ethical goals for children and families, and acting in a developmental and critical partnership with other organisations in their locality. This model of leadership clearly demands a distinct set of skills, competencies and understandings of the leadership task. In a useful paper by Demos/NCSL (2004) some of these leadership competencies and tasks are identified, including the capacity of leaders:

1. To generate collective vision and shared purpose which all organisations can identify with and sign up to.
2. To support leadership capacity-building by distributing leadership opportunities.
3. To create a climate of *'professional generosity'* and exchange, opening up professional practices to external scrutiny and for wider adoption.
4. To have an openness to see that there will be multiple perspectives on a situation.
5. To enable the development of autonomy in the system while promoting shared vision.
6. To support learning and continuous improvement by creating feedback loops.
7. To maintain an open and vibrant learning culture.

We offer these skills, competencies and understandings for Pedagogic System Leaders as a starting place and stimulus for deeper and more critical reflection about what governments engaged in transforming ECEC systems are demanding of the leaders within it. There is clearly no one-size-fits-all approach to system development and so the responses of system leaders need to be pedagogic, i.e. concerned with learning, and localised, culturally embedded and multi-faceted.

Portraits of Pedagogic System Leadership

The following English and Irish case studies focus on three ECEC leaders who are working with us on a system leadership course designed to develop their Pedagogic System Leadership. The portraits are offered, not as a guide for others' development, but as illustrations offered to shine a spotlight on the real challenges, struggles and opportunities that system transformation brings for those with the courage to lead within them. Each case study will focus on the leaders' responses to one or more of the system shifts which were identified earlier in this chapter. They are written by the system leaders themselves and convey a personal journey of development and critical reflection on their developing system leadership capacity.

Ali Irvine's portrait

Ali works in England and her portrait focuses on her responses to two system shifts:

System Shift 1: ECEC is undergoing a period of rapid and significant development and is receiving continuing policy attention and investment.

System Shift 3: There is a persisting structural and organisational split between care and education which means that systemic coherence within ECEC and between ECEC and primary schooling is lacking.

Ali writes

I wish to begin with this thought from my Personal Journal:

> Managing change, it's what we do now. Nothing remains consistent. It is a volatile and uncertain time in the history of children's centres. Many of us view ourselves as small-time leaders in this ever-changing global system, a system where local, national and international politics impact on the public services that we deliver. There appears little time for reflection or consolidation in this culture of change, but one thing remains certain, our leadership is valuable and the child will remain at the centre of all we do.
>
> (Personal Journal, 23 January 2017)

In this extract I have tried to encapsulate the concept that it is no longer possible to consider ourselves as leaders in isolation. Current political shifts worldwide, coupled with the economic strains being placed on individual countries across the globe, has created an environment where leaders on every level must now consider one another in any process of change, bringing together their individual strengths and shared visions for the future and for the future of their children.

We are certainly moving through a period of fast and furious change and this statement appears to echo the thinking of many current writers and scholars considering the concept of system leadership and its role within the modern world. I question how effectively I would be able to lead my team if I chose to work in autonomy, without considering the position of individuals within the staff team, partners or indeed the families and children with whom I work. It is important to consider that all of those groups mentioned here are also functioning within the cycle of continuous change. I believe these ideas and thoughts must continue to shape me as a leader and influence decisions I make on a local level and within the framework of a 'global' society.

Bush (2011), when considering leadership within the educational system, writes '*The shift to self-management in many countries and the associated requirement to collaborate with many groups and individuals has made it more difficult to sustain a closed system approach*' (p.45). I would argue that this concept can also be related to organisations and systems on a global as well as local level, adding pressure on leaders to reconsider their own place within the wider context of change management and their relationships with other leaders, '*How do we move forward as leaders amongst leaders?* (Personal Journal, 26 January 2017).

Undertaking the 'mapping' exercise with a group of colleagues on the course was a very useful tool. On completion of this activity, I later took the opportunity to personally reflect on my own role as a leader within the Children's Centres:

> over the past three years, I have not only successfully adapted my own leadership role and style to complement the changes that have taken place, but I have managed the team of early years leaders and practitioners from across the locality, through a challenging and uncertain time. I have seen them emerge stronger and equally as passionate and committed to their work and developing roles across the group as they were previously. This feels good.
>
> (Personal Journal, 20 January 2017)

It may appear that through the inclusion of this extract, I have considered my work done. On the contrary, this thought, this idea, coupled with my emerging knowledge and understanding of system leadership and change management, led me to the realisation that there is so much more to accomplish and that in this time of significant change, I need to also consider theories and models that are new to me, bringing fresh ideas to support not only my own team but the wider Children's Centre Community. The 'mapping' exercise during the course has encouraged me to look further afield in my own knowledge and understanding of change and given me ideas on how I might reach out to my commissioners, partners, fellow professionals, families and children to consider how we develop services that are fit for purpose, unambiguous, certain and clear in vision and purpose, supporting us all to move forward together as our familiar worlds are changing.

The implementation of system leadership as a concept is worthy of consideration during this time of great change and within the area of early intervention it would appear to be the natural way forward. It offers me and leaders from all agencies the opportunity to come together. Ghate, Lewis and Welbourne (2014) explain the aim of system leadership by suggesting that working across and through multiple organisations together will result in positive social change. However, while considering this as an idea and reflecting upon the strategies I may need to use in order to become a more effective leader under this model, I also began to consider,

> Have theories of system leadership been created by leaders whose long-term vision is to bring about effective change in public services for the greater good of families and children within our society, or, for a more political and controlling effect to bring about greater performance and public accountability to services as a money saving exercise during these times of austerity?(Personal Journal, 12 February 2017)

As is apparent in this written reflection, I am at times sceptical of such theories, believing that we should continuously question and challenge ideas in order to ensure that the child and family remain at the forefront of all we do. However, I also recognise that in order to manage rapid change well in these times of austerity there is a need for efficient, effective evidence-based systems that support the needs of the wider societal changes that are coming about as a direct response to the current economic climate.

I will now consider what I have come to understand are the skills necessary to be an effective system leader and manager of change. From the reading I have undertaken, it is clear that in order to support the development of the Children's Centre agenda in the current political and economic climate, leaders will need to be flexible, innovative and collaborative in their approach to managing change. This collaboration will need to reach out further than before and partner agencies and other interested parties will need to be included in planning and delivering services which will best meet the needs of families and children within local communities. It will take a skilful leader to be able to negotiate in collaboration with other professionals while also being confident, open and fair enough to share responsibilities and ideas. Leaders will need to identify individual skills and expertise across the team and draw upon these, thereby, adding value to individual colleague's contributions. There will be little time for autocratic leaders who wish to 'hold the baby' themselves. Leaders must accept their own limits and recognise the value of their colleagues.

Considering the reading I have undertaken and reflecting on my personal feelings and emotions, I have come to the realisation that I should not look upon my leadership as a position of isolation. Through methods of distributed leadership, drawing upon the strengths of the whole team, I will be better equipped to bring about successful change. Viewing myself and my position as not an isolated professional, or as Aubrey, Godfrey and Harris (2012) describe, a 'traditional leader', but as a leader who utilises the power of collaboration and teamwork.

Delia Goodman's portrait

Delia works in Ireland and her portrait focuses on her responses to three system shifts:

System Shift 4: Regulation and quality assurance of ECEC services to secure, promote and develop quality are increasing.
System Shift 5: Expectations of the role, level of professionalism and qualifications of the ECEC workforce is increasing.
System Shift 6: ECEC curriculum guidelines are increasingly common and include provision for the under threes.

Delia writes

In the last 20 years, the early years sector in Ireland has experienced significant developments which have included:

- revised Child Care Act 1991 (Early Years Service) Regulations in 2016;
- minimum qualification of staff in all services to a QQI Level 5;
- development of Síolta, the National Quality Framework for Early Childhood Education in 2006, and Aistear, the Early Years Curriculum Framework in 2009;
- introduction of the free preschool year (ECCE Scheme) in 2010;
- the quality agenda which includes an eight-point plan to improve the quality of ECEC in Ireland.

With these changes happening there has been little guidance about the coordination and access to resources to support their implementation in the ECEC sector.

In this portrait of my leadership development I will consider how my multi-agency working can begin to bring about a unified approach to accessing training and resources in developing quality across the early years sector. In my readings, I have read how 'multi-agency working can help generate new ideas, indicate future needs and directions for all partners as well support the implementation of national policy at local level' (Gasper, 2010, p. 90). I intend to consider this statement and explore how my system leadership supports multi-agency working and collaboration.

Let me begin this portrait with my understanding of integrated system leadership. My theory is based on my reading, the learning from taking part in the activities during the training course and my reflections. There was one paper I read which I found particularly inspirational entitled The Dawn of System Leadership by Senge, Hamilton and Kania, (2015, p. 28) where it is suggested that those with the core capabilities of system leaders can '*build relationships based on deep listening, and networks of trust and collaboration start to flourish*' and where three core capabilities are identified which system leaders must develop: '*fostering collective leadership*', '*fostering reflection*' and '*co-creating the future*'. This theory of Senge et al. (2015) was evident in many of the readings I have explored, and while they may use various descriptions, the theory is similar. In my Personal Journal, I noted the following: 'Everything I have read about system leadership comes back to having a vision, developing relationships outside of our organisation and developing new learning to enhance our work' (12 November 2016).

Therefore, my understanding of integrated system leadership is about developing relationships outside of my organisation and having a collective vision that fosters new learning and future work. This is taking my leadership to the next level, developing my knowledge, skills and credibility as a leader outside of the organisation, becoming a system leader.

The broader aim of the national organisation in which I work is to bring coordination, cohesion and consistency to provision of state funded ECEC and ensure quality supports work in alignment with statutory ECEC systems. From research and from my reading I understand the importance of investing in high quality ECEC which can yield positive outcomes for children and families, especially for those living in disadvantaged areas (DCYA, 2013, p. 16). At a policy level, there is a recognition of the importance of ECEC Better Outcomes Brighter Futures National Policy Framework' which states, 'All children will benefit from investment in early years care and education. Indeed, children in early years care and education are shown to out-perform those without it' (DCYA, 2014, p. 15).

In Ireland, there has been increased investment in the provision of services and the upskilling of the early years workforce, with all early years practitioners having to meet the minimum qualifications requirements. Not only do the qualifications of practitioners impact on the quality of practice, but also the content of the day to day practice (theory) influences quality. We have two national frameworks to support and enhance the quality of practice for children from birth to 6 years (Síolta and Aistear). However, the knowledge, awareness and access to these national frameworks has been limited, with little funding to support their implementation. It is at this point where I began to consider how I can support our organisation to build more awareness of these frameworks in the sector.

When taking part in the course activity on *mapping community cultures with a locality system*, I reflected on which agencies I could begin to work with. I developed a taxonomy of these relationship in my Personal Journal using the headings in Figure 12.1.

I reflected on agencies at all levels of this taxonomy, taking into consideration their partnership and their role in the sector. I considered the relationships from an integrated system leadership perspective. Looking at this theoretical framework, I thought about the vision,

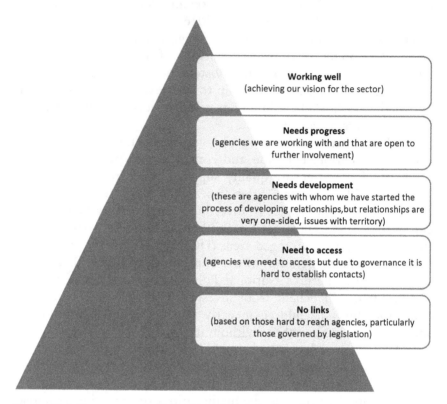

Figure 12.1 Taxonomy of relationships (Personal Journal, Goodman, 2 November 2016)

what their purpose or vision is, are there opportunities for joint working and can we begin, or have we already begun, to contribute to each other's work as professionals? This reflective process towards developing integrated working is illustrated in Figure 12.2.

In my readings as part of the course I read that 'knowledge and needs of a multi-agency team is crucial as it enables you to understand and work more efficiently with individuals from different professional backgrounds' (Ang, 2011, p. 295). This was important to consider for many reasons, knowing which agencies are open to developing a partnership, and identifying agencies with similar values and vision. Senge et al. (2015) argues that we should recognise that real change starts with a recognition that we are part of the systems we seek to change. I agree with this statement: it isn't about

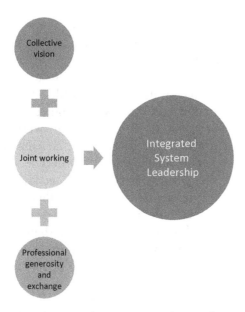

Figure 12.2 Integrated System Leadership (Personal Journal, 29 September 2016)

our organisation alone addressing the awareness and access to the national frameworks but other agencies in the sector identifying they are a part of the change process.

Judith Parr's portrait

Judith works in England and her portrait focuses on her responses to three system shifts:

System Shift 1: ECEC is undergoing a period of rapid and significant development and is receiving continuing policy attention and investment.

System Shift 2: Multiple policy aims for ECEC are increasingly common and expected outcomes from investment are wide-ranging.

System Shift 5: Expectations of the role, level of professionalism and qualifications of the ECEC workforce is increasing.

Judith writes

I had until recently believed that certain people were born to be leaders – surely the ability to be a leader must be defined by certain pre-existing qualities rather than something that could be learnt and developed over time? This never sat comfortably with me, as I never felt that I fitted this mould. In my mind I had 'drifted' into my current role purely by chance – I believed that I happened to deliver a set of convincing answers in a job interview. However, I am starting to realise that this is not the case. Rowley (1997) in her article discussing whether academic leaders are born or made, suggests that there are certain traits which are recognisable in many leaders – such as intelligence, initiative and self-assurance. However, she goes on to develop the point that leaders are generally able to be flexible in their styles depending on the situation and the team around them, and that their styles are influenced by their own values and beliefs, confidence and, interestingly, their stress levels.

Related to this is what I learnt through my reading about the 'imposter phenomenon' (Clance and Imes, 1978). It wouldn't be an understatement to identify this theory as being an epiphany for me in terms of understanding my own feelings of anxiety and inadequacy at many stages of my life, when I thought I would be 'found out' as not being capable of roles I was undertaking. Understanding a little about this has enabled me, to some extent, to move past it and recognise that I am worthy of my career progression to date. I need to recognise that perhaps leadership is a tangible process, rather than only recognition of personal attributes and qualities. Giltinane (2013) describes three styles of leader – Transactional, Transformational and Situational. Reading through the descriptions initially led me to suppose that I primarily use a transformational style – I am able to create vision, work democratically and recognise individuals within the team (Bass, 2008). However, on further reading I came to realise that I am, in fact, a situational leader – I am able to adapt my style to suit the situation I am faced with.

> I'd never given much thought to what 'style' of leader I am, or what elements of leadership I am using at any given point...I hadn't considered that I can change style depending on the circumstance, but I can see now that I do.
>
> (Personal Journal, 22 October 2015)

Goleman's (1998) identification of leadership styles also clarified for me where my strengths and areas for growth lie. I am aware that I work well when I am able to use his Democratic and Affiliative styles. I am also able to be visionary at times, although long periods of this would not be conducive to my own well-being.

For the last six months I have undertaken the role of Children's Centre Co-ordinator, with responsibility for access to services, at a busy Children's Centre in a town bordered by two cities. I also have responsibility for a satellite centre ten miles away in a rural, generally affluent location. I lead alongside another co-ordinator, who has responsibility for measuring the impact of our services. Our team is made up of Outreach Workers, Early Years Practitioners and Administrators, and we share the time of a Qualified Teacher and Safeguarding Lead who work across all the Local Authority Children's Centres as well as a Service Manager who strategically leads two Children's Centre areas. Following re-structure of services in our Authority this year, I re-located to this area and took on the leadership of a group of staff, the majority of whom were also new to this particular Children's Centre. As a result, the last few months have been a time of great change.

We are also half way through our first year as a Local Authority commissioned service. It is a perfect time to pause in the busy-ness of the work to reflect, individually and collectively, on where we have come from, how we have got to where we are now, and where we want to go from here. I felt that it would be beneficial to help my team reflect on the work they have done, the issues they have faced and their opinions on how best we can move forward. Rodd (2006) emphasises that in this stage, when conflict often occurs, staff need recognition of their contribution to the team, in an environment of mutual support and encouragement. Without this, she feels there can be an increase in stress, power struggles and destructive criticism. Personally, I am finding that my team seem to be responding well to my leadership, but I am aware of some background discontent around new expectations and methods of working, which they perceive I am 'inflicting' on them. I need to help them understand and 'own' these concepts and create an environment where opinions are valued and heard, even when they may go against the grain of what my team think I want to hear. As a result, my aims in my learning contract of coaching, managing conflict and leading with greater emotional intelligence are brought sharply into focus.

In terms of my initial goals, as set out in my learning contract, I can now reflect on how well I feel I have achieved these and my thoughts are mixed on this. 'To lead with greater emotional intelligence' was the first of my aims. I feel that generally my emotional intelligence is increasing and the way in which I interact with my team is changing. I feel that I am demonstrating to greater effect the five competencies outlined by Goleman (1998) of self-awareness, self-regulation, motivation, empathy and social skills. I am excited and re-invigorated by the fresh understanding of how my own skills development can only promote a more effective, efficient working environment, and give leadership to those in every role. Intertwined with this outcome is that of developing my coaching skills, to support individuals in their own development as well as that of the wider team. My last area for development was that of managing conflict. This is my weakest area of growth, due to my own subconscious reluctance to raise current issues, and the fact that the opportunity was not appropriate to force discussion of uncomfortable matters. Perhaps I could have more overtly highlighted the issue of team conflict within the work I did? On reflection my team is not yet in a place where they can focus on and address the 'storming' issues effectively. This, I feel, shows my increased levels of emotional intelligence – a while ago I may have just leapt in to try and 'solve' what I perceived to be the 'problem'. I now appreciate that this is not always conducive, often there may be steps to be taken beforehand which can address the issue without antagonism, defensiveness or feelings of there being 'winners' and 'losers' (Kline, 1999).

My development as a leader still has some way to go – in fact, I would argue that the journey is endless, and there will always be room for growth. However, this course has clarified for me where I need to go next with my development. I still have work to do on acknowledging that I have effective system leadership skills and that I am adept at putting them into practice. I need to work on accepting the meaningful critique of others and learning from it. I also need to recognise that conflict is a natural and inevitable part of working life – in itself it is not a problem, unless it is not approached and managed effectively (Rodd, 2006). I will, over the next months, be taking steps to undertake more personal study and further training around the areas of managing conflict and coaching others. I don't yet feel confident in these areas, and I feel it would have a significant impact on the development of my team if I could address these further. At this point I feel revitalised by my growing self-awareness and am anticipating the future with the knowledge and growing understanding that my ongoing self-reflection and personal development could have long-lasting positive effects for my team and ultimately for the ever-changing system in which we work.

Note

1 www.crec.co.uk/integrated-system-leadership

References

Ang, L. (2011). Leading and managing in the early years: A study of the impact of a NCSL programme on children's centre leaders' perceptions of leadership and practice. *Educational and Management Administration and Leadership*, 40(3), 289–304.

Argyris, C. (1993). *Knowledge for action. A guide to overcoming barriers to organizational change*. San Francisco, CA: Jossey Bass.

Argyris, C., & Schon, D. (1996). *Organizational learning II: Theory, method and practice*. Reading, MA: Addison Wesley.

Aubrey, C., Godfrey, R., & Harris, A. (2012). How do they manage? An investigation of early childhood leadership. *Educational Management, Administration and Leadership*, 41(1), 5–29.

Bass, B. M. (2008). *The Bass handbook of leadership: Theory research and managerial applications* (4th ed.). New York: Free Press.

Bush, T. (2011). *Theories of educational leadership and management* (4th ed.). London: Sage Publications.

Clance, P., & Imes, S. (1978). The imposter phenomenon in high achieving women: Dynamics and therapeutic intervention. *Psychotherapy Theory, Research & Practice*, 15(3), 241–247.

Craig, J., & Bentley, T. (2005). *System leadership*. London: Demos/NCSL.

Demos/NCSL. (2004). *System leadership and governance: Leadership beyond institutional boundaries*. London: The Innovation Unit and NCSL.

DCYA. (2013). *Supporting access to the early chilhood care and education (ECCE): Programme for children with a disability*. Dublin: Government Publications.

DCYA. (2014). *Better outcomes, brighter futures: The national policy framework for children and young people 2014–2020*. Dublin: Stationery Office.

Economist Intelligence Unit (EIU). (2012). *Starting well: Benchmarking early education across the world*. Hong Kong: Economist Intelligence Unit.

Eurydice. (2014). *Key data on early childhood education and care in Europe, Eurydice and Eurostat report* (2014 ed.). Brussels: EACEA.

Formosinho, J., & Oliveira Formosinho, J. (2012). Towards a social science of the social: The contribution of praxeological research. *European Early Childhood Education Research Journal*, 20(4), 591–606.

Freire, P. (1972). *Pedagogy of the oppressed*. Harmondsworth: Penguin.

Friedman, M. (1962). *Capitalism and freedom*. Chicago: University of Chicago Press.

Gasper, M. (2010). *Multi-agency working in the early years: Challenges and opportunities*. London: Sage Publications.

Ghate, D., Lewis, J., & Welbourne, D. (2014). *System leadership: Exceptional leadership for exceptional times*. London: Virtual Staff College and the Leadership Forum.

Goleman, D. (1998). *Working with emotional intelligence*. London: Bloomsbury.

Giltinane, C. L. (2013). Leadership styles and theories. *Nursing Standard, 27* (41), 35–39.

Kline, N. (1999). *Time to think: Listening to ignite the human mind*. London: Cassell Illustrated.

IEA. (2016). International Early Childhood Education Study. Retrieved from www.iea.nl/fileadmin/user_upload/Publications/Electronic_versions/ECES-policies_and_systems-report.pdf

OECD. (2012). *Education at a glance 2012: OECD indicators*. Paris: OECD.

Pascal, C., & Bertram, T. (2012a). *The impact of early education as a strategy in countering socio-economic disadvantage*. London: Ofsted.

Pascal, C., & Bertram, T. (2012b). Praxis, ethics and power: Developing praxeology as a participatory paradigm for early childhood research. *European Early Childhood Education Research Journal, 20*(4), 477–492.

Pascal, C., & Bertram, T. (2016). *Early childhood policies and systems in eight countries: Findings from IEA's early childhood education study*. Hamburg: The International Association for the Evaluation of Educational Achievement.

Pascal, C., Bertram, T., Delaney S., & Nelson, C. (2012). *A comparison of international childcare systems: Evidence to childcare commission*. London: Department for Education.

Rodd, J. (2006). *Leadership in early childhood*. Maidenhead: Open University Press.

Rowley, J. (1997). Academic leaders: Made or born? *Industrial and Commercial Training, 29*(3), 78–84.

Senge, P., Hamilton, H., & Kania, J. (2015). The dawn of system leadership. *Standford Social Innovation Review, 13*(1), 25–33.

Sylva, K., Melhuish, E., Sammons, P., Siraj-Blatchford, I., & Taggart, B. with Hunt, S., Jelicic, H., Barreau, S., Grabbe, Y., Smees, R., & Welcomme, W. (2008). *Effective pre-school and primary education 3–11 project: Final report from the primary phase (DfE Research Brief 061)*. London: DfE.

UNESCO. (2012). *Institute for statistics: International standard classification of education ISCED 201*. Montréal: UNESCO.

EDITORIAL PROVOCATIONS
Engaging readers and extending thinking

Sandra Cheeseman

The final section of this book considers the broader systems context of educational leadership. The chapters of this section draw on international contexts to look critically at how cultural, regulatory and economic systems can both enable, but also disable possibilities for early childhood programs. Of note is the impact that systems have on the work of individual practitioners.

Chapter 10 outlines the Finnish early childhood reform agenda and notes that alliances between policy planners and policy implementers rely on trust. Trust, as foundational to systems leadership, then permeates the section with all three chapters highlighting the significance of the individual in interpreting and responding to systems-wide initiatives. This chapter asks important questions about how systemic policy is interpreted and enacted by the individual teachers in relation to the children s/he works with. To what extent do we as educational leaders and practitioners see ourselves as having the power and authority to apply contextually relevant interpretations of systems policy?

Quite a different context is presented in Chapter 11, where Singapore's nascent development of the early childhood sector is explored. Moving early childhood education and care from the individual responsibility of families to a shared responsibility with the State and the mixed market of early childhood providers offers a different lens to consider systems influence. Educational leadership in this context is subject to many and at times conflicting pressures. Describing herself as an 'octopus', one principal notes how she juggles the multiple needs of administration, teachers, children and parents. The introduction of the Singapore Pre-school Accreditation Framework (SPARK) is provided as an example of a system wide initiative that provides both a positive framework for ECEC provision but also a demanding layer of expectations for educational leaders. How do we as leaders negotiate the good intentions of system change against the ever-increasing pressures on leaders to be the responsible persons? What are the possibilities for networks of professional support and communities of practice? Should we be advocating for all system change to be accompanied by a consideration of the implications for leaders in thriving rather than simply surviving change?

Chapter 12 provides an international overview of the rise of ECEC as government business and notes the complexity of systems according to a county's economic circumstances, marketised provision and priority on the policy agenda. Highlighting globally the significant differences between early childhood education provision and that of the schooling sectors, the complexity of the early childhood leader's roles is brought to the fore. The chapter notes that, as systems transform, old models of ECEC leadership may be lacking in their capacity to meet the challenges of the changing sector, particularly in delivering the socially just outcomes that we know to be possible for all children.

Concluding this first edition in the series – *Thinking about Pedagogy in Early Childhood Education*, this section has provided a provocation to the reader to think critically about leadership in complex and rapidly changing contexts. While many of the leaders showcased in this section identify their need to address their own challenges and need for on-going professional learning, there is a strikingly clear need for systems to take account of the demands on leaders in a changing context. How much more can be gained by a focus on building the capacity of early childhood leaders to effectively negotiate the complex and competing demands of the sector? Is it not a mistake to leave to chance the importance of leadership in realising the goal of giving all children the best start in life?

CODA

Thinking forward

This volume has drawn together established ideas and images of early childhood as well as a variety of emergent themes and concepts. The two concepts that have conflated in this volume are simultaneously both well-established and emergent. The notion of 'Pedagogy' as a space for teaching and learning has been inherent in teacher education programs since they began, variously defined and sometimes hidden in a space between teaching practice and curriculum, whereas 'Leadership' was often something which sat between management and administration. The co-location of these constructs into Pedagogical Leadership which has been evolving over time, creates a contemporary, dynamic and interesting learning space.

The authors of chapters in this volume and the carefully constructed provocations from the volume editors have offered insight, examples and challenges for those seeking to be pedagogical leaders as well as those who are already in roles incorporating this responsibility. Readers have been given opportunities to redefine personal conceptions of both pedagogy and leadership and the spaces in which these domains intersect. Inspiration has been offered from authors who live and work in different contexts from your own, but which offer possibilities for exploration and growth. You may have been most intrigued by people in situations familiar to your own or perhaps by those working in contexts quite different from what you know.

Throughout the volume, children are seen as active protagonists alongside educators juggling responsibilities shaped by pedagogical issues within diverse communities and ever-changing systemic frameworks. These offer the reader an opportunity to listen in on conversations that extend the scope and range of pedagogical leadership and may transform personal beliefs and site-based philosophies. Rich versions of pedagogical leadership are exemplified from mega perspectives – ranging from Australian big data sets to Canadian systemic innovations, through site-based examples in New Zealand and Finland, to individual examples of conversations and/or situations that demonstrate pedagogical leadership from a range of people in varying roles. You may be inspired to look for other work that these authors are engaged in, seeking out publications to extend your knowledge and deepen understanding of these important ideas and initiatives. We hope that you will pursue the provocations that have been offered, talking with colleagues and asking questions that are yet to be explored.

So where does this journey take us? The volume suggests a future that encompasses leadership as incorporating the ethics of professional behaviour as well as the primacy of relationships and connectedness. Unpacking the role of pedagogical leaders has highlighted the importance of critical reflection – not only on events and contexts, but on personal beliefs and site-based philosophies. Complex relationships with national structures and curriculum frameworks sit alongside examples of resilience and perseverance of children, families and educators.

The implication for existing and prospective pedagogical leaders is to become resilient, challenge orthodoxies, redefine personal conceptions of both pedagogy and leadership, and examine the spaces in which these intersect. We therefore hope you take inspiration to do just that, accepting the invitations for further growth and professional exploration.

Michael Reed & Alma Fleet

INDEX